THE NEW CENTRAL TEXAS GARDENER

The New Central Texas Gardener

Cheryl Hazeltine & Barry Lovelace

Illustrations by Kate Bergquist
Photographs by Jeffrey Lava

Texas A&M University Press
COLLEGE STATION

Library of Congress Cataloging-in-Publication Data

Hazeltine, Cheryl, 1942–
    The new central Texas gardener / Cheryl Hazeltine and Barry Lovelace.
        p.   cm.
    Includes bibliographical references and index.
    ISBN 0-89096-848-9 (cloth). — ISBN 0-89096-871-3 (pbk.)
    1. Gardening—Texas.   I. Lovelace, Barry, 1938–   .   II. Title.
SB453.2.T4H39   1999
635'.09764—dc21   98-34626
                                                            CIP

For Susannah ·

Contents

List of Illustrations, *ix*

Preface, *xi*

CHAPTER

1. The Climate Where We Live, *3*

2. Soil and Its Conditioning, *11*

3. Tools of the Trade, *21*

4. The Home Landscape: Planning, Selection,
and Some Special Gardens, *28*

5. Lawns: Establishing and Maintaining Them, *37*

6. Alternatives to Lawns, *48*

7. Tree and Shrub Planting and Care, *57*

8. Trees: A Checklist, *67*

9. Shrubs: A Checklist, *87*

10. Vines and Climbers, *106*

11. Flowers, *113*

12. Vegetables, *144*

13. Trouble in the Garden, *167*

14. Gardening Calendar for Central Texas, *178*

Bibliography, *187*

Index, *189*

Illustrations

A landscape plan	*page*	29
Grasses		38
Ground covers		51
Pampas grass		53
Century plant		55
Planting a balled tree		59
Pruning a large limb		62
Cedar elm		71
Crape myrtle		73
Live oak		75
Southern magnolia		78
Texas mountain laurel		79
Texas persimmon		80
Texas redbud		81
Weeping willow		82
Windmill palm		83
Abelia		89
Azalea		91
Camellia		92
Cenizo		93
Gardenia		95
Burford holly		96
Japanese yew		98
Juniper		99
Waxleaf ligustrum		100
Common oleander		101
Pittosporum		102
Pyracantha		103
Jasmine, asiatic		108
Chinese wisteria		109
Wild grapes		112
Annuals		121
Perennials		123

Bulbs   125
Wildflowers   137
Hybrid tea rose   140
Sample vegetable garden   147
Rosemary   164
Insects   175

COLOR SECTION

A Central Texas spring garden   *following page* 162
Xeriscape shrubs
Shade garden
Shade shrub
Pond
Small-space garden
Creating a view
Wildflowers
Raised-bed vegetable garden
Garden retreat
Sunny border
Any place can be a garden
Novel combinations
Classic mixed border
Textures in green
A classic spring border

MAPS

1. First and last freeze dates   *page*   6
2. Average length of the warm season   8
3. Soils of Central Texas   13

TABLES

1. Annuals (Spring-Summer Blooming)   *page* 116
2. Annuals (Fall-Winter Blooming)   120
3. Perennials   126
4. Bulbs   133

ILLUSTRATIONS

x

Preface

*When once fully explored, however, such was the tempting
beauty of the landscape upon its borders, that no dangers could
deter the settlers from seeking an abode in a region,
that in appearance, realized their most seducing
dreams of a paradise upon earth.*

JOHN M. NILES

SOUTH AMERICA AND MEXICO

WITH A COMPLETE VIEW OF TEXAS

This is not a theoretical book. It is a basic gardening text for Central Texans, containing expert advice tempered by the authors' more than fifty years of shared experience in a glorious but challenging land, a land of withering heat, blue northers, floods, and drought—in short, a microcosm of Texas.

Our purpose is to provide new gardeners and gardeners new to Central Texas information and advice about landscaping design for function and esthetic appeal; wise plant selection, from trees to turf to tomatoes; and garden practices that work. Along the way we hope also to provide useful information to experienced gardeners who know, as we do, that gardening is a continuous learning process. We especially hope that all our experience will guide the reader to the successful and joyful gardening that has brought us so many hours of pleasure—without having to repeat all of our experiments and mistakes.

The changes in gardening in Central Texas since the appearance of *The Central Texas Gardener* in 1980 are astonishing. At that time little gardening information for the area was readily available, and since much gardening lore and information was passed down from generation to generation, newcomers to the area were left to much trial-and-error gardening. Today, lack of information is less a problem than its organization, selection, and use.

Other changes are the area's population explosion (most newcomers are from other areas of the country); the shifts in environmental attitudes and recreational interests of gardeners; and the shrinking time available in busy lifestyles. Interest in gardening has increased substantially, and personal attitudes and goals for gardening have changed almost as dramatically. Our houses today are built on smaller lots, and many of us would prefer a landscape design that frees us from tedious mowing chores. We are more conscious of efficient water consumption, and more of us wish to include birds, butterflies, and other wildlife was well as flowers and vegetables in our gardens. Plant growers have responded to these demands with a broader variety of plants to grow in our gardens and landscape.

More people, more plants, more information, more choices. In *The New Central Texas Gardener,* we aim to respond to these changes with practical and realistic information that is easy to use. Acknowledging that the vast majority of us acquire started plants at garden centers, we have eliminated the chapter on propagation of plants and we have added a new chapter, "Tools of the Trade." While covering all of the basic equipment a gardener needs to get started, that discussion is not limited to the shovel, hoe, and rake. "Tools of the Trade" also includes what we believe are superb print resources, helpful Internet locations, and references to the many excellent resources available through state agencies, county horticultural extension agents, and Texas A&M University Extension Service.

We know from hearing from readers of the first edition that most people use this as a reference book, reading at any given sitting only the chapter relating to their garden issue of the moment. That is why we emphasize the importance of appropriate plant selection, correct siting, and cultural practices by repeating this information throughout.

Included in our selections are a few plants that are less than ideally suited to Central Texas conditions. Some of these plants are extremely popular and would be missed if omitted; a very few are, admittedly, a nod to personal favorites. We have tried to qualify their use in our area.

We garden quite differently than we did when we started out. Interests wax and wane, plants and ideas come and go, and personal philosophies change. But we garden more avidly than ever, always learning, always looking forward to the new. While the act of gardening may be solitary, learning about gardening is not. Learning about gardening involves dialogue and active listening. Hence we acknowledge those gardeners who have given of their time and sage advice. Bill Koenig shared his considerable knowledge about trees. Trey Wyatt and Barbara Ballard educated us on new turfgrass and lawn maintenance. Marilyn Good shared her knowledge of the "green industry" and emerging horticultural trends. Richard Hazeltine provided support and technical assistance. We are also grateful to David A. Anderson, professor at the University of Texas School of Law, Carl Morgan, climatologist with the U.S. Weather Service, and reporter Chuck Lindell of the *Austin American-Statesman* for their valuable aid. Ted Fisher, the amiable extension horticulturist in Cherokee County, provided advice and support when he was stationed in Travis County. And then there are the gardeners we know, neighbors and friends and members of local garden clubs, who have shared with us their experiences and secrets about enabling gardens to grow—wisdom and knowledge we in turn now share. We are grateful for the editorial assistance we received from Joann Lovelace and Sue Thornton, whose keen eyes, not to mention encyclopedic knowledge of grammar and form, have made this book more readable. The authors, of course, accept responsibility for any errors. We thank our photographer, Jeffrey Lava, for his generous gift of time and talent, and Kate Bergquist for her charming illustrations.

Most importantly, we are indebted to Joan Filvaroff. Her enthusiasm, energy, and graceful writing made *The Central Texas Gardener* happen almost twenty years ago, when gardening in Central Texas was a new adventure for us. We are also grateful for her helpful and valuable contribution to *The New Central Texas Gardener.*

Brilliant though he was, Thomas Jefferson, our third president, acknowledged that as a gardener he was constantly learning. We hope this book helps to make you a more knowledgeable gardener; writing it has done the same for us.

THE NEW CENTRAL TEXAS GARDENER

❦ 1 ❧

The Climate Where We Live

In the spring I have counted one hundred and thirty-six
different kinds of weather inside of twenty-four hours.
MARK TWAIN, "NEW ENGLAND WEATHER"

Most Central Texans agree that they live in the best part of the country, if not the world. Ample sunshine, an abundance of greenery, and a great expanse of beautiful skies delight the natives and attract an increasing number of migrants from the north.

One of our friends insists that summer is the only sure season in Texas—sure to be hot; the rest of the year, almost anything can happen. Another popular saying here is, "If you don't like the weather, just stick around for twenty-four hours." Both maxims speak to the great and sudden shifts in weather, particularly in winter when northers—cold winds out of the north—appear, often dropping the temperature fifty degrees Fahrenheit in a matter of hours. While all of Central Texas shares this fickleness of weather, there are noticeable variations in the general climate from north to south and from east to west, even in this relatively limited area. Within our subtropical region, Dallas and Fort Worth are more apt to have a taste of snow in the winter or, worse yet, of the ice that comes when it's too cold for rain. The northern part of our region is also likely to be somewhat cooler in the summer.

From May through September warm, humid, tropical air, swept in from the Gulf of Mexico by prevailing south-southeasterly winds, dominates the Texas weather scene. Moving across the hot land, the warm air gives rise to those glorious cumulus clouds so characteristic of the Texas summer sky. This same tropical air mass that is responsible for our thundershowers and an occasional hail storm also prevents air pollutants from accumulating in Central Texas.

These climatic conditions strongly affect gardening in Central Texas. To be more precise, which plants grow and how well they grow is determined largely by three major climatic factors: temperature, water supply, and light (length of day and intensity of sunlight). Two of these factors, temperature and light, are beyond the control of the backyard gardener, and her or his success will increase with the acknowledgment of that fact and the attempt to work in harmony with these realities. These elements are interrelated and so variable—especially in Texas—that gardening is a different experience every season. Perhaps that's why we always have something to say about the weather.

TEMPERATURE

The Central Texas climate is really dominated by two features: prolonged high temperatures in summer and sudden shifts of temperature in winter. Temperatures in our region top 90 degrees Fahrenheit on between 87 and 116 days annually, whereas there are only 24 to 44 days in winter when the mercury drops to 32 degrees or lower. But those 90-degree days tell only a partial story. Many warm areas of the country see their temperatures fall significantly at night (e.g., Wichita, Kansas; Albuquerque, New Mexico; Sacramento, California), giving plants much relief from the blistering heat. In Central Texas, though, minimum temperatures for July and August rarely dip below 73 degrees, and this is at night.

High average temperatures and the frequent abrupt changes we have in our weather influence our plant selection and care. Because cold fronts often arrive overnight, depart just as suddenly, and may follow each other in quick succession, plants may not have time to provide their own natural defenses. If they fail to go fully dormant or if they bloom prematurely, for example, a quick hard freeze can kill them. Even evergreens are more likely to be damaged by a sudden drop in temperature than by a slower drop, which would give them time to acclimatize. Nonetheless, unless a freeze is unusually long, hard, or sudden, even bulb plants such as ranunculus and anemone, which may appear before their prescribed time, will survive nicely in the mild Central Texas winter.

Although Central Texas is best suited to semihardy and subtropical plants, one is constantly tempted by occasional minor successes and attractive offerings at the nursery to try one's hand at varieties better adapted to other temperature zones. Gardeners in San Antonio may be fooled into thinking that they can consistently grow bananas after one or two atypical harvests, while Dallasites may eschew wise advice to regard tulips as annuals if several successive cold seasons result in successful blossoms. And in Austin, ever-hopeful residents frequently try for the best of all possible worlds, planting species from the tropical, semihardy, and hardy categories. Some years it works, but don't count on favorable results over the long term.

While gardeners cannot change the temperature at will—don't we wish—there are several techniques we can use to cheat the temperature and improve chances of carrying plants through until our warmer weather arrives. Site selection can make a big difference in plant survival. A light-colored stone or brick wall, for example, will absorb heat during the day and radiate it out at night, protecting nearby plants. And if you combine a heat-absorbing wall with a southern exposure, chances for survival increase even more. Similarly, fences, hedges, and other plants can provide protection. So, when selecting a site for a plant, consider winter conditions.

Protective coverings can also insulate tender species. Garden centers and supply houses carry row covers or garden quilts to be used with wire supports to drape over plants for some freeze protection. You can also use sheets and blankets from the house. Do not, however, use plastic. Plastic will transmit rather than ward off the cold, and you will end up causing more damage than you set out to prevent. There are other products on the market (e.g., a water-filled plastic teepee that fits around young tomato plants and protects them at below-freezing temperatures) that can help during cold snaps. Check with your local garden center for new products.

While temperature is an important consideration for all plants, it becomes a more significant concern for the vegetable garden. Temperature defines the growing season, which lasts generally from the last to the first freeze (see map 1 for first and last freeze dates in Central Texas). Not all plants, however, do equally well through the whole growing season. For each species there is a minimum, optimum, and maximum growth temperature. The optimum temperature will vary according to the growth stage of the plant; seedlings have lower optimum temperatures than the same plants at a more mature stage. Thus temperature affects not only which plants are ideally suited for a region but also when they should be planted. (see map 1.)

Information about optimal temperatures is seldom available to the average gardener, and certainly it is not our intention to burden you with statistics and jargon. But it is helpful when you are selecting varieties, particularly vegetable varieties, to understand that these differences in temperature tolerances are why

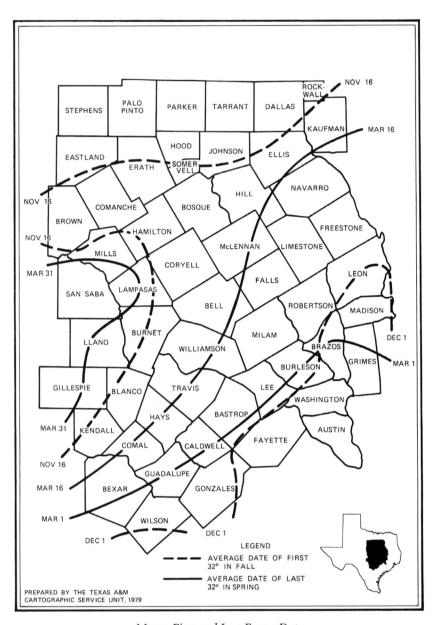

STEPHENS · PALO PINTO · PARKER · TARRANT · DALLAS

ROCK-WALL · NOV 16

KAUFMAN · MAR 16

EASTLAND · HOOD · JOHNSON · ELLIS

ERATH · SOMER-VELL

NOV 16

NAVARRO

HILL

COMANCHE · BOSQUE

BROWN

NOV 16

FREESTONE

HAMILTON

McLENNAN · LIMESTONE

MILLS

CORYELL

MAR 31

LEON

SAN SABA · LAMPASAS

FALLS

BELL · ROBERTSON · MADISON

BURNET · MILAM

DEC 1

LLANO

WILLIAMSON

BRAZOS

GRIMES · MAR 1

BURLESON

GILLESPIE · BLANCO · TRAVIS · LEE

WASHINGTON

HAYS · BASTROP

AUSTIN

MAR 31 · KENDALL

COMAL · CALDWELL · FAYETTE

NOV 16

GUADALUPE

MAR 16 · BEXAR · GONZALES

MAR 1

WILSON

DEC 1

DEC 1

LEGEND

- - - - AVERAGE DATE OF FIRST
32° IN FALL

———— AVERAGE DATE OF LAST
32° IN SPRING

PREPARED BY THE TEXAS A&M
CARTOGRAPHIC SERVICE UNIT, 1979

Map 1. First and Last Freeze Dates

some vegetables are classified as cool-season crops and others are warm-season crops. Those that are cool-season crops put on their best growth while temperatures are moderate in the spring and fall. Warm-season plants will do best when planted so that peak summer temperatures occur during their growth stage. In Central Texas, generally high summer temperatures over an extended period favor planting warm-season crops. Cool-season crops must be planted more judiciously.

Since Central Texas covers a large region, with variation in altitude and proximity to the Gulf Coast and substantial differences in distance from the equator, there are important variations in the growing season for areas even within this region. Map 2 sketches three zones within Central Texas based on average length of the warm season. (see map 2.)

The growing season in Central Texas is long. At our northern boundary, Dallas–Forth Worth, the season lasts 240 days, with the average first frost occurring about November 12 and the last frost on March 17. Austin has a 260-day season, with the first frost expected near November 22 and the last frost about March 7. In Waco, first frost comes about November 18, and the average last freeze date is March 16. In San Antonio, the average first freeze comes around November 26, and the last about March 3, giving that area an average frost-free period of 268 days. The extended growing period our area enjoys means that vegetable gardeners get a chance to put in two crops a year (for planting dates, see chapter 12, "Vegetables").

LIGHT

Light affects the growth as well as food and seed production of plants. As there are warm-season and cool-season plants, there are also short-day and long-day plants—that is, plants that need more or fewer hours of sun each day. Goldenrod, hibiscus, and spinach are examples of long-day plants; salvia, asters, and chrysanthemums prefer shorter periods of daylight. Asparagus, narcissus, and foxglove are not especially sensitive to the length of day. Our suburban fall garden, surrounded by tall trees, always fades as the days gro{ /horter and the light from a lower sun is blocked by the house and trees.

Gardeners obviously cannot add hours to the day or subtract them, but we can use siting to influence the amount of sun plants receive. Plants recommended for full sun in many gardening books and on seed-packet instructions can often do well in Central Texas in partial shade, particularly if it comes in midafternoon.

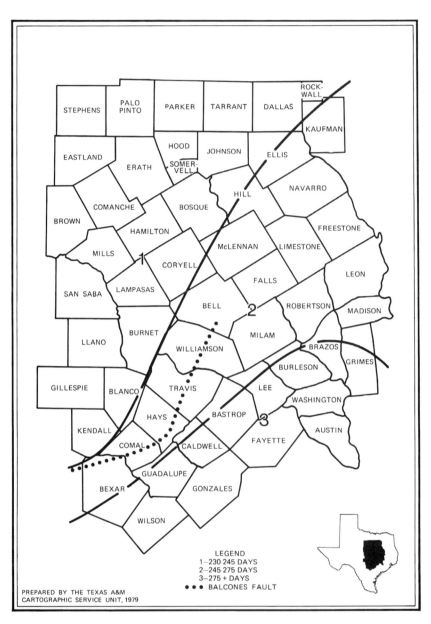

LEGEND
1 — 230-245 DAYS
2 — 245-275 DAYS
3 — 275 + DAYS
● ● ● BALCONES FAULT

Map 2. Average Length of the Warm Season

WATER

Many ornamental plants and vegetables we want to grow would not survive our climate if we were not able to affect their water supply. Heat, periods of low humidity, and wind increase the rates of evaporation and transpiration (the process by which water and carbon dioxide are exchanged through cells in the leaves), meaning that plants experience a moisture deficit. Plants growing in soils with little capacity to hold water (especially sandy soils) will need watering more frequently than those in better soils. This is another reason why the gardener must pay attention to where plants are sited, in order to assure convenient watering. It may even be a good idea to consider installing an underground watering system before beginning a lawn and basic landscaping (see chapter 4, "The Home Landscape").

Rainfall in Texas is just as erratic as the sudden changes in winter temperature already discussed. Not only is the rain unevenly distributed through the state; the amount may vary tremendously from year to year. In the Hill Country, rain tends to come in torrents with long dry spells in between. Generally in Texas, precipitation increases as one goes from west to east. The average annual precipitation range for our section of the state is twenty-seven to thirty-six inches. However, during the last decade, climatic changes associated with El Niño in 1991–92 and again in 1997–98 have brought annual rainfall 150–160 percent of the norm.

April, May, and June are our wettest months, with September often spilling rains from dissipating tropical storms. Winter precipitation often comes in the forms of drizzle, light rains, and fog. In other seasons, violent thunderstorms, occasionally accompanied by hail, are common. On September 9 and 10, 1921, for example, Thrall, Texas, experienced the worst rainstorm ever recorded in the continental United States, when 38.2 inches of rain fell in a twenty-four-hour period.

Current theories hold that torrential rains occur when warm, moist air masses from the Gulf of Mexico collide with drier, cooler air from the north and west. These heavy cloudbursts occur more frequently along the Balcones Escarpment, a geological fault zone roughly paralleled by Interstate Highway 35 from San Antonio to Waco. Formed about forty million years ago when rock strata fractured, the fault is the site of numerous limestone springs that have long provided the water to attract human settlement. Native Americans camped along the fault line long before Europeans entered Texas.

Topographical features also determine how runoff from heavy rains is dissipated. Where natural drainage channels are gently sloped and valleys are flat and broad, runoff is relatively slow. This situation is more typical east of the Balcones Fault. In the Hill Country, where soils are shallow and slopes steep, runoff tends to be rapid and much of the water is consequently lost.

Weather in Central Texas is nothing if not capricious. One ill-timed frost, hailstorm, tornado, hot spell, or whatever can bring an entire vegetable season to a halt and can do severe damage to trees and landscape plants. The wise gardener therefore considers climate both in the original selection of plants and in the care taken to make the plants, especially non-natives, prosper.

🌿 2 🌿

Soil and Its Conditioning

Our soil belongs also to unborn generations.
SAM RAYBURN, "ON CONVERSATION"

Soil—a miraculous mixture of minerals, air, water, and organic matter—as old as the ages, ever changing, continuously renewed. How well it performs depends on its texture, structure, and chemistry. Ideally, it is composed of 45 percent inorganic minerals, 5 percent organic matter, and 50 percent pore space shared equally by air and water. The solid-matter particles should be balanced in size to permit good drainage, adequate aeration, and proper nutrient intake by vegetation. Soil of this quality rarely occurs in nature; most soil is, instead, a mix of three basic types.

SOIL TYPES

Clay is composed of minute, tightly arranged particles. When wet, it becomes sticky and plastic. Water drains slowly; erosion and water runoff become serious problems. Water replaces air in the pore space and slows the release of nutrients to the plants. During the dry season, clay hardens and cracks, upsetting root systems and hastening evaporation. Easily compacted, it is referred to as heavy soil.

Sand particles are large, as much as twenty-five times larger than clay particles. Sand drains too rapidly, causing nutrients to leach away before they can be used by plants.

Loam, a mixture of large and smaller particles, provides moderate drainage and good aeration. It is good for fast and deep root development and nutrient retention. Because well-drained soils tend to harbor fewer diseases, loam is a healthy soil.

Of the ten distinct vegetational designations of Texas, four converge in Central Texas, each with its own well-defined soil characteristics (see map 3). The eastern counties occupy regions identified as the Blackland Prairies and the Post Oak Savannah. These fertile prairies are extensively cultivated. Blackland Prairie soils are largely calcareous (containing calcium) clay, although there are large sections of acid, sandy loams. The Savannah soils are acid and generally loamy. Some sections of the rolling north-central Cross Timbers contain a large portion of rock fragments. There the sandy to clay loams are neutral or slightly acid. The soils of the Edwards Plateau, or Hill Country, are mainly clay on top of limestone. They range from fairly deep in the eastern section to very shallow with a good percentage of rock fragments in areas west of the Balcones Escarpment.

IMPROVING THE SOIL

How difficult it is to improve your soil depends on the kind of soil it is, its depth, and the number of rock fragments you have to remove. For example, in clay soils the seemingly overwhelming problems of poor drainage, inadequate aeration, and limited nutrient retention can be corrected by spading or rototilling in sand, gypsum, and organic matter (peat moss, compost, or manure). The sand and gypsum help create air spaces and lighten the soil. Organic matter benefits soil by holding the fine clay particles together in large "crumbs" and by releasing nutrients as the matter decays. This decomposition takes place rapidly at first, then slows considerably as the organic material becomes humus (an advanced state of decomposed organic matter). Since humus eventually breaks down into elements, organic matter must be added repeatedly to maintain good soil structure.

If you live in the Hill Country, you may also hit caliche—crusty layers of calcium carbonate in some of our soils. The depth of the caliche may vary from several inches to several feet. If it's too deep, you may want to plant in another location or in a raised bed. Shallow caliche can be broken up with a pickax and discarded.

Having come to terms with rocks and caliche, you are ready to attack the clay. First, rototill or dig the soil to about one spade's depth, eight or nine inches, if possible. Spread sand or gypsum to a depth of two inches and organic matter to a depth of four inches, and incorporate them by digging or rototilling

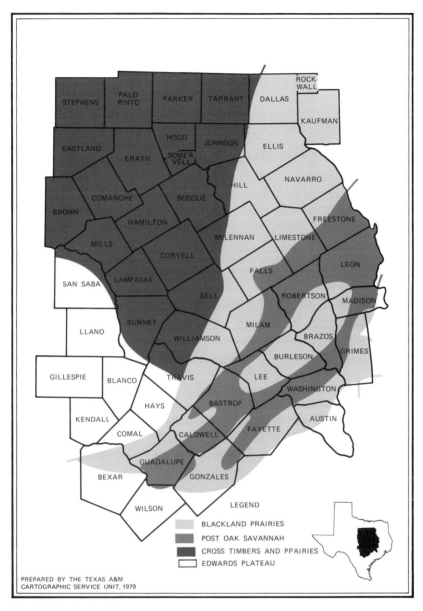

ROCK-
WALL

STEPHENS PALO PARKER TARRANT DALLAS
PINTO
KAUFMAN

EASTLAND HOOD JOHNSON ELLIS
SOMER
ERATH VELL

HILL NAVARRO

COMANCHE BOSQUE
BROWN FREESTONE
HAMILTON
MILLS McLENNAN LIMESTONE
CORYELL LEON
FALLS
SAN SABA LAMPASAS
BELL ROBERTSON MADISON

BURNET MILAM
LLANO BRAZOS
WILLIAMSON GRIMES
BURLESON

GILLESPIE TRAVIS LEE
BLANCO WASHINGTON
HAYS BASTROP
KENDALL AUSTIN
COMAL FAYETTE
CALDWELL
GUADALUPE
BEXAR GONZALES

WILSON LEGEND

BLACKLAND PRAIRIES
POST OAK SAVANNAH
CROSS TIMBERS AND PRAIRIES
EDWARDS PLATEAU

PREPARED BY THE TEXAS A&M
CARTOGRAPHIC SERVICE UNIT, 1979

Map 3. Soils of Central Texas. From Frank W. Gould, Texas Plants:
A Checklist and Ecological Summary, *MP-585/Revised (College Station:
Texas Agricultural Experiment Station, 1975).*

again. Your labors will be well rewarded when you're able to prevent the formation of hardpan, an impervious layer of soil particles so tightly packed together that drainage is impossible. A deadly condition for plants, hardpan is a serious problem in clay soils that receive heavy foot traffic, particularly in wet seasons.

Should you live in one of the few pockets of sandy soil that our region contains, you can improve your soil's ability to retain moisture and nutrients by adding two to three inches of compost or humus and working it well into the soil.

If these chores sound arduous, don't despair. Turning heavy clay into friable soil (crumbling easily when damp) that supports and sustains thriving plants is one of gardening's great satisfactions.

While expensive, importing good garden soil can be an appropriate alternative, especially for small areas and to create raised beds. Beware of bargains and make sure what gets delivered to your yard is what you ordered. Ask your dealer about the soil's origin and whether it is weed free. Many dealers now offer a variety of mixes adapted to the plants you wish to grow—suitable for roses, for example, or for vegetables.

The particle composition of soil is not the only characteristic to affect gardening. Among other factors are the pH level and availability of nutrients.

MAKING SOIL

While this chapter, and indeed the entire book, are devoted to gardening in the soil, there are times when gardeners may need to make their growing medium. Soil is needed for potted plants and hanging baskets, plants being "grown out" for planting in beds around the house, and for potting tender plants so they can be brought in for protection from the winter. In each of these cases a lighter soil provides the best environment. One of the best recipes we have found comes from Doug Blachly, a renowned Austin gardener. His formula meets all of the criteria for soil: soil matter, fertility, and air space. It is a simple, but effective, mix:

2 parts compost or potting soil (or part of each)

1 part peat moss

1 part perlite

Try the mixture. It has worked well for us as it has for Doug, which is why we call it Blachly's Blend.

SOIL pH

The acidity or alkalinity of soil is measured on a pH scale from 0 (most acid) to 14 (most alkaline); pH 7 is considered neutral. When the pH is too high or too low, the availability of nutrients to the plants is reduced, and the resulting deficiencies lead to poor growth. Although most things will grow in soil with a pH between 4 and 8, most fruits, flowers, and vegetables do best in soil with a pH between 6.5 and 7.0.

In many areas of Central Texas, the soil is very alkaline, with a pH of 7.5 to 8.5. At these levels iron is unavailable to plants, and the resulting deficiency, iron chlorosis, is a common but treatable problem. Symptoms of iron chlorosis are easy to identify: yellowing leaves with green veins. Copperas, compost, sulfur, iron sulfate, or cottonseed meal should be added to the soil to help reduce its pH.

Excessive acidity can be quickly reduced by adding lime, but this is not a common problem in Central Texas.

Soil pH should be checked before you embark on any major planting. Also, find out the pH preference of the plants you wish to grow and decide whether you want the extra trouble of maintaining the proper soil pH. If not, substitute plants more tolerant of the native soil. Keep in mind, too, that the water of much of this area is alkaline.

PLANT NUTRIENTS

Plants require sixteen nutrients. The three primary nutrients, which are needed in the greatest quantities, are nitrogen (N), phosphorus (P), and potassium (K).

Nitrogen stimulates growth and the production of plant protein and gives plants rich green color. It is especially important for leafy vegetables and large-leafed plants. However, it is an element that quickly gets leached away. Plants that suffer from nitrogen deficiency may yellow, and their older leaves may drop. Stunted growth, delay in bud opening, smaller leaves, fewer flowers, and smaller fruit may also result from a lack of nitrogen.

On the other hand, beware of the consequences of nitrogen oversupply: too-rapid growth that results in spindly, weak stems, too much leaf growth, and plants that bloom too late in the season.

Phosphorus stimulates vigorous growth of seedlings, the production of fibrous roots, and seed production. It is important for efficient use of soil moisture by plants and for production of plant sugars. Plants deficient in phosphorus display symptoms similar to those of nitrogen deficiency. However, the leaves of phosphorus-deficient plants are usually dull green, tinged with purple. Often the entire plant is dwarfed. Happily, there is little danger of plants suffering from excess phosphorus.

Potassium's role in plant nutrition is less easily defined than that of nitrogen or phosphorus. It is believed that potassium contributes to normal cell growth through cell division and that it acts as a catalyst in the formation of proteins, fat, and carbohydrates. Plants are heavy users of potassium, and a lack of it results in leaves that turn ashen and have curled tips and edges.

Calcium, magnesium, and sulfur are secondary nutrients, generally supplied by soil. The eight remaining nutrients—iron, zinc, manganese, boron, molybdenum, copper, sodium, cobalt, nickel, and chlorine—are trace elements. In our alkaline soils, iron and manganese are present but frequently inaccessible to plants, as previously mentioned in the soil pH section.

Soil testing kits are available that measure soil pH and indicate the amounts of nitrogen, phosphorus, and potassium your soil needs. Accuracy may be hard to achieve because it depends on the tester's ability to match the colors of the tested soil to a color chart. We think your best bet is to take advantage of the comprehensive soil testing service available through your county agricultural extension agent and performed at Texas A&M University. For a nominal fee, your soil is tested for nitrogen, phosphorous, and potassium, for trace elements, and for pH. Recommendations for soil improvement will be made according to its intended use: lawns, vegetables, or flowers.

For analysis, send soil samples to: Soil Testing Laboratory, Texas Agricultural Extension Service, College Station, Texas 77843. Special mailers are available at your county agricultural extension agent's office. To find the office, check your local phone book (blue pages in most directories, business pages in others) under the county in which you live. It will be found in the county government listings.

FERTILIZER

Even a casual reading of gardening literature quickly reveals a plethora of recommendations for fertilizing. The confusion this causes is only compounded when your nursery doesn't carry the particular formula you ask for but offers a substitute that you are not sure is comparable. Inevitably an old-timer appears insisting that his or her magical concoction works wonders for every living thing, or an organic gardener insists on only organic fertilizers. Confronted with a blur of fact and lore, most of us who garden for pleasure are left completely frustrated.

Generally, 5-10-5 is a good formula for a balanced fertilizer. The numbers refer to the percentage of nutrients contained in the fertilizer mixture. Since the numbers always are given in the same order—nitrogen (N), phosphorous (P), and potassium (K)—a hundred-pound bag of 5-10-5 would contain five pounds of nitrogen, ten pounds of phosphorous, and five pounds of potassium. The remaining eighty pounds are inert materials used to "carry" the fertilizer. While 5-10-5 is an excellent balanced fertilizer for many garden needs, certain circumstances require special mixes, which we discuss later.

Fertilizer applications should be made according to the kind, age, and special needs of the plant(s), but guidelines for 5-10-5 fertilizer offer a good general picture and a basis for comparison.

Flower beds	3–5 lbs. per 100 sq. ft.
Bulbs	1–3 lbs. per 100 sq. ft.
Vegetables	3–5 lbs. per 100 sq. ft.
Evergreen shrubs	3–6 lbs. per 100 sq. ft.
Evergreen trees	2 lbs. per inch diameter of tree at chest height
Deciduous ornamental trees	2–4 lbs. per inch diameter of tree at chest height

Ideally, soil should be moist and foliage dry when fertilizer is applied. Always water thoroughly after fertilizing.

Organic vs. Inorganic Fertilizers

Before petrochemicals were introduced to agriculture and gardening, farmers and gardeners met their crops' and plants' nutrient needs with manure, cottonseed meal, bone meal, and blood meal. While many gardeners today insist that these organic sources are preferable to inorganics such as superphosphate, iron chelate, and ammonium sulfate, it is difficult to find experimental evidence of differences in plants nourished by organic versus inorganic nutrients. Releasing their nutrients more slowly, organics are longer lasting than chemical fertilizers and are usually formulated in lower concentrations, reducing pollution runoff in our waterways. They are also more expensive. Whether you use organic or inorganic fertilizer, it is important to remember always to refer to the application recommendations on the label. It is tempting to think that if one scoop is good, using a bit more will be better, or to broadcast just a few extra handfuls. Wrong. Too much fertilizer will result in "burning" your plants and injury to soil organisms such as earthworms; too little and your plants will fail to thrive.

Recently, foliar feeding has gained popularity. This method involves mixing water-soluble chemicals with a prescribed amount of water and applying the mixture directly to the entire plant with a watering can or sprayer. Because leaves absorb most efficiently in the morning, it is best to apply foliar fertilizer at that time of day. Be sure to wet both sides of the foliage thoroughly. To be most effective, this method of feeding flowers, vegetables, shrubs, and small trees should be practiced every ten days to two weeks from the first feeding in early spring until the end of September, when most growth (fall vegetable and flower gardens being the exceptions) begins to slow.

COMPOST

Mix a pile of damp leaves, grass clippings, and some vegetable wastes from the kitchen, and within several months you can be harvesting a crop of "black gold." We have already discussed the importance of organic matter to soil structure and chemistry. Compost is the least expensive and most readily available source of organic matter.

Making a compost pile is a pleasure. Its appeal is easily understood, for composting is the ultimate recycling and can be practiced on a very simple level. Composting is a dynamic process—the decomposition of organic matter by microorganisms—and an understanding of what goes on inside that heap of vegetative wastes can prevent you from coming up with just another pile of soggy leaves at the end of the year.

Two types of bacteria decompose organic matter: aerobic bacteria, which live in the presence of air, and anaerobic bacteria, which live in a wet, airless environment. Anaerobic bacteria tend to smell bad and work more slowly; they are responsible for many people's fears about a compost pile. Fortunately, they can be replaced by the aerobic variety by keeping the pile moist, but not soggy, and by turning the compost to introduce oxygen. Confining composting materials in a bin (roughly four feet square and four feet high) constructed of hardware cloth or wooden slats prevents leaves, grass, etc., from scattering and allows sufficient heat buildup. For convenience, compost bins, usually of black vinyl, are readily available at nurseries, garden centers, and hardware stores.

Bins range in design and price from simple and inexpensive to sophisticated and pricey. They tend to keep things neat and, given the proper ratio of ingredients, cooking right along. They are excellent where space is limited.

Heat is generated by the multiplying organisms; its presence indicates that the compost pile is functioning. The optimum temperature range for a compost pile is 104 to 140 degrees Fahrenheit. At around 158 degrees, the pile will suffer "thermal kill" and will cool to somewhere within the optimal range. It is a delight on a frosty morning to see the steam rise when you wiggle that aerating stick in the middle of the bin and know that everything is going just fine.

Moisture is another critical factor in the environment of bacteria. A healthy compost pile will be between 40 and 60 percent moisture, or as damp as a squeezed sponge. Below 40 percent, the rate of decomposition will decline; above 60 percent you risk having anaerobic bacteria, with their accompanying odors, take over.

Carbon and nitrogen present in organic matter provide the fuel and building materials for bacterial growth. The proper proportions of these two elements—expressed as the carbon/nitrogen or C/N ratio—are essential to composting success. Too little nitrogen will result in failure of the compost to heat up and a slow rate of decomposition. The optimal ratio is in the range of twenty-six to thirty-five parts carbon for each part nitrogen.

What to Add to the Compost Pile

Because the C/N ratio is the most important aspect of composting, we provide a list of carbonaceous and nitrogenous materials suitable for use:

C (carbonaceous)

leaves
hay, straw
sawdust
wood chips
chopped cornstalks

N (nitrogenous)

vegetable kitchen waste—when using kitchen waste, be sure
    to bury it well into the pile to avoid attracting vermin
    and wildlife
weeds—do not use any that have gone to seed
plant residues from garden and grass clippings

Grinding organic materials (particularly cornstalks and the woody parts of plants) is helpful but not necessary. It speeds the decomposition process. A variety of textures provides for air circulation and prevents compaction. Finished compost has a dark, rich color, an earthy odor, and a fluffy structure. Often the origin of the materials can still be identified.

You can see from the list that nitrogenous materials tend to be green, succulent, or leafy in comparison with woody, drier carbonaceous materials. If the compost seems to be working too slowly, you can add a little nitrogen in the form of fertilizer or some more grass clippings.

What Not to Add to the Compost Pile

What you do not add to a compost pile is as important as what you do use.

Avoid chemically treated wood products. Sawdust from tree pruning is fine, but it is best not to use sawdust from construction sites. Wood used in construction can be chemically treated, sometimes with very undesirable materials such as arsenic, copper, and chromium.

Don't add poisonous plants such as poison ivy.

Avoid diseased plants and weeds that have gone to seed. Your home compost pile may not reach the temperature of 140 degrees required to kill off seeds.

Don't use animal products, including pet manures and meat products. Meat wastes are attractive to wildlife and neighborhood pets and are certain to spell trouble. Pet manures may carry organisms dangerous to people.

From time to time, we do see insects in the outermost layers of the pile, but they never appear in the finished product. Earthworms, on the other hand, are frequently a bonus product of compost.

All composting methods are based on the requirements discussed, which bear repeating:

1. C/N ratio
2. moisture
3. aeration
4. sufficient size for heat retention

Chemical analyses show nitrogen levels of compost to be between 1 and 3 percent and phosphorous and potassium levels under 1 percent. For this reason, compost should never be considered a substitute for fertilizer. Instead, it should be used as a soil conditioner to increase water-holding capacity, to provide air space and nutrients for soil microorganisms, and to improve soil texture. Compost is also an excellent mulch.

❦ 3 ❦

Tools of the Trade

Though an old man, I am but a young gardener.
THOMAS JEFFERSON

Since the first budding gardener sharpened a stick, dragged it across the ground, and created a planting furrow, the eternal question has been asked: "I wonder if I could put an engine on this thing?" The search for that proper tool, be it equipment or knowledge, continues. Thomas Jefferson's admission that he needed more information about horticulture—more tools for this trade—was written to a friend when Jefferson was eighty-one years old. In this chapter we explore the tools gardeners can use to create and maintain a garden, from the trusty trowel to the Internet.

EQUIPMENT

Today's gardening implements are but sophisticated improvements on that sharp stick. Indeed, the dibble, a wooden shaft with a metal point used to plant bulbs, is the current version of the sharp stick. A gardener can create an equipment inventory that includes gas or electric powered mowers, blowers, mulchers, trimmers, edgers, and other exotica. And yet, the dibble and the equipment that soon followed—forks and shovels—are still necessary components of any gardener's toolshed. The following inventory we consider minimal for tending your yard and garden:

HOSES. All plants need water, and unless you have an extensive irrigation system you will need water hoses. Measure from your faucets to the farthest reaches of your yard and buy appropriate lengths of hose. Garden hoses can be left outside most of the year except when it freezes. When a freeze is imminent, coil the hoses and put them in a warmer location. The garage will be fine.

Should you want to avoid hauling hoses and sprayers from garden bed to garden bed but also avoid installing a full-fledged irrigation system, you can use porous soaker hoses. They drip, or leak, water at the ground level and are more efficient than sprayers. Soaker hoses come in hard and soft versions, depending of the type of material used for construction. Like conventional garden hoses, they should be brought in when a freeze is forecast.

SPRINKLERS AND NOZZLES. Hose-end lawn sprinklers come in a variety of shapes, sizes, and patterns at various prices. What kind to use depends on your yard's geometry—square, rectangular, or irregular. Less water is lost to evaporation when delivered in heavy drops close to the ground. For all yard chores from watering flower beds to washing windows, we like nozzles with several settings. Rotate the head and you can go from gentle spray to sharp water jet, which is perfect for knocking those pesky aphids from your plants.

SHOVELS. You will need at least two kinds of shovels. A sharpshooter has a long, slender, rounded shovel blade with a short handle. It is used for chopping, trenching, moving small plants, and general purpose work. A round-point shovel has a longer handle and, as its name implies, a blade "rounded" to a point. It is used for digging holes and moving soil. Remember, shovels are for digging, and given our heavy soils, they need to be sharp. Periodically sharpen your shovel with a metal file.

FORK. If you turn soil, and you will if you garden, a four-tined fork is essential. It is used for loosening, turning, and mixing soil and for working in soil amendments. The fork also is handy for coaxing stubborn roots when transplanting small trees and shrubs.

HOE. This is an indispensable tool for weeding, making planting rows, tamping soil, and other odd jobs. Some newer models have a curved metal piece, called a swan neck, from the end of the handle to the blade. This eases some of the chopping and digging action required to dig weeds or form raised beds.

RAKES. A leaf rake is necessary unless you have no trees in your yard. Even if you don't have trees your neighbors probably do, and on a windy day your neighbor's leaves will become yours. So get a leaf rake. A garden rake is a necessity to rake soil, to smooth turned or tilled areas, and to adjust garden contours.

MOWER. Assuming that you do have grass but don't have goats, you will find a mower a real necessity. There are two types of mowers (powered and manual) with two types of actions (reel and rotary). The reel mower's blades revolve against a cutting bar and cut the grass against it. This provides the most uniform cut and comes either gas powered or gardener powered (that is, you push). These are best for zoysiagrass. The rotary mower's blade revolves on a horizontal plane. As the blade turns at high speeds, the sharp ends shear off the grass. These mowers come in either gas- or electric-powered models and are best for buffalograss, St. Augustinegrass, and bermudagrass. Most new models are constructed to mulch grass, eliminating the need for a catcher. A rotary blade dulls quite quickly under normal use and should be sharpened regularly (every six to eight weeks during the mowing season). Grinding wheels that fit on power drills are available at hardware and garden stores. After sharpening, make sure that the blade is balanced so it won't damage the engine.

EDGER. After mowing, edging is the finishing touch that many people overlook, but one that makes the yard look trim and well kept. You have three choices in edgers. The first is manual—more of the sharp-stick technology. This type of edger does not do well with our tough southern turfgrasses. The two other choices are either gas powered or electric. They, in turn, come in two cutting types: blade and string. The former has a metal blade that spins at high speed and trims grass evenly; this type works best along driveways, walks, and other hard-surface-to-grass areas. In the string edger, a length of plastic line spins at high speed, shearing the grass. This can work along hard-surface-to-grass areas and can also be used with care around trees and other areas in the yard. Be sure to avoid slashing tree bark and shrub stems. Always don protective eyewear when using edgers—they routinely throw up small rocks and other debris.

SAWS. At least one good pruning saw is handy to have for removing dead and diseased limbs from trees and for shaping trees and bushes. If you leave most of the riskier work to professional tree trimmers, the saw you need can be small and compact.

PRUNERS. Shrubs, bushes, and small tree limbs periodically need to be trimmed back. There are two types of pruners. Anvil types have a blade that comes down upon a cutting bar, which tends to crush the limb. The pass-through type are like scissors with two cutting blades passing alongside each other. We prefer the pass-through type because it cuts more cleanly. If you have larger limbs to cut you can purchase a lopper, essentially a pruner with long handles to provide more leverage.

HAND TOOLS. When you work in a garden bed two tools are essential: a trowel and a cultivator. A trowel's blade looks like a small, thin round-point shovel. Make sure you buy one that has a thin blade and a sharp edge. You will need these features to cut into garden soil. A cultivator is a three- or four-tined tool used to loosen soil and dig up weeds.

This inventory will get you through many gardening seasons. But if you are like most gardeners, you will soon want more. Before long you will find yourself drifting toward the garden tool display thinking, "If only I had that flat-bladed shovel I could . . ." You have been properly warned, and we do not accept responsibility for your actions.

SOURCES OF INFORMATION

If there are increasingly sophisticated and specialized items to choose from in gardening equipment, this is even more the case with the burgeoning information now available in various forms.

An important source of information specifically geared for our area is the Agricultural Extension Service at Texas A&M University, which produces some of the highest quality gardening literature anywhere. And it's free, to boot. Drop by your local county extension office and check the pamphlets that are in their inventory. You will find short articles on a wide variety of topics. And if the county horticultural extension agent or a volunteer master gardener is around, you can probably get some free advice as well.

Books

At the end of this book is a bibliography. We want the reader to know, however, that there are a few books we consult regularly when we are in need of information and when we are curious about a particular plant or want to look at some nice pictures for ideas about plants and landscapes. Like Jefferson, we too are young gardeners. This short list of important books (presented in alphabetical order by author) is quite personal, reflecting our own gardening interests as well as our preferences for certain writers.

Geyata Ajilvsgi. *Butterfly Gardening for the South.* Dallas: Taylor Publishing Co., 1990, 242 pages. Being limited to the South is a major strength of this book. The author explores in depth various stages of the butterflies' lives, the plants that support them, butterfly-friendly pest controls, and organizations that support butterfly conservation. Excellent color photographs make butterfly identification easy.

Better Homes and Gardens. *Step by Step Landscaping.* Des Moines: Meredith Corp., 1991, 336 pages. This is an easy-to-follow guide to planning, shaping the land, and building basic garden structures.

Sam Cottner. *The Vegetable Book.* Waco: TG Press, 1985, 421 pages. In this complete guide to vegetable gardening in Texas, a chapter is devoted to each of the vegetables we can grow in the state. The author is head of the horticultural program at Texas A&M University.

Joe Eck. *Elements of Garden Design.* New York: Henry Holt and Co., 1996, 164 pages. An inspiring and elegant book that explores the basics of garden design while conveying the magic and mystery of the garden.

Penelope Hobhouse. *Color in Your Garden.* Boston: Little, Brown and Company, 1984, 239 pages. Inspiring and gorgeous, this authoritative tome by Great Britain's doyenne of gardening tells you everything you ever wanted to know about color—from the color wheel to uses of color in the garden throughout the seasons. While the plant materials are not always appropriate for Central Texas, the reader will learn much about color from the discussion and photographs.

William E. Knoop. *The Complete Guide to Texas Lawn Care.* Waco: TG Press, 1986, 136 pages. This is a concise work on turfgrasses that grow well in Texas. It starts at the beginning, with soil preparation, and moves on through to lawn maintenance. The text is enhanced with informative illustrations and photographs.

Stephen W. Kress. *The Bird Garden* (National Audubon Society). London: Dorling-Kindersley Publishing Co., 1995, 176 pages. An ornithological writer tells how to select vegetation that will attract birds. In this beautiful volume you will learn which birds are attracted to specific plants and how to plan for food, water, and shelter needs as well as nesting sites. The entire country is covered, region by region.

Helen Nash. *The Complete Pond Builder.* New York: Sterling Publishing Co., 1996, 144 pages. In a field crowded with information, this beautifully illustrated guide to pond gardening covers it all—site selection, construction, plant and fish selection—very succinctly.

Scott Ogden. *Garden Bulbs for the South.* Dallas: Taylor Publishing Co., 1994, 250 pages. If you want to grow bulbs and you live in Central Texas, then this book is a must. Find out why you've never had luck in our area with many traditional fall-planted bulbs and learn about some great new alternatives.

Neil Sperry. *Complete Guide to Texas Gardening,* 2nd edition. Dallas: Taylor Publishing Co., 1996, 388 pages. This is a comprehensive review of gardening in Texas. It is a good reference book for your gardening questions about soils, flowers, trees, and shrubs.

Elizabeth Stell. *Secrets to Great Soils.* Pownal, Vt.: Storey Communications, 1998, 224 pages (paperback). The author elaborates well on the saying "old as dirt." Since many of our soils are so difficult, we heartily recommend this book, which gives the whys and hows of our gardens' number one ingredient. How to develop fertile soil, the benefits of mulch and compost, and soil-working tools are entertainingly covered here.

Sally Wasowski with Andy Wasowski. *Native Texas Plants: Landscaping Region by Region.* Houston: Gulf Publishing Co., 1991, 408 pages. An extensive guide to native flowers, trees, shrubs, and ground covers, this handsome volume is extremely helpful to those who might wish to learn about Texas flora as well as those who garden. Their newer *Native Texas Gardens,* Houston: Gulf Publishing Co., 1997, 208 pages, is equally authoritative and attractive.

William C. Welch. *Perennial Garden Color.* Dallas: Taylor Publishing Co., 1989, 268 pages. This is a comprehensive review of perennials that grow well in the South, including Central Texas. The explanations are direct and informative and most of the photographs (there is at least one for each plant listed) will provide the gardener with an idea of how the plant will look when grown and in bloom.

Modesty precludes us from including *The New Central Texas Gardener* in this list. But, since you are obviously reading this book, why not just go ahead and put it on anyway?

Magazines

Numerous periodicals are devoted to gardening, of which two are particularly appropriate for Central Texas gardeners. (Annual subscription rates may change.)

Texas Gardener (P.O. Box 9005, Waco, TX 76714, bimonthly, subscription $16.95) tends toward propagation and vegetable gardening, although there are articles on annuals and perennials that do well in Texas.

Neil Sperry's Gardens (400 W. Louisiana, McKinney, TX 75069, ten issues per year, subscription $23.50), published in north Texas, focuses on landscape design and shrubs, trees, and flowers.

Internet

Providing access to outstanding university research programs, chat rooms, and shopping, the Internet has enlarged the gardener's world. We know firsthand that gardeners prefer moving dirt to surfing the Net, but days that are rainy, too hot, or too cold are perfect for going online. Since web sites come and go, and may get infrequent updating or may simply be abandoned, we have provided some major sites that have been up and active for a while, and we suggest that you search within by keyword. You will discover a whole new world in the process. You can find commercial sites offering seeds, plants, tools, and other garden items as well as the latest on plant research. Here are some sites we check out regularly, along with mailing addresses where appropriate.

Aggie Horticulture (http://aggie-horticulture.tamu.edu). We love this site. Maintained by the Horticulture Department at Texas A&M, it has information on all kinds of plants for Texas, including new varieties that are being tested and will be in nurseries in a few months or years. Click on "extension" for a link to your county extension agent. Be sure to link to Earth-Kind Environmental Landscape Management website (http://aggie-horticulture.tamu.edu/earthknd/earthknd.html). An educational program of Texas Agricultural Extension Service, Earth-Kind promotes resource conservation and environmentally aware gardening and landscape practices.

Austin Pond Society (http://www.ccsi.com/~sgray/austin.pond.society/apshome.html). Whether you want to install a pond or just wish to dream about it, this website has it all—chat rooms, commercial links, personal pond pages, and links to pond organizations worldwide. An outstanding resource.

Extoxnet (http://ace.ace.orst.edu/info/extoxnet/). Maintained cooperatively by University of California-Davis, Oregon State University, Michigan State University, and Cornell University, this site offers objective, science-based information about pesticides written for the nonexpert. Its convenient search and browse format is easy to use.

Lady Bird Johnson Wildflower Center (http://www.lnstar.com/mall/wildflower/index.html). To list but a few of the items offered here—you'll find visitor information; programs and services; a catalog of native plant materials, including a fact sheet catalog by region; hyperlinks to other native plant organizations; and native plant seed resources. Mailing address: 4801 LaCrosse Ave., Austin, TX 78739.

Texas Parks and Wildlife Department (http://www.tpwd.state.tx.us/). This site offers Texas Wildscapes, part of its Nongame and Urban Program, giving information on and even certification in gardening for wildlife. Mailing address: TPWD, 4200 Smith School Road, Austin, TX 78744.

The Neighborhood's Garden (http://www.tpoint.net/neighbor/Aus.html). Jim Parra, a horticulturist at the Zilker Botanical Garden in Austin, has maintained this delightful site for years. He offers great information from the general down to the neighborhood scale. Weather, plants, problems, local events, organizations, and excellent hyperlinks to gardening resources are among Jim's generous offerings.

We could go on forever, but these tools and reading matter should do for a start, and you will be able to get almost anywhere via hyperlinks offered at the Internet locations mentioned. Every day is truly a new day for a gardener. So pack up your tools and get gardening.

❧ 4 ❧

The Home Landscape

PLANNING, SELECTION,
AND SOME SPECIAL GARDENS

*To own a bit of ground, to scratch it with a hoe, to plant seeds,
and watch the renewal of life—this is the commonest delight of
the race, the most satisfactory thing a man can do.*

CHARLES DUDLEY WARNER, *MY SUMMER IN A GARDEN*

The traditional urban landscape has taken on a new look. Foundation plants lined up in a row against the house and wide, spacious lawns no longer rule. Smaller lots, water conservation awareness, interest in native plants, and gardening for wildlife are changing the appearance of our neighborhoods. Decks and patios extend our outdoor living space, bringing new creativity to container gardening and creating a demand for year-round interest in our gardens.

Since a well-designed landscape does much to enhance the value of one's home, you may want to consider the services of professional landscape architects and designers. But whether you plan your own landscape or hire out, a knowledge of the basics is not only helpful but will give a greater appreciation for the art of design.

THE PLAN

A scale drawing of your property—including any utilities, property lines, outbuildings, existing walks, drives, trees, and shrubs—is an excellent way to de-

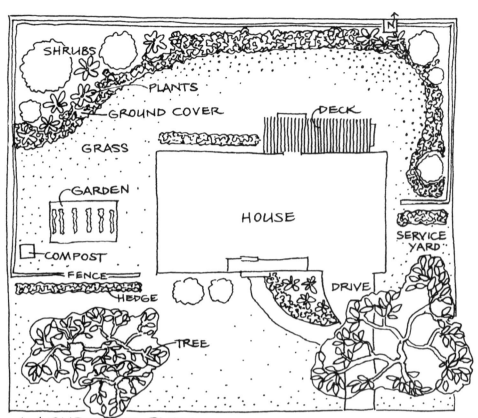

A LANDSCAPE PLAN

termine the exact location of such features and how much space they occupy. These things are surprisingly easy to misjudge from visual memory. Be sure to include the compass orientation of the house to determine exposure to the sun, and note the slope of the land. Our frequent flash flood conditions are no small matter. How your site drains is an important factor in planning your landscape. Steep slopes are easier to maintain if they are planted in ground cover rather than lawn. Mark windows and doors in the house to remind you of the views you will have from inside. Don't forget to provide for roof over-hangs and drip lines; easy to ignore, they can bring a lot of grief. The soil be-tween the drip line and house will require irrigation if planted, and without gutters the drip line itself will be compacted into a lifeless strip of dirt. A path of mulch, gravel, or decomposed granite in this space can be a useful alterna-tive to difficult-to-maintain plantings. (Decomposed granite is the loose ma-terial you often see on hike-and-bike-trail surfaces. It is quarried in Central

Texas and crumbles into tiny particles when dug. Its texture and mineral content also make it an ideal amendment.)

How will your site be used? Do you need play space, an area for pets, or a place for entertaining around a pool? How much of the area is devoted to activity and foot traffic, how much to plants? Consider screening service areas that may contain a storage building or compost pile. If you are considering an automatic sprinkler system, it should be included in your plans. If you have large flower beds or a vegetable garden, the requirements in these sections will be different from those of your lawn. For beds, a low-pressure drip irrigation system may be superior to overhead sprays.

Consider environmental factors. Shade-loving evergreens planted on the north side supply shelter against cold winds. Deciduous trees provide shade in summer and let in light during winter. You can learn a lot about which plants do well in a given exposure by taking a drive around the neighborhood. (It's also a very good way to collect design ideas.) Give particular attention to deeply shaded areas. We are always saddened to see glorious Indian hawthorns grown straggly and wan at the shady north entrance of an elegant home.

If your home is in a dramatic Hill Country setting, where soil is thin at best, the slope steep, and the deer population abundant, you may achieve a more appropriate look and save a lot of maintenance work by enhancing the natural vegetation with suitable native plant materials. As native plants have become more widely available, exciting new design possibilities have been created.

To complete a good balanced view of what your landscape needs, look at your lot from the street or from a neighbor's house and take photographs that you can review as you plan. Is your plan for the front or public side in balance with the appearance of the neighborhood? Do any elements in the plan conflict with neighbors' views or your own property usage?

As you make your plan, remember that there is a strong rationale for taking time in carrying out a landscape design. We think installing those elements that comprise the framework and then living with them while sorting out other possibilities has much to recommend it. This is especially true in the case of refurbishing an existing landscape.

With use needs defined, existing plants noted, and maintenance requirements considered, your challenge is to create a pleasing, harmonious relationship between your home and its site. This is a good time for a soil test, before choosing your plants from the wide selection of trees, shrubs, ground covers, and vines. Remember that unlike interior design, the landscape is a dynamic system. Well-executed and cared for, it will look better as it matures.

When considering a particular plant, first ask yourself, "Will this plant contribute to the scene or distract from it?" Then ask, "How large will it be when fully grown?"

Particularly handsome or dramatic plants—Texas mountain laurel, crape myrtle, Japanese yew, or multitrunk yaupon, for example—are excellent accent plants. Use such accents sparingly to avoid visual confusion.

Use color to direct the eye. Cool colors such as blues, grays, and violets tend to recede, heightening a sense of distance. Conversely, the warm reds, oranges, and yellows appear to foreshorten distance.

Group plants according to cultural requirements, such as water and sun, and for a more natural look.

Use generous proportions when planning flower beds and paths to avoid a constricted look. Beds along fences should be at least half to two-thirds as wide as the height of the fence. Paths, paved or unpaved, are more inviting and useful if they are three to three and a half feet wide.

Scale is as important in the garden as in the living room. Use dwarf or compact varieties instead of squeezing large shrubs into small spaces. Not only do these plants have a smaller ultimate size, but they also grow more slowly, reducing the need for frequent trimming.

Simplicity is good; be aware that our tendency is to overplant. It is easier—and cheaper—to add than to subtract.

SELECTION

Appropriate and careful selection of plants is the single most important factor in determining if your garden will thrive, survive, or be a pack of trouble. We know that most plants, especially flowers, are often purchased on impulse; we would never deny the joy of unabashedly scooping up some beauties from the season's first new shipment of bright, cheerful flowers. When it comes to expensive and permanent plants such as trees and shrubs, however, it's important to be as knowledgeable as possible.

You need to know the cultivation needs of the plants you intend to buy. Consider carefully soil conditions, water and light requirements, and temperature hardiness. While plant labels provide much of this information, often they are written by a giant grower, perhaps from California, and they tend to include the broadest parameters possible. Even if the label suggests that a given plant will just love its new home in your garden, microenvironmental conditions usually not noted need to be taken into consideration. Use of common names often can be confusing, too. "Coneflower" can refer to one of several species of the genus *Rudbeckia* or *Echinacea purpurea,* the purple coneflower. These are good reasons to shop at a garden center where the staff is knowledgeable and helpful.

Today, everyone seems to be a purveyor of plants. Consumers are confronted by an enormous selection at supermarkets and megastores as well as at traditional retail nurseries and garden centers. Variety, quality, service, and price can vary greatly at different locations. If you are purchasing expensive trees or shrubs, you may need expert advice and delivery or installation service. At other times, a tempting hanging basket of petunias at the supermarket may be just the right purchase. Smart customers get the best buy when they know their needs and thoroughly inspect the merchandise.

Nowadays, dormant fruit trees are usually purchased in bare-root condition in late winter to early spring; larger-caliper (the diameter of a tree measured in inches at chest height) trees are often field grown and offered for sale with roots balled and burlapped. The overwhelming majority of plants are sold in plastic containers. When selecting your plant, a careful look can often reveal much about its condition. You may ask the nursery staff to lift the plant out of the container so that you can inspect the root system. You should see an abundance of healthy, white root tips tightly packed on the outside of the soil ball. If thicker, older roots are circling around the root ball, the plant is considered root-bound and in danger of dying if the main root girdles the stem. If the soil ball is loose and crumbly, the shrub may not have been in the container very long and the root system has not had time to develop. The soil should be damp and well drained. If the soil has withdrawn from the sides of the container, this means that the plant has been allowed to dry out between waterings.

Be sure to inspect the entire plant before buying. Lack of space at the retailer necessitates plants being presented in a tightly arranged sea of green. Separate out your candidate and give it a good looking over. Branches can be broken in crowded conditions, and shrubs that have spent a long time at the garden center may have lost considerable leaf mass on their lower branches or may be misshapen.

Be savvy when shopping for native plants. Be sure to ask the nursery staff if your selection is native to your specific area of Texas. More than once we have arrived home with our new "native perennial," only to discover that it was native to Montana or Indiana.

While shopping for plants you are likely to have picked up a few bags of mulch, fertilizer, and other soil amendments. If you can't store these items in a dry, protected space, it is best to purchase only what you intend to use in a short time. Stored outside, plastic sacks break down rapidly in sunlight, and insects, particularly ants, are quick to invade mulch.

One last word of caution: now that you have that perfect plant, be sure to pack it carefully in the car. Don't drive home listening to the plants rolling around the trunk, spilling soil from the containers, crushing flowers and branches.

Keep an eye out for local garden club sales. These wonderful events, often held as club fund-raisers, offer great opportunities to pick up interesting species at reasonable prices and to get good growing advice as well. Of course, sharing with gardening friends is a always blessing.

SOME SPECIAL GARDENS

Xeriscape Gardening Principles

Fifteen or so years ago a new word appeared in the gardening vocabulary—*xeriscape*. From the Greek word *xeros,* meaning dry, xeriscape refers to water conservation through creative landscaping. Developed in Denver, Colorado, the concept quickly spread to other dry states, including Texas. Originally xeriscaping was strongly identified with the use of native plants, and, to some, the two became synonymous. Fortunately today a broader definition prevails, so that the idea includes many excellent drought-tolerant varieties. In Texas, where drought is common and water supplies are under constant assault, all gardeners should be aware of the seven xeriscape principles. Even if a xeriscape is not in your plans, these are excellent landscaping guidelines that can be modified to fit your needs.

START WITH A GOOD DESIGN OR PLAN. Follow the above general principles of good garden design.

IMPROVE THE SOIL. Almost all Central Texas soil can be improved by the addition of organic matter, which aids in retention of soil moisture.

USE MULCH. Mulches discourage weeds, keep soil temperature lower, and improve moisture retention.

LIMIT LAWN AREAS. Since turfgrass, especially St. Augustine, is often the biggest water consumer in the yard, consider reducing the size of your lawn. There are many attractive drought-tolerant plant alternatives and handsome nonplant materials, such as light tan or gray gravel (not white—it's too reflective; and not too dark—it's too heat absorbent).

CHOOSE LOW-WATER USE PLANTS. Most plant growers and retailers tag their products to indicate water requirements. Nursery staff should be able to assist you.

WATER EFFICIENTLY. Most low-water plants can do well with an inch of water per week. Be sure to group plants according to similar water requirements. Soaker hoses and drip irrigation systems are excellent means of delivering water directly to plants, reducing evaporation and runoff. They are particularly useful in vegetable gardens and flower beds and on slopes. Check your automatic sprinkler system periodically to ensure proper operation. If your system is programmable, you will probably want to use different settings for flower beds, vegetables, and lawns. Generally, lawns require more frequent watering. If you use an end-of-hose sprinkler, choose one that delivers large water drops close to the ground. Sprinkling early in the day reduces water loss through evaporation.

PRACTICE GOOD MAINTENANCE. Do not overfertilize. Weed as needed. Raise the lawn mower height so as not to cut more than one-third of the total grass height, and leave grass clippings. It is essential to understand that, like all other plants, xeriscape plants require regular watering during the first year as they become established. Too often people water once or twice after planting, leave the plants on their own, and then are disappointed when they fail.

Dry shade is the most demanding condition for the xeriscape garden. Be sure to choose plants carefully for this situation. Some excellent plants are yaupon, nandina, aspidistra, American beautyberry, English and Algerian ivies, liriope, cedar sage, Hinkley columbine and Turk's cap.

Attracting Butterflies and Hummingbirds
Thanks to an increased environmental awareness and the educational efforts of conservation organizations, many gardeners have come to realize the richness other living creatures bring to their world. Glorious in their beauty and fascinating in their behavior, butterflies and hummingbirds are a gift to any garden. They are easy to entice, but gardening for butterflies requires, at the very least, an understanding that the butterfly is a complex creature. Its life is spent in various stages, each with particular requirements.

Perhaps learning to tolerate and respect caterpillars is the biggest adjustment gardeners must make if they are not to act at cross purposes. In the caterpillar or larval stage, the butterfly is a voracious consumer of vegetation. It is important to set out plants that are attractive to caterpillars and to forgo chemical efforts to rid the garden of caterpillars. Systemic pesticides and *Bacillus thuringiensis* (a microbial insecticide that kills caterpillars) should definitely be avoided. Field guides can help you identify butterfly caterpillars, many of which are truly spectacular.

During the butterfly stage, which for many species is short-lived, the insects feed on the nectar in flowers. Some species are very particular in their tastes, while others feed from a variety of flowers. Wildflowers are superb candidates for butterfly gardens. We are fortunate in Central Texas to have many spectacular butterfly species pass through. Monarchs, queens, red admirals, painted ladies, the Gulf fritillary, and several swallowtails, sulphurs, skippers, and hairstreaks are all common. Butterfly populations are sporadic, and there may be years when a given species may fail to appear.

Plants that appeal to caterpillars and are commonly found in gardens are dill, parsley, radish and ruellia. Pentas, butterfly bush, many species of milkweed, lantana, passionflower, summer phlox, verbena, and zinnia are some flowers that are easy to grow and that will attract a wide variety of butterflies. We encourage you to use the many readily available resources, including Internet groups, conservation organizations, and butterfly gardens in local parks, to explore this exciting facet of gardening. Plant it and they will come!

We had been setting out hummingbird feeders for years before we became aware that feeders, especially in our hot summers, need to be cleaned and refreshed at least every three to five days to prevent harm to the birds from fermented sugar water. Not confident that we were willing to keep up that schedule, we decided to let flowers fulfill the needs of the hummers that were so enjoyable to watch. Not only would they get their nectar, but they might also find insects and an occasional spider.

Hummingbirds visit many tubular flowers in the red spectrum. Their favorites are the cardinal flower, butterfly bush, beebalm, abelia, coral bells, cupheas, salvias, phlox, and Turk's cap, but their interest is by no means limited to these flowers. Hummingbirds also are attracted to dripping or running water.

Ponds

Once found only on large estates or in public gardens, the pond is enjoying increasing popularity as we constantly expand our garden experience. As supplies and materials have become more affordable and readily available, more of us have been attracted to the many pleasures of a water garden. Bringing a new element into the garden, the pond offers an opportunity to enjoy fish, new kinds of plants, and the soothing sound of water. A garden pond can be as simple as an old bath tub or stock watering trough, or as elaborate as a concrete pool with a bridge and decking. Backyard pond gardeners have had great success with preformed polyethylene ponds, which come in a variety of shapes with liners of ethylene propylene rubber (EODM).

If you are thinking of adding a pond to your garden, there are several critical considerations.

PLACEMENT. For maximum enjoyment, the pond should be able to be seen from the house. Deciduous trees and ponds are not ideal companions. And water lilies require at least six hours of sun a day for optimum bloom.

RECOMMENDED DEPTH. Twenty-four inches is a good depth that will help to moderate temperature. Since light rays heat primarily the top twelve inches of water, the remainder has a cooling or temperature-stabilizing effect.

FILTERS AND PUMPS. A filter system and recirculating pump are necessary to the appearance and health of a small pond. They trap debris and aerate the water, which is especially important if you wish to stock your pond with fish. Both require regular attention and care. Be sure to get a pump that is up to the job. You can always restrict the flow on a large pump, but you can't increase it with a small one.

It is a good idea to seek the advice of a pond specialist or someone who has hands-on experience. Fortunately, pond gardeners are enthusiastic, ready to share advice and stories, and very well organized. A hit to the Austin Pond Society web page, http://www.ccsi.com/~sgray/austin.pond.society/apshome.html, (see chapter 3, "Tools of the Trade") will link you to their universe.

Finally, whatever garden style you choose to pursue, your home landscape should be a reflection of your own tastes and personality. Design principles and guidelines are intended to assist and enlighten, not to discourage and restrict. Use them imaginatively to create a place of your own.

✤ 5 ✤

Lawns

ESTABLISHING
AND MAINTAINING THEM

*I believe a leaf of grass is no less than the
journey-work of the stars.*
WALT WHITMAN, "SONG OF MYSELF"

To many homeowners, their house is their flagship floating in a sea of green—
their lawn, the subject of admiration to all who see it (at least, this is their
hope). Indeed the lawn is often the most prominent feature in a yard. It also
can consume more time, water, attention, concern, worry, labor, and money
than any other part of the yard. But to most homeowners it is worth all this
because, in spite of the resources required, the lawn is esthetically and emo-
tionally satisfying.

In addition, an attractive lawn makes positive contributions, such as cooling (grass reduces temperature around a house), preventing soil erosion,
muffling noise, reducing glare, contributing oxygen to the environment,
filtering harmful pollutants from the air, providing an inexpensive recreational
surface, and providing a framework for other elements in the landscape.

There are hundreds of species of grass that grow in Texas, but only a few are
suitable as turfgrasses. The four most commonly used in this area are St. Augustine, bermuda, zoysia, and buffalo. All are warm-season turfgrasses that grow
in the late spring, summer, and early fall. Ideally, all should be planted early in
the fall or very early in the spring.

GRASSES: ST. AUGUSTINE GRASS (Stenotaphrum secundatum) 2. BERMUDA GRASS (Cynodon dactylon) 3. ZOYSIA (Zoysia japonica)

GRASS TYPES

St. Augustinegrass *(Stenotaphrum secundatum)* is native to the Gulf Coast and the West Indies as well as to the west coast of Africa. It is a broad-leafed perennial with runners (stolons) on the surface. It grows well in this area and is also a favorite in coastal locations like St. Augustine, Florida, from which it derives its name. Either sod blocks (approximately twenty-four inches by thirty inches) or plugs (approximately four inches by four inches) are planted to start the lawn. Don't ask for seed when you buy St. Augustine, or you may be given carpetgrass, which is similar, but is actually field grass and not suitable for lawns in this area. St. Augustine should be mowed at a height of one to four inches.

St. Augustine is favored for its dense, thick turf, which crowds out many weeds and other grasses. It is easy to start and gives rapid coverage, taking about six months for complete coverage using sod blocks or plugs set six to twelve inches apart. St. Augustine stays green longer than bermuda and grows in either sun or shade. It is the most shade tolerant of the grasses discussed in this book.

On the debit side, St. Augustine is susceptible to diseases such as brown patch, St. Augustine Decline (SAD), and leaf spot. It is attacked by chinch bugs and white grubs, and it is more susceptible to iron chlorosis (iron deficiency) and needs more water than bermuda. In addition, its coarse texture is unappealing to some people.

A variety of St. Augustine called 'Floratam' (developed by the Texas and Florida agricultural experiment stations) is fast growing and vigorous; it resists both SAD and chinch bugs. It is not as cold tolerant as common St. Augustine and should be grown in areas close to the coast. 'Seville,' a semidwarf variety, is also resistant to SAD and chinch bugs but it, too, is not as cold tolerant as standard St. Augustine. 'Raleigh' is a variety that appears more cold tolerant and is resistant to SAD; it is also shade tolerant, but is not resistant to chinch bugs. This is the most common variety sold.

Bermudagrass *(Cynodon dactylon)* is very popular, although in much of Central Texas it comes in second behind St. Augustine. This narrow-leafed and vigorous grass was brought to our country from tropical Africa in the seventeenth century. It has stolons (surface runners) and rhizomes (underground creeping stems). Bermuda has a fine texture, drought tolerance, and generally good resistance to turf diseases. It is also easy to start and spreads quickly. Seed, sod blocks, or plugs are used for planting. For a dense turf, bermuda should be mowed weekly during the growing season at one to three inches.

Among its disadvantages, we find that bermuda doesn't grow well in the shade and that its underground stems make it a persistent nuisance in flower beds and gardens. Although both St. Augustine and bermuda tend to "brown out" in winter after a frost, bermuda goes dormant earlier than St. Augustine.

Common bermuda is the least expensive variety, but it is also the most invasive. The hybrids such as 419 Tifway (used on most golf course fairways) and Testurf 10 give a denser, weed-resistant turf when mowed close and frequently. And they can be mowed down to half an inch to two inches, lower than their common brethren. They need a bit more fertilizer and cost more.

Zoysiagrass *(Zoysia japonica)* is a native of Asia and has been known as Korean or Japanese lawn grass. There are two other varieties *(Z. matrealla* and *Z. tennuifolia),* but they are not as popular as the *japonica.* With proper care, zoysia makes an attractive turf that resists invasion by weeds and other grasses as well as damage from insects and disease. Zoysia has a deep root system, enabling it to find water and survive droughts. It is very tolerant of traffic.

Zoysia does not do well in dense shade, and it is a slow-growing grass. Older varieties started from sod blocks or plugs may take one to two years to provide the same coverage that bermuda or St. Augustine would give in three to six months. For this reason zoysia is not a pest in gardens. However, it turns brown with a frost and stays straw-colored all winter; it is also relatively expensive. In our climate zoysia should be watered regularly and mowed as often as bermuda at one to two inches, preferably with a reel-type lawn mower. Four newer varieties of zoysia—'Emerald,' 'El Toro,' 'Palisades,' and 'Ja Mur'—require less water and are more shade tolerant than the regular variety. These newer varieties cover much faster than the older varieties.

Buffalograss *(Buchloe dactyloides)* is the only native grass that is used as turf. It can be propagated from seed or sod, but the latter results in a more even lawn texture. It is best used in areas receiving full sun, although a new variety, '609,' is more shade tolerant and thicker than the prairie or native grass. The prairie grass also does not fare well in shallow soil.

Buffalo is best used in lawns with low traffic. It does not tolerate heavy use well, so if you have kids who want to use the yard for football or baseball, buffalo is not the grass of choice. It also does not like heavy irrigation. Because it is native, it will withstand most rainfall conditions in Central Texas. If we have a hot, dry summer it may turn brown but will green up after a rain. It should not be heavily fertilized. Once a year in fall will be sufficient.

A common cause of failures for this turf rests not with the grass but with the homeowner. Conditioned to watering, fertilizing, and mowing, homeowners frequently and unwittingly provide an environment hostile to buffalograss but prime for invasion by bermudagrass. Generally, the best management practice for buffalograss is benign neglect.

Two other grasses are sometimes suggested for Central Texas: fescue for shady areas, and rye for winter overseeding (seeding on top of existing grass). We do not recommend them for these uses. Fescue is a cool season grass. It will survive in Central Texas in shade if it is watered heavily, but even then it is being sustained on life-support and will not thrive. If you have a shady area that will not support one of the four major grasses, we suggest you use an appropriate ground cover (see chapter 6, "Alternatives to Lawns").

Overseeding with rye will result in a green lawn throughout the winter. But it also means winter maintenance. While we are avid gardeners, we do not relish mowing the lawn at Thanksgiving or Christmastime. Additionally, winter lawns need water and fertilizer. And the rye will interfere with the emergence of the summer grasses in the early spring.

A new home often brings the chore of putting in a new lawn. Sometimes the builder has accepted that responsibility; even then some supervision by the homeowner at planting time may prevent problems from developing later on. If you move into a pre-owned home, the lawn may need to be reestablished.

If your home is located in a newly developed, rocky area, the builder will probably have to bring in high quality topsoil. Whether or not topsoil is imported, make sure that building debris—stones, lumber trash—has been removed first and that the area has been properly graded to provide surface drainage. The ground should slope gradually away from the house, walks, and drive.

If the site has been neglected and invaded by weeds, it may be necessary to apply a glyphosate herbicide, e.g., Roundup, to kill off unwanted vegetation. Nonselective and broad spectrum, this product will kill every plant it touches, so be extremely careful to spray only those plants you want to eliminate. Always read pesticide labels carefully. After two weeks, rake up the dead plants, prepare your soil, and begin planting your new lawn. First you may want to take a soil sample and have it tested (see chapter 2, "Soil and Its Conditioning"). Some people merely add a well-balanced fertilizer by rototilling or raking it well into the soil. Be sure the lawn area is smooth and, if you are going to seed, that it is flush with walks and drives to prevent mowing and runoff problems. If you use sod, the lawn should be a bit lower because the sod will add height.

Although lawns may be started almost any time from March, after the last freeze, through September, some installers prefer fall to avoid intense summer heat. However, you should be sure to allow six weeks of growth before frost time, when the soil gets cold. If you choose spring to start a lawn, the grass will benefit from a longer growing season, but you must be sure to provide ample water and to protect it against the invasion of weeds.

If you use grass seed, buy a quality product with a high percentage of germination and purity. A reputable seed dealer can help you make the best possible selection. Some we talked to said that a 90 percent germination rate or higher (the rate is listed on the package) is a good buy. We suggest using a small seed spreader, but you may hand sow. Regardless of the method you use, we suggest you sow one half of the seed going in one direction across the yard (e.g. east to west) and the other half going in the other direction (e.g. north to south). This will result in more complete and uniform seed distribution.

If you have sown seed, it should be watered lightly and frequently to keep the surface moist. Sprouts will appear in two or three weeks. As seedlings develop, reduce the frequency of watering and increase the amount of water applied at one time. This allows a deep root system to develop. Sod blocks or sprigs should be watered every day for two weeks after planting.

MAINTENANCE

Lawns, like humans, must have five elements to keep alive and vigorous: air, water, light, food, and mowing (well, you probably get your hair cut regularly). Provide these elements appropriately and you will have a healthy lawn; provide them yourself, and you too will be healthy.

Air

Like all living organisms, grass needs oxygen. Other plants in your yard generally have ready access to air. They live either in beds that aren't disturbed or in pots that have holes in the bottom. But grass lives in an environment where it is walked on, rolled on, run on, played on, marched on, and generally stomped on most of the year. The soil in which it lives, then, can become compacted, which means that air cannot penetrate the compacted soil to reach the grass roots.

In order to get that air to the roots, the lawn needs to be aerated on a regular basis. For most lawns, once a year is sufficient. For heavy use areas more frequent aeration may be necessary. The best way to aerate a lawn is with a aeration machine designed especially for that purpose.

You may have seen ads for spikes that attach to shoes so you can "aerate as you walk." You can't. The spikes do not leave sufficiently large holes in the turf for air to get in and they tend to close over quickly. You may be tempted to try golf shoes. Don't bother, unless you want to use your yard for golf practice. The shoes won't help—at least, they won't help your lawn. There are small implements on the market that can be pushed into the ground like a fork or shovel. These might do the job if you have a small yard and lots of patience.

But the quickest, most effective procedure is the aeration machine. A normal-sized yard (90 by 110 feet with a house in the middle) can be aerated in an hour or less. And machines can be rented at most rental stores. Don't buy one—they are large, expensive, and not cost effective for the infrequent user.

When you aerate you'll notice small plugs of turf appearing as the machine moves forward (you'll be following and guiding it; it will do the work and drag you along). This is what you want to see. Those plugs (which will disappear as you mow and water) are opening up the soil to let in air, water, and fertilizer. If you live in a happy neighborhood, why not make the aeration a block event? Invite neighbors to share in the rent and the aeration. The appearance of your entire block will improve.

Water

Turfgrass (except buffalo!) likes water, *lots of water*. Turf is the most water-intensive user in your entire yard. For water conservation purposes you may want to limit the amount of turf you maintain. Rainfall in our Central Texas area is not always sufficient to keep turf alive and happy, and in dry periods, you'll have to supplement the rain with local water. This means a lot of watering.

We recommend applying one to two inches of water (including rain water) every week during the summer; a similar amount every two weeks during the spring and fall; and a similar amount each month during the winter. Yes, grass does need water during the winter months. During this period it is dormant, not dead.

Using these guidelines, each yard, depending on type of grass used, should receive from twenty-seven to fifty-four inches of water annually. The lower number, we believe, is marginal at best, and homeowners are better off trending toward the higher application rate. The average annual rainfall in Central Texas is about thirty-four inches, but it's not distributed evenly.

This means the lawn will have to be watered whenever there is insufficient rainfall and the grass starts to dry. How to tell if the grass is dry and needs watering? Here are a couple of guidelines. If it hasn't rained an inch or so in the previous period (one week in the summer, two in the spring and fall, one month in the winter), then you can probably guess that water is needed.

Also, check the grass blades. If they are curled, the grass is dry. And walk on the turf. If it's not springy but instead hard to the step, it's time to water. Check flower and shrub beds around the turf. If the soil in the bed is dry, then the soil under the turf will be likewise.

There are two basic ways to water. Haul out the hoses and sprays and commence. It is best to work out a watering plan that minimizes the amount of time you spend moving hoses and sprayers while at the same time watering all of the grass and, one hopes, little of the street, driveway, and sidewalk. This may take some time and a few different sprayers, but it is effort well spent. You will save both time and water in the long run.

The second way to water is by irrigation. This has become a cost-efficient investment for the homeowner. The new sprinkler systems are driven by computers (actually, chips and a circuit board), rather than by the older hydraulic mechanisms, and are now installed with plastic rather than copper piping. In all, the cost of most sprinkler systems is reasonable. And the turf gets the benefit of water on a regular schedule.

Light

Turf needs at least some sun daily. Depending on the type of grass, its needs may range from dappled sunlight to partial shade to full-day sun (the discussion of each grass type covers the sun requirements). If the area where you wish to grow turf does not receive enough sunlight, then consider abandoning grass and seeking alternatives. Ground covers and other alternatives to lawns are discussed in chapter 6.

Food

Grass is a living organism; it needs food. Compared with other plants, grass has a big appetite. It needs a good application of fertilizer in early spring to get off to a good start and again in the fall to last through the winter. It can also benefit from feeding in late spring and/or early summer. But by far the two most important feedings are the first and last (and St. Augustine generally needs only these two).

When selecting fertilizer, pick one that has a ratio of 4-1-2 or 3-1-2 (that is, in order, nitrogen, phosphorous, and potassium). Some fertilizers come with insecticides and weed killers. This is an individual choice, but we choose to focus on feeding and strengthening the grass rather than on attacking something that may or may not be harmful.

In fact, our first lawn fertilization of the growing season doesn't involve commercial fertilizer. Here's what we do. After mowing the grass for the second or third time in the spring, we aerate (as described earlier in this chapter). Then we apply a generous amount of composted sewage sludge. The City of Austin markets this product as "Dillo Dirt." Check with your municipal wastewater treatment facility. Many other Texas cities now sell treated sludge for lawns and flower beds (it is not recommended for vegetable garden use). We apply about two or three cubic yards of this compost to the entire yard area. If you water it in thoroughly, the next step is to make sure your lawnmower is in tip-top shape; it will soon get a good workout.

For some time, homeowners have used topsoil on their lawns in the spring. We advise against this. First, without knowledge of its origin, you may be applying soil that contains weed seeds (in composted sludge the seeds will be killed in the composting process). Second, application of too-heavy a layer of soil can actually kill grass roots by reducing available air and water. If you need to fill in a small patch (as contrasted with major landscape contour changes), add a little compost or sewage sludge and gradually build up the area. The compost or sludge, of course, can also be used for fill in applications at other times of the year.

If you do choose to use commercial fertilizer, we recommend the pelletized form. The fertilizer is encapsulated in small pellets and is released slowly into the soil. This both feeds the turf over a longer period of time and avoids the possibility of burning the grass with too much nitrogen. Always apply fertilizer at the rates recommended on the package. In this case "more" is not a good practice.

Mowing

Who among us doesn't look forward eagerly to Saturday morning when we can get out and mow the yard? Just kidding. Actually, lawn mowing need not be a burdensome chore if you follow some simple steps.

First, mow frequently, particularly in mid to late spring when the grass is growing vigorously. Never remove more than a third of the grass blades' length at a mowing (which means perhaps twice weekly, or three times every two weeks in the vigorous growing season). And, for whatever reason, if the grass gets too long and you must take more than a third, you should catch the clippings. If you don't, the longer clippings will tend to mat, keeping out water and air. Otherwise, don't catch the clippings, but let them return to the soil where they will compost.

Second, make sure your lawnmower is in top running condition and that the blade is sharp. Dull blades don't cut the grass, they bludgeon it and cause damage. Hardware stores and garden centers have electric drill attachments for sharpening lawn mower blades. This is a project that can be done in the family garage. Just make sure the blade is balanced after sharpening (the stores also carry inexpensive levels to ensure that blades are balanced). Otherwise the blade will wobble as it rotates and will damage, if not destroy, the mower engine. Finally, vary your mowing pattern so that the grass doesn't tend to grow in one direction.

Let us say something now about scalping a lawn: *Don't do it!* This has been a practice passed down through generations. Turf scientists, however, have undertaken extensive research showing not only that scalping does no good but that it can actually do harm. To scalp is to mow as closely to the soil as possible. The soil thus becomes exposed to the elements, as do the grass stolons, putting stress on the lawn at the time it needs energy to begin its early spring growth. So, we repeat: *Don't scalp your lawn!* Consider a modest "buzz haircut," but don't go any lower. And when you give the lawn that buzz cut, catch the cuttings; in the process you will pick up dead thatch left over from the previous year.

We have already indicated the best heights for mowing lawns, ranging from one to three inches or more. When to do what? Simple. Start out early in the spring mowing at the lowest recommended height and gradually move up to the highest recommended height. Thus, if you have St. Augustine, you might start at one inch in March, move up to two inches by late April to mid-May, and be at the highest level when the heat of the summer hits around June.

TROUBLES

Proper watering, fertilizing, and mowing are also important for weed control. If that doesn't work, the next step is to hand pull the weeds—no fun, but it helps. Different herbicides are available for specific weeds; it's best to check with the county agent or a nursery expert on what can (and cannot) be used on your lawn.

If you've chosen St. Augustine, be on the lookout for trouble from cinch bugs. They are small (an eighth of an inch long) and black, with white wings folded over the back; they're particularly active in hot, dry summers. Watch for irregular brown patches in open, sunny areas of the lawn, especially along a driveway, sidewalk, or the house foundation. The grass turns yellow, then dies and turns brown. You can test for chinch bugs by removing the ends from a tin can, twisting it into the ground near the edge of the damaged area, and filling it with water. If the grass is infested, within five minutes the bugs will float to the top. If you have a bermudagrass lawn that appears stunted and turns brown, you may have bermuda mite. Check with your local nursery to obtain recommendations on appropriate treatment for each problem.

Another enemy of Texas lawns is the white grub, the larva of the junebug, which feeds on grass roots. If areas of sod can be easily lifted, a number of grubs may have severed the plant roots. To check, examine the roots and soil by digging up several sections of sod four inches deep. Treatment with an insecticide is indicated if you have more than four grubs per square foot. Watch for grubs beginning in June and throughout the summer.

Several diseases threaten lawns in Central Texas, particularly St. Augustine lawns. Circular yellow or brown patches several feet in diameter (the outside resembles a smoke ring) are symptoms of a fungus called brown patch. This disease is prevalent in the spring and early fall when the high temperature is between seventy-five and eighty-five degrees; the fungus stops growing at ninety degrees. A preventive fungicide may be applied beginning in early fall. It may also be needed for leaf spot diseases—indicated by brown to gray spots that turn into dark blotches on leaves and stems of St. Augustine and bermuda, particularly in shaded areas that remain damp for some time.

Just as in humans, a virus disease is the hardest to control in lawns. St. Augustine Decline (SAD) causes mottling of the leaf blade and an overall decline in lawn vigor. Since chemicals won't help, it is suggested that a SAD-resistant variety be added to an infected area, where it will eventually replace the ailing grass.

Despite all the obstacles to raising a good lawn, there are few greater rewards than a fine expanse of green covering your property.

✤ 6 ✤

Alternatives to Lawns

Pleasures newly found are sweet
when they lie about our feet.
WILLIAM WORDSWORTH,
"TO THE SMALL CÉLANDINE"

The use of alternatives to the great American lawn is perhaps the most significant recent change in landscape design. Four factors driving their increasing popularity are our increased awareness of the need to conserve water resources, the trend toward smaller residential lots, the desire for lower-maintenance yards, and the extension of living areas outdoors.

Alternatives may be a large, wide-ranging group of plants we call ground covers, other nonshrub plants such as ferns and ornamental grasses, or decks and patios, known in the nursery trade as "hardscape." (Since this book is about gardening, we limit our discussion here to plants. *Better Homes and Gardens Step by Step Landscaping* is an excellent source for hardscape. See chapter 3, "Tools of the Trade.") Not only are these alternatives effective problem solvers for difficult situations; they also contribute enormously to the visual interest of our home and community landscape.

The term *ground cover* refers to a group of low-growing plants used in places that otherwise would either have grass or remain bare. *Low-growing* is not a precise term, but we think of such plants as being under eighteen inches in height, although many of the new ornamental grasses reach much greater heights.

Ground covers come in many forms. Some are herbs and shrubs like rosemary; some are vines such as ivy; others are evergreen plants such as monkey grass and liriope; and some, such as plumbago or river fern, die back in winter. Happily there is a choice for almost every situation. Ground covers are superb on steep slopes where soil may be thin or erosion a problem; in wet, soggy areas; for narrow strips; and under trees where the shade may be dense or prominent surface roots interfere with mowing. Drought-resistant species such as junipers or trailing lantana thrive in the relentless summer sun.

Esthetically, ground covers provide color in foliage or flower, and they supply texture, relieving monotony and blending unrelated shrubs and flowers. They can soften the hard edges of paved walks and drives.

Two significant limitations to ground covers need to be mentioned here. First, they do not tolerate foot traffic. In situations of heavy foot use, nonliving materials such as stepping stones, decks, pavers, bricks, or decomposed granite may be more appropriate. Second, even a fast-growing ground cover will require at least two years with conscientious attention to a fertilizing and watering regimen to become established and provide good coverage. When selecting a ground cover, review both your site conditions and the plant's requirements.

Although ground covers and other lawn substitutes may solve certain problems, conserve water, and cut down on maintenance chores, they do not eliminate chores. Ground covers require care if they are to thrive, and most of the tasks must be done by hand. Obviously in our hot summers, many species (excluding succulents and cacti) require more attention than in more moderate climates. Like lawns, alternatives to turf require careful planning and preparation if they are to do the desired job.

If you wish to reserve a space for a cactus and succulent garden, be certain to pick a sunny spot and to provide excellent and fast drainage. To discourage those persistent weeds and grasses, try placing a sheet of black plastic over the prepared soil, fastening it with rocks, wires, or stakes, then cutting holes in it to insert the plants, and covering it with pebble mulch. Another effective use of pebble mulches is as borders for driveways and pathways.

Planting a ground cover requires preparation similar to that for planting grass. First, the ground must be properly graded. This is the time to install a sprinkler system if you are so inclined. Existing weeds need to be killed and the soil amended with organic matter. If you are planting a flat area, mound (or crown) the soil very slightly after amending it so that it is just an inch or so higher at the center to ensure good drainage. As the soil settles, it is best that the area slopes just slightly toward the edges to prevent a depression from forming in the center. Apply a balanced (1-2-2) fertilizer at the rate of twenty to forty pounds per thousand square feet.

Using the measurements given in the plant list at the end of this section, properly space the plants and set them into holes so that they are just slightly below ground level and will be in a position to catch water. On a slope, it's a good idea to prevent washouts by staggering the rows. Then the area should be mulched with wood chips, for example, or finely ground bark. This helps the plants retain the moisture critical for their survival; the stolons and runners of many ground covers need moisture to root. Mulching also keeps weeds out and makes the area more attractive. The final step, no surprise, is to water thoroughly.

When you plant ground covers, spacing is important, since you want coverage as soon as possible. A flat of thirty-two four-inch plants planted at twelve inches apart will cover approximately thirty-two square feet. Larger plants such as cotoneasters (see chapter 9, "Shrubs") and creeping juniper need to be three to four feet apart.

Once the ground cover is established, it requires fertilizing, weeding, watering, and as mentioned, mulching. Fertilize the plants in autumn and once more in early spring. Water regularly and thoroughly in spring, summer, and fall and occasionally in winter when it's dry. The Department of Agriculture suggests watering whenever the soil is dry to the touch and the tips of the plant wilt slightly at midday. As we have noted, you'll need to keep the area free of weeds and stray grass.

A list of popular ground covers and other alternative plants follows. Choose those with characteristics that best suit your needs. Ground covers include some vines and low shrubs, which are discussed in other chapters but are listed here to emphasize their potential use as ground covers.

FERNS

Ferns are particularly useful in shady situations. Their handsome foliage makes them valuable as accent plants or as a ground cover. Some are evergreen and some die back in winter. All appreciate moisture and lots of organic matter. Ferns tend to be sensitive to chemicals, so be extra cautious with fertilizer and pesticides.

Autumn *(Dryopteris erythrosora).* The fronds of this native of China and Japan emerge a beautiful bronze, later turning olive green. Generally, it is evergreen in the southern area of Central Texas.

GROUND COVERS: 1.ENGLISH IVY 2.AJUGA 3.VINCA MINOR

Holly *(Cyrtomium falcatum).* This handsome fern, its name derived from the holly-like shape of its leaves, is way up there on our list of favorites. An excellent choice in many situations, it stands well on its own or as a background for flowers such as impatiens. It appreciates supplemental watering and protection from direct sun in summer. Well-established holly ferns can grow to two and a half feet in height and three feet in width.

Japanese Painted *(Athyrium Goeringianum japonicum).* Small and delicate, the Japanese painted fern is prized for its silvered, almost filigreed foliage. It is deciduous and withers a bit in summer but is very striking. It will grow to one foot.

River or Wood Fern *(Thelypteris kunthii).* Native to Texas, this tall (to three feet), light-colored fern tolerates drier soil than many other ferns. After it freezes, cut it back to remove unsightly foliage. It spreads fairly rapidly if given water, and it divides well.

Southern Maidenhair *(Adiantum Capillus-veneris).* Known by all in Central Texas as the native fern that hugs our seeping limestone cliffs, the maidenhair is exceptionally lovely. Its delicately scalloped leaves of the truest green are offset by jet-black stems. Given its preferred habitat, we recommend this fern for shady crevices around ponds or in pots. It will die back in a freeze but return in spring.

ORNAMENTAL GRASSES

Ornamental grasses form a group that is enjoying great acceptance and popularity. Homeowners prize these new drought-tolerant plants, which work well in landscape plans for reducing the size of lawns. With graceful, arching leaves, ornamental grasses are particularly effective in softening the hard edges of buildings, walks, and driveways. Many also serve well as accents in perennial gardens. Most of them love full sun and require little maintenance. Some are native, some exotic. Some introduce subtle color, others give new meaning to flowering plants and seasonal interest, and almost all bring striking texture to the landscape.

Fountain *(Pennisetum seataceum)*. One of the showier grasses, fountain grass bears soft, fuzzy blooms from August to October. A purple variety, 'Atrosanguineum,' is also available. It grows to three to four feet.

Japanese Silver *(Miscanthus sinensis)*. Growing to five feet, this striking striped grass is available in several varieties. It has a wide, arching habit. *M. sinensis* 'Zebrinus' has broad horizontal white or yellow stripes, and the dwarf variety, 'Yaku Yima,' grows to eighteen inches.

Lindheimer's Muhly *(Muhlenbergia lindheimeri)*. Growing in gently arching clumps, this native is tough, drought tolerant, and not very fussy about soil conditions. It has blue-gray foliage and grows to three to four feet.

Little Bluestem *(Schizachyrim scoparium)*. We have admired this handsome native for years on walks in the Hill Country. Stiffly upright and attractive all year long, its foliage turns from green to blue-gray to reddish bronze in fall.

Mondo Grass or **Monkey Grass.** See following section, "Other Ground Covers."

Pampas *(Cortaderia selloana)*. For some time the only grass offered as an ornamental, pampas grass continues to be widely used in our Central Texas landscapes. Growing to eight to ten feet, it requires a large space so as not to dominate other plantings in the area. It is an excellent screen and windbreak. Razorlike leaf margins make it a candidate for places away from play areas, doorways, and other activities.

PaMPaS GRaSS (Cortaderia selloana)

OTHER GROUND COVERS

Ajuga, also called **Carpet Bugle** *(Ajuga reptans)*. One of the more striking ground covers, ajuga has green, purple, or variegated evergreen foliage, which turns a reddish bronze in fall; it has spiky clusters of small blue flowers in spring. The plants should be set six to eight inches apart in spring. They will multiply rapidly by sending out stolons; the new plants can be divided from the parent plant after new spring growth. Ajuga likes rich, moist soil, does well in the shade, but is subject to nematodes and fungus.

Asiatic Jasmine *(Trachelospermum asiaticum)*. See chapter 10, "Vines and Climbers."

Cast Iron Plant *(Aspidistra elatior)*. Flourishing in the most difficult of all environments—dry soil and deep shade—this broad-leafed member of the lily family holds a special place in our hearts for thriving where nothing else will even grow. It has little tolerance for sun and will easily sunburn. In wide open exposure its leaves may suffer wind damage and a severe freeze will cause it to die back. In protected areas such as under eaves and along fences or walls, it cannot be beat.

Century Plant *(Agave americana)*. The agave, with its barbed, fleshy leaves, is a large evergreen plant at maturity and should be given ample space and full sun. It cannot tolerate wet soils. Ascending to a height of twenty feet or more, the stalk resembles a giant asparagus, which then bursts open, exposing its yellow blossoms. Flowering but once after twenty years of growth, the dramatic succulent then dies. More shade tolerant, the very striking Queen Victoria Maguey *(A. victoria-reginae)* has fewer spines, and is more compact.

Creeping Juniper *(Juniperus horizontalis)*. Short, stiff, narrow bluish green leaves on firm woody branches give this shrubby ground cover a rugged appearance. It works best as a cover for large areas in full sun. This plant is susceptible to red spider mite and bagworms.

Ivy *(Hedera* spp.). The **Algerian** *(H. canariensis)* and **English** *(H. helix)* ivies are superb ground covers. See chapter 10, "Vines and Climbers."

Liriope *(Liriope muscari)*. An evergreen, grasslike perennial that grows up to a foot tall and forms a dense covering for the ground, liriope produces small white or purple flowers on spikes in summer. Similar to lily turf, only hardier and thus a better choice farther north, it makes a fine border plant and ground cover under trees. It tolerates heat and drought once established and thrives in soil improved with compost or peat moss. Preferring semishade, it can suffer sunburn in long exposure to the bright summer sun. Many attractive cultivars of liriope are available, especially the variegated varieties such as 'Silver Dragon' and 'Silvery Sunproof.' Possessing the same characteristics, and growing to three feet in height and width, giant liriope is a superb choice for an accent in shady areas of flower beds, borders, or other appropriate locations.

Mondo Grass or **Monkey Grass** *(Ophiopogon japonicus)*. Only six inches high, mondo grass nonetheless grows densely in grasslike mounds, making it especially useful under trees or as a border plant. It likes organically enriched moist soil and does well in half-day sun to quite dense shade. A dark green all year long, in early summer it has small lavender flowers followed by clusters of blue berries. It is an excellent backdrop for spring-blooming bulbs. Once established, monkey grass is drought tolerant. It will take a light mowing in spring if a very uniform appearance is desired. The plants should be set six to twelve inches apart since they spread rapidly. Dwarf monkey grass (*O. japonicus* 'nana') is more compact and, like all dwarf varieties, grows more slowly. It grows to three inches.

Periwinkle, Vinca *(Vinca minor)*. This southern European native is very

CENTURY PLANT (Agave americana)

much at home in our hot, dry climate. It has glossy, dark green or variegated white and green foliage and funnel-shaped purplish-blue flowers in early summer. Plant twelve to eighteen inches apart, preferably in light shade and enriched, moist soil. Once established, it requires little care and will grow to a height of one foot.

Periwinkle, Common, also called **Creeping Myrtle** *(Vinca major)*. An excellent and popular evergreen ground cover that grows up to one foot high but prefers light shade, this vinca needs little care. It has dark, lustrous leaves about two inches long and flowers in lavender or white ('Alba' variety). Hardier than *V. minor,* it is an excellent ground cover. Plant in the spring or early fall, twelve to eighteen inches apart. The plants may be divided or cuttings taken at any time. Its trailing growth habit makes it a fine selection for use around trees or on slopes. Recommended for northern Central Texas.

Red Hesperaloe, also called **Red Yucca** *(Hesperaloe parviflora)*. Bearing a striking resemblance to the true yuccas, this stemless evergreen plant has slender, dark green leaves and long red spikes of conspicuous flowers that bloom throughout the summer. It is slow-growing yet wide-reaching and brings the flavor of the Southwest to its setting. Plant it in full sun.

Texas Sotol *(Dasylirion texanum)*. Resembling the yuccas, the evergreen tufted lily has leaves that are more slender than those of the yuccas. Its trunk frequently is located underground, giving the shrub the appearance of a clump of long grass. This hardy native grows from three to six feet and requires full sun. In spring, flowers are put out on long spikes.

Wintercreeper, also called **Euonymus** *(Euonymus fortunei)*. This evergreen vine forms a dense carpet of oval-shaped, serrated leaves that turn an attractive purplish red in fall. It rarely grows more than six inches tall. Preferring sun, it will tolerate partial shade. Euonymus should be planted at about twelve-inch intervals. It is a good choice for erosion control in rocky areas, especially if the soil is enriched with organic matter.

Yucca *(Yucca spp.)*. These natives of the American Southwest are characterized by their long, thick, evergreen, daggerlike leaves. Singular in appearance, yuccas do equally well as accent plants and grouped with other succulents. The **Aloe Yucca** *(Y. aloifolia)* grows to ten feet. Showy white flowers on twelve- to eighteen-inch spikes appear in late spring or early summer. The **Twistleaf Yucca** *(Y. rupicola)* is a small, low-growing plant, sending up tall spikes of greenish white flowers in late spring. The **Spanish Dagger** *(Y. treculeara)* is a spectacular tree of five to twenty-five feet, with a simple or branched trunk. Extravagant flowers on a one- to four-foot spike appear in spring. Its distinctive and exotic appearance makes it a popular specimen plant.

❧ 7 ❦

Tree and Shrub Planting and Care

Now 'tis the spring and weeds are shallow-rooted;
Suffer them now, and they'll o'ergrow the garden.
SHAKESPEARE, *HENRY VI*

For gardeners, cruising a nursery can be exhilarating. Every turn down a new aisle offers opportunities for finding plants one has never seen before. Regardless of your plant-shopping skills, however, the real work begins after the plant—in this case a tree or a shrub—is purchased. For it is the planting and care that make the purchase grow, thrive, and become a treasured occupant of the yard.

PLANTING

Late fall and winter, when trees are dormant, is the best time for container and/or balled-and-burlapped tree planting; this gives the root system a chance to get established and ready for the big growing season in spring, and for the debilitating hot weather that follows. Bare-root trees are best planted before the last frost in March while still in dormancy. In Central Texas you can plant most shrubs at any time of the year when they are available, although your job will be more difficult in the midst of a hot spell. If you plant then—and plant then only if you must—be certain to water deeply (and daily, if possible) for several weeks thereafter for best results.

To plant any tree or shrub, first dig a hole about twice as wide as the root ball. If the plant is in a container, cut the container from top to bottom on both sides to ease plant removal and minimize damage to the root system. If the plant is balled and burlapped with natural burlap (it will be brown), do not disturb the wrappings. However, if the burlap is made of synthetic material (it will be green), all of it should be removed from the root ball immediately before planting. Synthetic material will not rot, and planting while it is still around the root ball will restrict root growth. Carefully cut the material away from the root ball, trying not to damage any of the root system. Make sure the root ball is damp so that there is a better chance of it staying intact during the planting process.

Before moving the plant, decide which profile is best and how you wish to position it. Trees and shrubs, like humans, have a good side (where the leaves are at their fullest), and that is the one to present. If the plant has bare roots, form a low cone of soil in the middle of the hole and put the center of the tree on the center of the cone. Spread the roots out in a natural manner down and away from the center of the cone. Center your balled and burlapped plant in the hole; be sure it is standing straight. Plant the tree at the level it was growing. The discolored ring near the base of the trunk indicates the original soil line. Begin backfilling the hole with the soil dug to create it. Do not fill the hole with any special soil or soil mix. The plant needs to send its roots out to obtain air, water, and nutrients. If you fill the planting hole with special soil or soil mix, the roots will stay there absorbing the nutrients and will not spread. The tree then is subject to being toppled by strong winds since it doesn't have any roots out in the surrounding soil and thus has no broad-based anchor for support.

Tamp the soil with your feet to eliminate air pockets as you backfill. Do not, however, stomp the soil in too firmly. That will compress it, cutting off oxygen to the roots. When the hole is about two-thirds full, fill it with water. After the water has soaked in, if you have a root ball burlapped with natural burlap untie the burlap and pull it gently away from the top of the soil ball. You can spread it out a bit and leave it to disintegrate in the soil. Finish filling in the hole with soil.

Build a ridge of soil three to six inches high around the edges of the hole to form a watering saucer, and fill it with water. An application of root stimulator—a moderate-phosphorus, low-nitrogen fertilizer—is often recommended at this time to overcome "root shock" and to get the tree off to a good start. No other fertilizing will be necessary for the first year. Remember, if there's no rain, fill the saucer with water several times a week for the next few weeks. After a year or so, it helps to fill the depression with an organic mulch of compost or

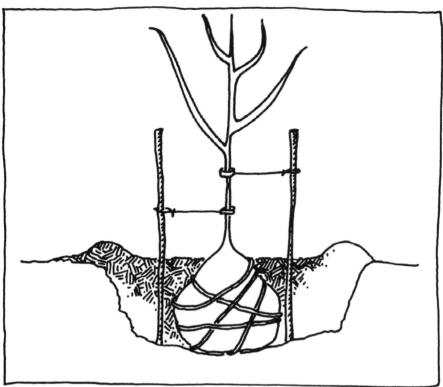

PROPER PLANTING OF A BALLED TREE

bark chips to preserve moisture and discourage weeds. Finally, cover an area up to six feet in diameter around the tree with organic mulch up to four inches deep. The mulch will help retain water and promote root growth.

TRANSPLANTING

Transplanting trees and shrubs from one location to another requires special care. Chances for survival are best if the plant is moved at the proper time— late fall or winter—before the growing period begins. Avoid transplanting during the summer months at all costs. During this season the rate of transpiration (the exchange of moisture and gases) is high, and many plants will not survive the shock suffered if they are moved.

The smaller the plant, the easier it is to remove from its original site without major damage to its root structure. The moving of trees with a trunk diameter of two inches or more should be left to experts. Not only do these professionals possess the skills, but they also have the necessary heavy-duty equipment, which few of us keep in the garage or toolshed.

When moving a tree, remember that its root system roughly parallels its branches, and that digging should begin outside the drip line. Try to take as much soil with the roots as possible. To achieve this, water several days before you move the plant. The soil should be moist so that it holds well when dug, but not so wet that it is mucky.

After transplanting the tree, remove dead and damaged branches. Do not, however, remove healthy growth. There is a common misconception that trees should be pruned to reduce the amount of system the roots support. However, pruning healthy limbs removes a source of energy for the tree. The tree is better off keeping the energy source. So when replanting a tree, leave it in the same condition as it was when acquired, except for dead and damaged portions.

Transplanting should be completed as quickly as possible; roots must not be allowed to dry out. If the tree cannot be replanted immediately, take steps such as covering the roots with wet peat moss to prevent loss of moisture, and spraying the roots and leaves with the garden hose as regularly as possible.

Trees that have long taproots, such as pecans, are especially difficult to transplant, and you should attempt to move them only if necessary and when the tree is small. If a taproot tree is to be transplanted, cut the taproot when the tree is very young. This will allow the tree to develop a strong lateral root network. When removing the tree, dig a hole larger than normal to reduce stress, and make sure that the receiving hole is also dug larger than normal.

To give a newly planted tree adequate support through harsh weather, stake the tree to two six-foot poles with guying wires. Be sure to insert the wire through segments of garden hose where it touches the tree to prevent it from cutting into the trunk. The wiring system should not be tight or it will constrict the movement and growth of the tree and may result in girdling (constricting the natural growth of the tree). The wiring system should be removed after one year, if not sooner, to permit the tree to grow strong and withstand wind gusts.

Keeping the root zone of a fruit tree evenly moist for its first year is important for a good start. Remembering that the tree's root system roughly parallels its branch system, water slowly from the branch line inward. A soaker hose works well here. Hoe the saucer you formed at the time of planting to prevent the soil from cracking and to discourage invasive weeds and grass. Mulch the saucer to a depth of two to three inches with compost, bark chips, or other organic mulch. Fruit production of mature trees will be more abundant and of better quality if the trees can be spared the devastation of severe drought. Watering deeply is the important point to remember.

Follow the same basic planting procedure for shrubs as for trees, but don't use guying wires. Instead of a root stimulator, work some slow-release fertilizer into the soil before planting. Use only peat moss as a planting medium for azaleas and half peat moss, half sandy loam for camellias, gardenias, and other acid-loving plants (see Azaleas and Camellias in chapter 9).

FERTILIZING

Fertilizing and pruning are the two basic maintenance procedures for trees and shrubs; both are extremely important to young plants. If they are done properly early in the plant's life, the plant will grow healthy and attractive with little need for more than occasional assistance from you.

Plants in need of fertilizer will lack terminal growth and have many dead branches, and the leaves will be yellow or a paler-than-normal shade of green. Since most trees are in yards that are fertilized, mowed, watered, and (we hope) aerated, there is some question about fertilizing trees. Our own experience is that regular lawn maintenance also enhances tree maintenance, and fertilizing specifically for trees is not necessary.

Shrubs are a different matter. Generally they are located in beds and do not receive the same treatment as lawns. Application of a good slow-release fertilizer in early spring and again in the fall is recommended. Shrubs should be mulched for moisture retention in summer and root protection in winter.

While most evergreen ornamentals require less fertilizer than do deciduous plants, maintaining proper soil acidity is a special concern for broadleaved evergreens, such as magnolia and loquat. At the very onset of chlorotic symptoms (yellowing leaves with prominent green veins), these plants should be given applications of iron sulfate or chelated iron. Foliar spraying is the most efficient method of application.

The heavy bloomers—azaleas, camellias, and gardenias—should be fed with an 8-12-4 fertilizer at six-week intervals from April to August. For hints on the special care of roses, see chapter 11, "Flowers."

PRUNING

Whether pruning is an art or a science is a debate that will not be resolved here. It does, however, come with its own nomenclature and an arsenal of im-

3rd CUT
2nd CUT
1st CUT

PRUNING A LARGE LIMB

pressive, specialized tools. Despite its considerable potential for good or harm on the landscape, few people understand pruning or take the principles seriously. To most of us, pruning means the removal of unwanted limbs and branches. Actually, proper pruning rejuvenates older plants, contributes to general plant health, determines the shape of the plant, and affects the number and size of blossoms and fruit.

There are four reasons for pruning: to remove growth that is interfering with utility lines and other structures; to eliminate wood that is damaged, dead, or diseased; to correct structural problems (e.g., limbs in danger of breaking under stress); and for improved appearance. After pruning diseased wood, always wash your tools in a ten-to-one water-bleach solution before going on to prune healthy branches.

Two basic pruning techniques are heading and thinning. Heading, or cutting the branches back to the buds, will produce a bushy look and may be just right for controlling a rangy plant, such as elaeagnus. It is, however, a method to be used judiciously because it can alter the shape of a tree or shrub radically. In thinning, one removes entire branches back to the main stem. This technique opens up growing space and encourages a natural line of growth. A clean cut flush with the branch collar (that rounded portion of the limb that intersects the branch and the main stem) is the desired end of the pruning cut. The result will be satisfactory in terms of both aesthetics and healing.

Trees

Prune at the proper time. This varies with the species, but a few basic rules can be stated here. Late winter, when a plant is dormant and its framework exposed, is the best time to prune deciduous summer- and fall-flowering trees and shrubs. Trees that are inclined to "bleed" heavily (ooze a lot of sap) when cut should be pruned in late summer or fall, not in late winter or early spring just as the sap is beginning to flow. Evergreens can be pruned from January through March and again in midsummer, leaving the new growth ample time to harden before the first killing frost. When they are three to four inches long, pinch out new shoots that are not desired as branches. This method, repeated every six weeks throughout the growing season, encourages shapely growth.

Oaks should be pruned in midwinter if possible, or in the middle of summer. Avoid other times of the year. The beetles that spread oak wilt are most active during temperate weather. They hibernate during winter and tend to stay out of the heat during midsummer (prompting one observer to suggest that beetles are far smarter than Central Texas gardeners).

Do not top trees unless they are diseased. Topping will destroy the natural growth lines of trees. Prune suckers at the base and watersprouts on branches. Both forms of growth are easily identified. Watersprouts, which are common on fruit trees, shoot straight up from, and are different in appearance than, other branches. Suckers grow from the roots at the base of the tree or shrub. Both are rapid growers, are visually undesirable, and drain from the plant energy that can be better used elsewhere.

Large limbs should be done in sections or with the aid of a rope for support. A heavy limb may tear before the cut is completed, stripping the bark and increasing the size of the wound. Never twist a pruning tool; twisting will tend to tear the bark. In most cases, unless you are agile and have a good deal of confidence and the proper tools, it is advisable to hire a professional to prune larger trees. Here the adage that you get what you pay for is true. The mere fact that a person has a pickup and a few tools does not imply much knowledge about trees. Often, these operators take off far too much leaf area in order to impress homeowners that they are indeed getting their money's worth. Check with your local nursery owner or a reliable and experienced friend to find out who the good tree people are.

To paint or not to paint? The controversy over painting pruning cuts with a wound dressing has been raging for decades. At one time it was believed that wound dressing sealed a cut, preventing damage from pests and disease. This thinking is unsubstantiated by scientific research. It is currently thought that wound dressing may actually slow a tree's natural healing process, and is now not recommended—with one major exception. In areas where oak wilt is present, a wound dressing should be applied to oak trees to prevent the spread of the disease by the bark beetle through the cut surface.

CONIFERS. Conifers should be pruned, if at all, after new growth has been completed and before it has become woody. "Candles," as the new shoots of pines are called, should be cut at about one-half the length of their new growth. The central candle of the top and the branches should be left longer than the side shoots.

FRUIT TREES. When it comes to pruning fruit trees, specific knowledge of the tree type is essential: pruning will affect the abundance and size of fruit produced. Your county extension agent is the best source of such information. Generally, a pecan tree's central leader is encouraged by pinching off the soft buds of the side limbs. Branches growing on the lower third of the tree should be removed, allowing permanent limbs to grow at the height of five feet. Tip prune the limbs by three inches in January through March to encourage new growth.

Three scaffold limbs form a basic network for a producing peach tree. After three years, 40 percent of the wood is removed annually, with the center receiving the heaviest pruning to allow the sun to penetrate. Unlike many fruits, the peach does not ripen once it is picked from the tree, so a California peach in the supermarket will never compare in flavor to a superb tree-ripened fruit from Central Texas.

The pear, with the exception of its susceptibility to fire blight, is the easiest fruit tree to maintain. It requires no pruning or fertilizing; these would, in fact, result in excessive, unwanted growth.

Light summer pruning and pinching back of terminal growth are particularly recommended for flowering fruit trees and ornamentals. Done routinely, these steps can make extensive dormant-season pruning unnecessary.

Perhaps in Eden, perfect fruit fell from the trees in great abundance; however, having been cast out of Paradise, humankind must work hard for those fruits. Pruning, watering, and routine schedules of spraying and fertilizing are necessary for fruit and nut production and for the flourishing of other trees and shrubs. Following these practices will result in a yard you will enjoy.

Shrubs

Because shrubs are put to so many different uses, it is difficult to state hard and fast rules for pruning them. While pruning in the correct season is essential for flowering shrubs, broader latitude is possible for evergreens. Spring-flowering plants, which form their buds during the previous growing season, should be pruned after flowering.

Larger and fast-growing plants, such as photinia, elaeagnus, and ligustrum, should be kept under control by regular thinning and pinching back throughout the growing season. These shrubs can lose irretrievably their desired shape if trimming chores are neglected for too many seasons. When buying shrubs, keep in mind your landscape needs and the ultimate size of the plants in question. Many of the best-looking ornamentals—nandina, crape myrtle, abelia, several hollies, and yaupon for example—are available in dwarf form. The dense foliage and compact growing habits of these shrubs make them highly desirable in many of our area's landscape situations, besides reducing pruning chores.

We have noticed a trend in recent years to prune back crape myrtles severely, to just a few limbs. The practice, called "dehorning," results in a tree or shrub with several stubs protruding from the trunk. This ruins the natural appearance of an otherwise outstanding plant. The human equivalent would be clipping one's fingernails starting at the first knuckle. This technique assaults the tree, renders it susceptible to attack by disease, creates an unsightly product, and reduces flowering. Instead of dehorning, we suggest that homeowners follow these practices: prune away the smaller limbs (the flowers appear on new growth), shape the plant vertically, and let it grow naturally.

Two commonly observed pruning errors to avoid are cutting back winter-killed branches prematurely, and tapering shrubs, particularly hedges, inward at the base. Eager to assess damage and to rid the landscape of unsightly blackened branches, gardeners often prune plants back to green growth too early. There are two reasons not to do this. First, the ability of many plants to revive as soon as spring arrives is astonishing and makes such pruning unnecessary. Second, early pruning increases the shrubs' vulnerability to possible late frost damage. Wait until all danger of frost is over or until new growth appears before correcting winter's crimes.

For some reason, gardeners love to cut back the frequently sparse or straggly lower branches of shrubs—thus unknowingly compounding the problem they seek to remedy. Lower limbs must be given adequate air and sunlight if foliage is to be encouraged. The base of a shrub always should be wider than the top. When clipping hedges, taper the shrub slightly toward the top of the plant. This will provide more light to the lower branches and reduce the probability of spindly lower branches reaching out for the sun.

So let caution be the byword when pruning or even thinking of pruning. Pruning mistakes cannot always be remedied. Once a limb is gone it can't be glued back. Tempering your enthusiasm is difficult on a beautiful spring day, when it feels so good to be outdoors and working in the garden, but rein yourself in. It pays. We know from firsthand experience. And, again, for big projects seek the services of trained professionals. As a rule of thumb, if you have to climb a ladder or into the branches of a tree to prune, let a professional do it. We, fortunately, do not have broken appendage stories to emphasize this point, but we have friends who do.

❧ 8 ❧

Trees

A CHECKLIST

*I like trees because they seem more resigned
to the way they have to live than other things do.*
WILLA CATHER, *O PIONEER!*

Large and conspicuous, trees are a yard's most prominent feature, deserving our admiration and respect. The character of an old, twisted oak or stately elm cannot be duplicated during one's lifetime. Realizing the monetary value of fine old trees, many homebuilders have abandoned the clear-cutting approach to site preparation and now take pains to leave standing the more distinguished specimens of our state's many handsome native trees.

There are, however, times when you need to select and plant your own trees. And it is precisely because trees are a long-term investment, dominant and permanent, that careful selection, placement and planting are important. Tree planting is not an impulsive act. Consider first the function of the tree in the landscape. Is it to provide shade, privacy, or accent? Think about its year-round appearance. Deciduous trees (which shed leaves at the end of a functional period) work well in a southern exposure, providing shade in summer and allowing light in winter. Redbuds and flowering fruit trees give us welcome spring color, and the red oaks bring fall color to the area. Evergreen trees (with leaves that remain green and functional through more than one growing season) are effective screens against cold north winds as well as visual intrusion.

Be aware that most trees grow outward as well as upward more rapidly than we anticipate. As they grow, they affect the entire landscape design. The southern magnolia is an example of a magnificent tree that will quickly dominate a small yard. Remember, too, that the cooling shade, so desirable in our climate, will influence where flowers and vegetables can be grown. And practically speaking, small saplings casually placed can interfere surprisingly soon with utility lines (both above and below ground), fences, eaves, and neighbors' yards as well as with one another.

When selecting a tree from our enormous variety of shade, fruit, and flowering trees of many sizes and shapes, take the long view and consider the tree's importance in your landscape. Often the larger-caliper (the diameter of a tree measured in inches at chest height) tree planted by an experienced nursery staff or tree service can be the prudent buy.

SHADE AND ORNAMENTAL TREES

While the distinction between a large shrub and a small tree can become rather fine, we think of trees as plants with single trunks that attain a height of at least fifteen feet. However, even with so broad a definition, exceptions do appear. Climatic and soil factors and the gardener's preference can make a difference in the form a plant assumes. For easy reference, we have listed here some shrubs that are sometimes used as trees; their descriptions are given in the next chapter.

Included are some indigenous trees that you will seldom if ever see for sale at the nursery, such as the hackberry or the Ashe juniper (often mistakenly called a cedar), but which are plentiful in our city, suburban, and rural landscapes. For gardeners who wish to give the required time and attention to achieve the unexcelled quality and pride that fruit- and nut-bearing trees can provide, we have included a list of the best choices.

Ashe Juniper *(Juniperus ashei).* This medium-sized evergreen with an irregular shape and small, scalelike leaves has played a historic role in Central Texas. It has been the economic mainstay of the Texas cedar chopper and is the only acceptable habitat of the endangered golden-cheeked warbler. Although slow-growing, it is so prolific on Central Texas rangelands that it will soon take over if not controlled. The pollen of the male tree is the source of discomfort for many sufferers of "cedar fever." Frequently, smoky gray stripes ring its shaggy bark. The small, pale blue berries produced by the female are an important food source for many wildlife species. It is often confused with the eastern red cedar, which is more commonly found east of Interstate Highway 35. Evergreen, it grows to thirty feet.

Afghan Pine *(Pinus eldarica).* This fast-growing evergreen is the best pine for alkaline soils. Reaching twenty-five to thirty feet, it is an excellent windbreak or visual screen.

Arizona Ash *(Fraxinus velutina).* Inexpensive and fast-growing, the Arizona ash was almost obligatory for every new home not too long ago. But it is short-lived (twenty-five to thirty years), and its weak wood can pose a danger in high winds. It has four- to five-inch compound leaves and grows to fifty feet. Today improved varieties are available. Deciduous.

Arizona Cypress *(Cupressus arizonica).* This native evergreen of the Southwest has scalelike foliage similar to that of the red cedar. Its silver-gray bloom makes the young tree attractive. However, when crushed, the leaves have a strong odor. In its youth, this cypress has a dense, conical crown, but it changes shape as the branches spread with age. Usually twenty to forty feet at maturity, it is rapid-growing and long-lived. Evergreen.

Bald Cypress *(Taxodium distichum).* A regal denizen of Big Thicket and other moist environs, this deciduous conifer now is appearing at Austin shopping malls and on the city streets of Fort Worth, as landscape architects discover its adaptability to a range of conditions. Tall and conically shaped with wide, drooping branches, its pale green, feathery foliage adds color and textural variety to any setting and turns red-orange in the fall. It grows at a moderate rate to about sixty to ninety feet.

Blackjack Oak *(Quercus marilandica).* Often found bravely standing alone in soils too poor for other trees, this slow-growing, medium-sized oak is best identified by its wedge-shaped, leathery leaves and very rough, almost black bark. The broad, stout branches of this native form a rounded crown, giving the tree a symmetrical appearance. It is appropriate for areas east of the Balcones fault line. Deciduous, it grows to sixty feet.

Black Locust *(Robinia pseudoacacia).* Although this ornamental tree has graceful, white, fragrant flowers in late spring, its sharp thorns, its need for deep, well-drained, moist soil, and its susceptibility to locust borers make it less than satisfactory for our area. Rapidly growing to forty to sixty feet, it is upright, with an open habit. Its long, feathery compound leaves are pleasing to the eye. Deciduous.

Bradford Pear *(Pyrus calleryana* 'Bradford'). Masses of snowy white flowers in spring and crimson leaves in fall make this deciduous, nonbearing ornamental an excellent choice. Its upward-growing branches and narrow habit are ideal for smaller areas. It will grow to its maximum height of twenty-five feet at a moderate rate. Deciduous.

Bur Oak *(Quercus macrocarpa)*. Twenty years ago a friend at Austin's Natural Science Center gave us one of the large, distinctive acorns from which this native, deciduous shade tree gets it species name, *macrocarpa* (large seed). Today the resulting tree graces the playground of an Austin elementary school with its beauty and shade. A high-branched tree with heavy, spreading limbs, the bur oak has a broad crown and simple alternate leaves with five to nine lobes. Growing at a medium rate to a height of up to 130 feet, the bur oak looks best in a generous space.

Catalpa *(Catalpa speciosa)*. Because of its enormous simple leaves (six to ten inches), and long seed pods (eight to sixteen inches) that remain on the tree during winter, this deciduous native is easy to identify. Conspicuous clusters of white flowers with purple or yellow make it a desirable spring-blooming tree. Its height of up to fifty feet and its large features make it a suitable tree for a large yard. Susceptible to worm and insect infestations, the catalpa may require care if it is to live a long life.

Cedar Elm *(Ulmus crassifolia)*. Possessor of a straight trunk and graceful branches, the region's most common elm is prized as a hearty shade provider and a handsome specimen tree. Of moderate growth rate, this deciduous native can attain a height of ninety feet, but it is often much shorter in the limestone hills of Central Texas. It has small, oval leaves with serrated margins. In fall its leaves turn a glorious filigree of gold.

Cherry Laurel *(Prunus caroliniana)*. See chapter 9, "Shrubs."

Chinaberry *(Melia azedarach)*. An all-too-successful garden escapee in the South, this Asian native is often seen on roadsides in urban and suburban areas. It is easily identified by its yellow, globular but poisonous fruit and large compound leaves (ten to thirty-two inches long). Messy and invasive, it is not considered a desirable ornamental tree. It grows at a moderate rate to forty feet and is short-lived.

Chinese Parasol Tree, Varnish Tree *(Firmiana simplex)*. The distinctive large, three-to-five lobed leaves, green bark, and unusual fruit—small, pealike seeds protected by five leafy pods—give this tree an exotic look. An Asian native, it grows quickly up to thirty feet tall. It is deciduous.

Chinese Elm *(Ulmus parvifolia)*. Tolerating a variety of soil conditions, the Chinese elm quickly reaches forty to sixty feet. Its handsome spreading branches and durability make it a good choice. Deciduous.

Chinese Pistachio *(Pistacia chinensis)*. Its capacity to withstand heat, drought, and poor soils makes this broadly spreading Chinese plant a good

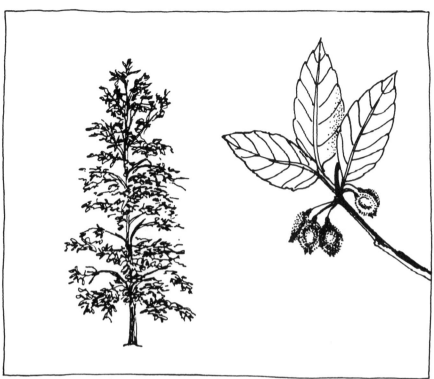

CEDAR ELM (Ulmus crassifolia)

shade selection for our area. Deciduous, it provides scarlet to yellow fall color. It grows to thirty feet.

Chinese Tallow *(Sapium sebiferum)*. Once popular for its pleasing heart-shaped leaves, which provide excellent fall color, the deciduous Chinese tallow was almost wiped out in Central Texas during the freezes of 1983 and 1989. In recent years it has been denounced by the Nature Conservancy for its invasiveness. It drops a messy waxy white fruit. It grows from twenty-five to forty feet.

Chinquapin Oak *(Quercus muhlenbergii)*. Loving well-drained terrain, this moderately sized oak is well adapted to Central Texas limestone soils. Its growth rate is moderate and wildlife welcome its acorns. Deciduous, it grows to sixty feet.

Cottonless Cottonwood *(Populus deltoides)*. A welcome sight to thirsty westward pioneers, this large, fast-growing, handsome tree indicated a nearby source of water. Just the rustle of its large leaves psychologically drops the temperature several degrees. "Cottonless" refers to the cultivar that does not produce large quantities of airborne seeds, which can be an irritant to allergy suffers. Its

TREES

roots, however, can be a problem for sidewalks, buildings, and other structures within a few years. Deciduous, it reaches ninety feet.

Crape Myrtle *(Lagerstroemia indica).* Blooming all summer long, the crape myrtle has won the "most popular" title for ornamental tree. It is available in white, lavender, and almost every shade of pink and red. New cultivars have greatly reduced the problem of powdery mildew so common years ago. The crape myrtle thrives in hot, dry weather. Tolerant of heavy pruning, it has long been the victim of unsightly dehorning, a practice intended to control height and promote a full, bushy top. Left to follow its nature, the crape myrtle will develop into a tall, gracefully elegant tree of twenty-five to thirty feet. Deciduous and thus showing off its smooth, pale bark, it can also be stunning in the winter landscape. Consult your nursery staff for size, color, and form.

Desert Willow *(Chilopsis linearis).* Another good tree for small spaces, the desert willow needs full sun and good drainage. Its showy pinkish flowers are delightful. A slightly wild appearance makes it a good choice for informal naturalized gardens. Deciduous, it grows to twenty feet.

Dogwood *(Cornus spp.).* The species *C. florida,* so prized for its white and pink blossoms, is a native of East Texas, where it is most often found in rich, moist soil under the protection of a tall pine or oak. It survives in Central Texas only if planted in rich, acid soil, kept moist, and given adequate shade. Its deciduous, oval leaves are shiny on top and paler underneath. This dogwood reaches thirty feet tall and has a spreading habit with a flat crown. The **Rough-leaf Dogwood** *(C. drummondii),* also deciduous, is a shrub or small tree (to fifteen feet) indigenous to Central Texas. Although its white flowers are comparatively inconspicuous, in late summer it produces a fruit that is relished by at least forty bird species.

Eastern Red Cedar *(Juniperus virginiana).* Settlers confused this juniper with a cedar, hence its name, and many of us today still confuse it with the Ashe juniper. It has a variable shape and seldom grows to more than fifty feet. Birds depend on it for its fruit. Found all over the eastern United States, in Texas it is more likely to occur east of Interstate Highway 35.

Flowering Peach *(Prunus persica).* This is a small but striking specimen when its double flowers (white, red, or variegated) appear in spring. Its small, narrow leaves are deciduous. This fast-growing, ornamental peach tree has a broad, rounded crown and reaches twenty to twenty-five feet.

Fruitless Mulberry *(Morus alba).* Once popular for fulfilling its promise as a quick shade provider in poor and dry soils, this rangy tree is no longer widely

CRAPE MYRTLE (Lagerstroemia indica)

used. Subject to bacterial blight that deforms leaves and branches, it is not considered a desirable ornamental tree. During dry spells it sheds its large, deciduous leaves as early as August. It grows to forty feet.

Ginkgo, Maidenhair Tree *(Ginkgo biloba)*. While this tree prefers a more temperate climate, there are specimens in our area. Another Chinese native, the deciduous ginkgo has been in this country since the eighteenth century. *Biloba* refers to its two-lobed leaves, which resemble those of the maidenhair fern. The pale yellow fruit is highly prized food in China and Japan; however, the female fruits have an unpleasant odor and are messy when they fall. The tree is grown primarily as an ornamental in this country and is usually under thirty feet. While full and round-headed in its maturity, it has a gawky yet interesting branching habit during its first twenty years.

Goldenrain Tree *(Koelreuteria paniculata)*. This is a particularly interesting tree in late summer and early fall because of its long, flowing clusters of yellow flowers, which are followed by the appearance of pinkish, bladder-shaped pods. A deciduous native of China and Japan, it is on the small side (under twenty feet tall) and grows fast. It is vulnerable to severe freeze.

Guadalupe Palm *(Erythea edulis)*. Thriving in areas with temperatures from below freezing to desert heat, this upright fan palm from Mexico is excellent as a specimen tree or as a filler in a shrubbery design. Unlike that of many other palms, its fan-shaped foliage remains green year-round. This palm grows slowly to thirty feet.

Common Hackberry *(Celtis occidentalis)*. Few kind words have been spoken or written about this persistent native. Overwhelmingly invasive, it is plagued by insect pests and fungi and rarely presents a healthy appearance. Easily identified by its warty bark, the deciduous hackberry produces a dark purple fruit relished by many bird species, perhaps its main value. While it can reach ninety feet, it more commonly grows to forty to fifty feet in Central Texas.

Thornless Honey Locust *(Gleditsia triacanthos* var. *inermis)*. This tough, fast-growing ornamental grows well in a variety of climatic and soil conditions, making it a suitable tree for urban and suburban locations. Its loose, open crown and deciduous, graceful compound leaves give it an airy appearance. It grows to thirty feet.

Honey Mesquite *(Prosopis glandulosa)*. For many the word mesquite evokes the image of scrubby bushes invading rangeland; this is an accurate vision as far as it goes, but mesquite is far more versatile in its habit. A handsome accent tree with delicate, fernlike foliage, this deciduous legume contrasts well next to broad-leafed plants. Its craggy, drooping branches begin a short distance above ground, giving the mesquite a shrubby appearance. A slow grower, it will reach thirty feet.

Huisache, Acacia, Sweet Acacia *(Acacia farnesiana)*. When found near the coast, the huisache is a multistemmed bush, but in Central Texas, its most common form is a single-trunk tree of up to twenty feet. Thorny branches, extremely fragrant yellow flowers, and feathery compound leaves are its outstanding features. A popular ornamental in tropical and subtropical countries, it blooms most reliably in the more southerly areas of Central Texas. This fast-growing native has been used for medicinal purposes, fence posts, and as a winter forage plant. Honey from pollen of huisache blossoms is distinct and desirable. Deciduous.

Japanese Black Pine *(Pinus thunbergii)*. This pine is an imported evergreen that has won praise for its vivid green foliage and irregular branching, which give it eye appeal and character. To thrive in areas of shallow limy soil, it may

LIVE OaK (Quercus virginiana)

require the addition of soil acidifiers and iron. Although the tree is slow-grow-ing, some older specimens are more than twenty feet tall. It has medium-length needles and produces a small cone.

Live Oak *(Quercus virginiana)*. Perhaps no other tree better expresses the rugged beauty of its native land than this magnificent oak. Classified as ever-green, the live oak sheds its leaves in early spring, and within three weeks the new leaves are in place. The best examples have massive, low branches and dramatic, wide-spreading crowns. The live oak, which grows slowly, will even-tually get up to sixty feet and is an excellent shade provider. Since these are fairly expensive in nurseries, the homeowner who finds them on site should make every effort to keep and preserve them. The live oak is susceptible to oak wilt (see chapter 13, "Trouble in the Garden").

Lombardy Poplar *(Populus nigra* var. *italica)*. A fast-growing, short-lived, deciduous tree, the poplar can be used as a screen or windbreak. It seldom achieves its maximum ninety-foot height. Its leaves are wedge shaped. Like the

Italian cypress, it is a columnar tree, with branches that turn upward and grow close to the trunk. Unfortunately, it is apt to acquire cankers as it grows, which will leave the top of the tree dead.

Loquat *(Eriobotrya japonica).* Handsome and fast-growing, this broadleaved evergreen native of Asia produces clusters of aromatic flowers beloved by bees in October and November. Of medium height (to forty feet), it is good-looking, and its edible fruit makes a delicious, mild-tasting preserve. The loquat's slightly triangular habit is often concealed by a variety of pruning styles. It is susceptible to fire blight.

Mexican Buckeye *(Ungnadia speciosa).* Its persistence in limestone crevices and other difficult places make this small (to twenty-five feet) native of bushy appearance a desirable specimen plant where others refuse to grow. Peachlike or redbudlike spring blossoms are followed by a distinctive three-valved seed-pod in late summer or fall. If eaten, the mildly poisonous seeds can cause stomach disturbances. The leaves of this slow-growing deciduous tree are dark green, compound, and five to twelve inches long.

Mexican Plum *(Prunus mexicana).* A small, deciduous tree, this plum is a southwestern native and has an irregular, open crown. It has white flowers about an inch in diameter; light green, gently serrated leaves; and dark purplish red fruit, which varies in quality. Deciduous and growing at a moderate rate to about twenty-five feet, it is primarily an accent tree.

Mimosa *(Albizia julibrissin).* Fernlike leaves, conspicuous masses of delicate pink flowers in May through June, and a broad, open crown are distinguishing characteristics of this popular accent tree. Its messy dropping of blossoms, weak wood and susceptibility to mimosa wilt (a fungus that causes leaves to yellow and wilt and that ultimately kills the tree) make this attractive tree less than an ideal choice. Deciduous, it grows to twenty feet.

Monterrey Oak *(Quercus polymorpha).* An upright, handsome semievergreen (evergreen in warm winters but will defoliate all leaves in a cold winter) oak with oval leaves. It is a moderately fast-growing tree that will reach fifty to sixty feet. Indifferent to soil as long as it is well drained, the Monterrey oak is drought-tolerant once well established.

Oak. *See* Blackjack Oak; Bur Oak; Live Oak; Monterrey Oak; Post Oak; Shumard Oak; Spanish Oak.

Ornamental Date Palm *(Phoenix canariensis).* Given rich, moist soil, this handsome, hardy feather palm will grow from six to twelve inches a year until it reaches about twenty feet. Its straight, erect trunk is crowned by glossy, dark green leaves, giving the neatest of evergreen palms a stately appearance.

Palm. *See* Guadalupe Palm; Ornamental Date Palm; Texas Palm; Washington Palm; Windmill Palm.

Pecan *(Carya illinoinensis).* Towering and regal, our Texas state tree is valued for its dignified bearing as well as its nut production. The largest member of the hickory family, this handsome shade tree can grow to sixty feet. It is a fast-growing, deciduous tree with long (nine- to twenty-inch), dark, compound leaves. The fruit, which ripens in September to October, is smaller and has a harder shell than the familiar papershell commercial varieties (for nut-bearing varieties suitable for our area, see Fruit and Nut Trees later in this chapter).

Post Oak *(Quercus stellata).* Post oak is a good, hardy shade tree with stout limbs and a dense, round head. It slowly grows up to forty feet tall and has deciduous, five-lobed leaves. Its acorns, which are eaten by deer and wild turkey, are set in a cup and ripen in the fall. Its rugged exterior belies an inherent fragility that prevents it from tolerating construction damage or surviving transplanting.

Purple Plum *(Prunus cerasifera).* A small ornamental popular for its purplish foliage, this is a slow-growing tree, which in spring produces delicate pink blossoms. Unfortunately, it is subject to borers. Its large, deep purple leaves are deciduous. It has a narrow shape, with branches beginning close to the ground, and reaches twenty feet.

Red Mulberry *(Morus rubra).* A small native tree with a spreading crown, this mulberry has alternate, toothed leaves, three to five inches long and sometimes mitten shaped or lobed. Its bark is dark gray-brown, and its sweet, edible fruit is purple or black when ripe but does not keep well. Fast-growing, it is best planted as an ornamental away from sidewalks and drives, where the falling fruit would be a nuisance. Deciduous, it grows to twenty feet.

Retama, Jerusalem Thorn *(Parkinsonia aculeata).* Depending on humidity conditions, this deciduous native may bloom up to five times a season, making it an interesting ornamental. Growing rapidly to twenty feet, the tree has delicate compound leaves that cover its widely spreading branches. When young, the tree has green bark, making it easy to identify.

Shumard Oak *(Quercus shumardii).* Closely related to and often confused with the Spanish oak, this native, deciduous red oak is larger (to 100 feet) and most likely to be found in the deep soils east of the Balcones faultline. A superb shade tree, its deeply lobed leaves turn a lovely red in fall.

Silver Maple *(Acer saccharinum).* A water lover that grows fast and may reach ninety feet under optimal conditions, this maple is usually half that size in our area. This deciduous East Texas native has five-lobed, light green leaves that

SOUTHERN MAGNOLIA (Magnolia grandiflora)

are silver-white underneath. Its wide-spreading branches provide abundant shade. It is susceptible to insects and fungus disease and may suffer from leaf scorch and chlorosis in Central Texas. Maple fans still find much to recommend it, but choose it with caution.

Southern Magnolia *(Magnolia grandiflora)*. By any definition a glorious specimen tree, the southern magnolia grows to large and noble stature. It begins branching near the base of the trunk, usually does not top fifty feet, and has large, waxy evergreen leaves and extravagant blossoms. Although it naturally prefers the moist soils of East Texas, it is successfully cultivated in our area, where applications of iron sulfate may be required to prevent chlorosis. Magnolias drop their leaves at the end of their second year; this natural occurrence should not be a cause for alarm.

Spanish Oak *(Quercus texana)*. The source of striking red color in the Hill Country in fall, this slender, deciduous oak reaches from fifteen to thirty feet. Although drought tolerant and generally a tough tree, it is very susceptible to oak wilt (see chapter 13, "Trouble in the Garden").

Sycamore, American Plane Tree *(Platanus occidentalis)*. Tall, conical, and fast-growing, this deciduous native is one of the most popular shade trees. It has broadly lobed, simple leaves four to twelve inches across. The sycamore's size can be overpowering for small yards, and in alkaline soils iron chlorosis is a common problem. Deciduous, it reaches a hundred feet.

Texas Mountain Laurel, Mescal Bean *(Sophora secundiflora)*. An extravagant profusion of intoxicating flowers and lustrous, dark green leaves make this informally shaped large shrub or small tree a valuable accent plant. Slow-growing (to fifteen feet) but exceptionally well suited to Hill Country soils, the native evergreen is available at local nurseries. It blooms best in full sun.

Texas Palm *(Sabal texana)*. At home along the Rio Grande River, this tropical-appearing evergreen may reach forty feet in height with a trunk one and a half to three feet in diameter. Its fan-shaped leaves are three to five feet wide and are long. Like other sabals, the ornamental *texana* has a distinctive leaf, which is split down the middle, supposedly to make it wind resistant. The dead

TEXAS MOUNTAIN LAUREL (Sophora secundiflora)

TREES

TEXas PERSIMMON (Diospyros texana)

fronds on this and other palms should be removed for a neat appearance. While easy to propagate from seed, the Texas palm is difficult to transplant.

Texas Persimmon *(Diospyros texana)*. Slight and delicate with smooth, gray bark and intricate branching patterns, the deciduous native persimmon has small, leathery leaves and is a desirable accent tree. Its fruit is appreciated by a variety of birds and mammals. A slow grower, this small tree (to forty feet) can be best appreciated when not overshadowed by larger shade trees. The messy black fruit of this tree can be a nuisance around patios and sidewalks.

Texas Pistachio *(Pistacia texana)*. A hardy native reaching twenty feet in the dry limestones of the Hill Country and forty feet in deep rich moist soils, the handsome Texas pistachio falls into that ambiguous category of small tree/ large shrub. It has an open spreading habit, bears red fruit in fall, and is an excellent xeriscape choice.

Texas Redbud *(Cercis canadensis* var. *texensis)*. Central Texas' favorite spring harbinger displays masses of rose-purple flowers late in winter or early in spring, before it leafs out. Broadly spreading trees with dull green, oval leaves, mature redbuds can be good shade providers, although they are most often planted for their early spring blossoms. Rarely growing to more than twenty-five feet, this deciduous native is a good size for any yard and is readily available at nurseries.

Vitex, Lavender Tree, Lilac Chaste Tree *(Vitex agnus-castus)*. Preferring dry, sunny conditions, this long-blooming native produces great spikes of fragrant blue-violet flowers, often used in sachets. Its toothed, lance-shaped leaflets appear in groups of five or more. The deciduous vitex has many trunks and grows to twenty feet. It makes either a good accent or a good border tree.

Washington Palm *(Washingtonia filifera* and *W. robusta)*. Dedicated to President George Washington, *W. filifera* is a native of the Southwest, while *W. robusta* is a Mexican species. They are similar, although according to one local palm expert we know, *filifera* is hardier and less likely to freeze. This striking ornamental evergreen grows at a moderate rate into a tall tree (forty feet), with a cylindrical trunk up to three feet wide, which is often covered with dead pendant leaves forming a large skirt. The fan-shaped leaves are up to six feet long

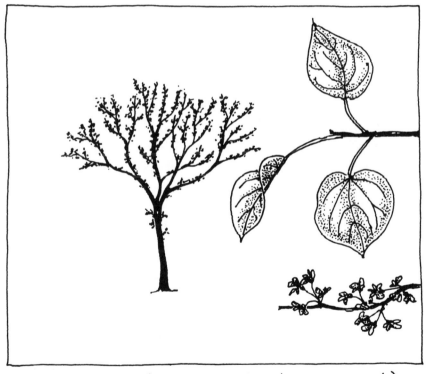

TEXAS REDBUD (Cercis canadensis var. texensis)

WEEPING WILLOW (Salix babylonica)

and five feet across. This palm has small, black, berrylike fruit. There are many fine specimens around the Alamo.

Weeping Willow *(Salix babylonica).* A romantic-looking import from China, this willow is characterized by drooping branches. Fast-growing and deciduous, it may reach fifty feet in height. It requires much water and is best planted near a lake or stream. Insect borers can be a problem. In an urban setting, this willow can cause problems with water and sewer lines. An attractive curly-leaf variety called 'Corkscrew Willow' is sometimes available.

Western Soapberry *(Sapindus drummondii).* This deciduous native, growing to thirty feet, is frequently confused with the chinaberry. A good shade tree, it is slender with a rounded head. It has long, yellowish green, compound leaves and produces an abundance of white flowers in early spring. The translucent yellowish fruit has been used to make soap in Mexico.

Windmill Palm *(Trachycarpus fortunei).* This evergreen Chinese native owes its common name to windmill-like, fan-shaped leaves, about three feet in diameter, with stiff, dark green leaflets. One of the hardiest of all palms, it appears to prefer cooler climates, although it can be grown in Central Texas. Under good conditions, it will grow six inches or more a year, reaching a height of fifteen to thirty-five feet. The hairy appearance of the trunk comes from a thick mass of long, dark fibers growing from the leaf base.

Yaupon Holly *(Ilex vomitoria).* (Also see chapter 9, "Shrubs".) We like the evergreen yaupon in all its many forms. Small (twenty feet is its maximum height), slender, and usually multitrunked, this native holly is a perfect specimen plant and serves well in many situations. The leaves are small and elliptical and bright red berries are borne on the female in winter. Its curious species name refers to a former medicinal use. The **Possumhaw Holly** *(I. decidua)*, also reaching twenty feet, has a loose, rangy, almost nondescript appearance during the growing season. It is in winter, after having shed its leaves, that this holly becomes a glorious standout, with no greenery to disguise the bounty of red berries clinging to its scaffold-like branches.

WINDMILL PALM (Trachycarpus fortunei)

TREES

Full sun, good drainage, and soil high in humus all are crucial to good fruit production, but the single most important condition for fruit bearing is the "chill factor," or the number of hours below forty-five degrees Fahrenheit needed to set fruit. Because many fruit trees require seven hundred chill hours—a number most of Central Texas cannot guarantee—selection of varieties proven to produce in our climate is essential.

Because it is so important to get the proper variety for your area, it's essential to buy these trees locally. Most fruit trees are purchased bare-root and should be completely dormant when bought. Buy fruit trees as soon after they arrive at the garden center as possible. Don't wait for end-of-season bargains—it is crucial that the trees have strong, healthy root systems.

Proper pruning, training, fertilizing, spraying, and weeding practices are necessary for high quality and consistent fruit. If that is your goal, the county extension agents are the best sources for continuously updated material.

Following is a partial list of fruit and nut trees well adapted to the climate of Central Texas. All those mentioned are deciduous.

Apples

Generally apples need more cold weather than we can provide. However, there are several varieties that grow here, especially in the slightly cooler northern part of our region. You may need two varieties of apples for good pollination.

Braeburn. This versatile apple is good for eating, baking, and sauce. It is crisp and sweet-tart with yellow flesh. It keeps for six months or more.

Gala. Fragrant, sweet, and mildly tart, this is an excellent eating apple.

Granny Smith. Juicy, crisp and tart, the Granny Smith is a favorite baking apple.

Red Delicious. A good eating apple that is juicy, mildly tart, and crisp.

Figs

To get a good fig crop you need to pay attention to soil moisture. The fig tree is shallow rooted and prone to water stress during dry spells, which can result in fruit drop. It is best to mulch and irrigate consistently.

Celeste. Thriving in all areas of Texas, the Celeste fig is a high quality fruit for fresh eating or preserving. It ripens in late June.

Texas Everbearing. The most common fig in Texas, this medium-large fig of good quality ripens in late June. It does best in Central and East Texas.

Peaches

No peach tastes as sweet as a local peach and what could be more "local" than your garden? Peach production begins seriously in the third year. Plant the tree in well-drained soil and keep the soil beneath the tree weed-free with mulch.

Dixieland. A large freestone of excellent quality, this moderately bacterial spot–resistant variety ripens in mid-July.

Frank. Excellent for canning and freezing, the Frank has been producing consistent crops in Texas since the turn of the century. The fruit, a good-textured clingstone, ripens in August.

Redskin. Producing in mid-July, the redskin yields a large freestone peach.

Sentinel. This variety produces a large, semi-cling fruit in early June.

Springold. A good early variety, the Springold produces a small clingstone with yellow flesh. It ripens at the end of May.

Pears

With their upright shape and handsome foliage, pear trees are among the most attractive fruit-bearing trees in the home garden. They also are easier to maintain than other fruit varieties. The trees listed below are oriental hybrids that are more successful in Texas than the European hybrids of supermarket familiarity, such as Bartlett and Bosc.

Fire blight is a problem for many pear varieties and can seriously damage or kill trees. Branches and twigs get a blackened, scorched appearance. Affected parts can be cut out (at least six inches below the diseased area). Pruning tools should then be cleaned in a chlorine bleach solution. Planting resistant varieties is the best line of defense.

Ayres. This variety is highly resistant to fire blight and produces a medium-sized russet-brown fruit of excellent quality in August.

Warren. Highly resistant to fire blight, the Warren produces an excellent dessert quality fruit in August.

Plums

Small and pleasing in shape, the plum tree is a welcome addition to the home landscape. For fruit production it is best to grow two different varieties of plums to ensure pollination.

Methley. Self-pollinating and a moderately vigorous grower, the Methley is a good garden variety. This tree produces a medium-sized fruit that ripens in early June.

Bruce. This common commercial variety produces a large, juicy plum excellent for preserves. A pollinator is necessary for crop production.

Allred. This small plum has red skin and flesh. Its fruit ripens in early June.

Pecans

As prized for its majestic beauty as for its sweet nuts, the pecan makes an excellent yard tree if its preferred conditions for deep fertile soil, good drainage, and space can be met. While most pecan trees are purchased bare-root, container-grown trees are increasingly available. As with any bare-root plant, buy early in the season and take precautions to prevent the root system from drying out or freezing before planting. This may mean wrapping it in damp newspaper or placing it in compost.

Caddo. The Caddo has handsome foliage and produces a small nut of high quality. It begins to produce in five to seven years.

Desirable. A leading commercial (improved papershell) producer, Desirable yields a quality nut and is relatively disease resistant. The tree will bear in eight years.

Sioux. This yields a small papershell nut of excellent quality. Problems with fungus during periods of high humidity are a possibility.

❧ 9 ❧

Shrubs

A CHECKLIST

A bad bush is better than the open field.
ENGLISH PROVERB

There are shrubs for every yard—which means the real dilemma for the home-owner may be too many choices. Some shrubs are evergreen, giving year-round color; some are deciduous, shedding their foliage in winter. Others are chosen for their appealing blossoms; still others for their attractive foliage. Shrubs may be used as a hedge to mark off an area, to provide a windbreak, or to offer privacy; often shrubs serve as the main decorative element in a garden.

Usually we think of a shrub as a woody plant that is not too tall and has many stems, while a tree has one trunk and grows to a larger size. Yet nature doesn't draw definitive lines, and there are a number of plants (such as crape myrtle and mountain laurel) that are often listed under the heading of "shrubs or small trees." The pruning shears determine which form such plants will take in the garden.

Before selecting your shrubs, you might read through the list that follows and note the main features of different bushes. Then consider the main func-tions of the plants to be used in a certain spot in your garden. If, for example, you are planning a shrub border, you might begin from the back and select the tallest-growing shrubs first. Be certain that those chosen will eventually be tall enough to give the privacy you want but not so tall that they will eliminate sunlight and breezes or dwarf your house or yard. Size at maturity should be one of your most important considerations. Most of the time six- to eight-foot shrubs will do the best job.

With the tallest shrubs selected, you can fill in with smaller ones in front. As mentioned in chapter 4, it is generally preferable to use clusters rather than single plants in a row. If you use flowering shrubs (and we hope you will consider them), be sure to take into account blooming times and the amount of sun or shade in the planting location. If a plant requires sun, it won't blossom properly in shade, and conversely a shade lover may be sunburned or scorched in a site with full sun.

The decided preference for evergreen shrubs in our climate is understandable. On gloomy winter days there is some psychological reassurance in seeing a lush, green plant, oblivious to nature's extremes, thriving in the garden. We have a wide selection of evergreens and semievergreens (plants that generally lose about half their leaves in winter) in Central Texas. Many of them are attractive and easily maintained.

Having said this, we are quick to point out that special features of some deciduous shrubs make them very desirable too. For instance, the shape and the flowers of the crape myrtle are worth a little winter barrenness, and the attractive, exfoliating bark of the crape can only be appreciated when the plant is bare of leaves.

The following list of shrubs will prepare you to make your decisions. For other suggestions regarding selection of plants, planting, and care, see chapters 4 and 7. The height and width given here refer to the mature, unpruned plant. While shrubs may be maintained at any height and width up to the maximum with consistent pruning, using dwarf varieties in smaller spaces can substantially reduce maintenance.

Within the checklist, the term *specimen* refers to the use of the plant as a single individual as opposed to in a group planting.

Abelia *(Abelia grandiflora).* Preferring full sun but tolerating partial shade, this medium-sized evergreen with graceful, arching branches produces white-pink flowers from early summer to fall. Enduring a wide range of conditions, the abelia is also versatile in function, serving equally well as a hedge or a specimen shrub. In fall its simple, opposite leaves take on a bronze cast. Bees love it! Dwarf varieties are available. Standard abelia grows to four or five feet high and three or four feet wide.

Agarito *(Berberis trifoliolata).* An interesting evergreen native with stiff, slightly variegated, holly-shaped leaves, the agarito is a medium-sized shrub

ABELIA (Abelia grandiflora)

that thrives in Hill Country soils. It does equally well as a specimen or a hedge. The bright red berries that appear in late spring are excellent for preserves or for attracting birds. Because its leaves are sharp and thorny, agarito should be planted where it can do no harm to the passerby. Like many other thorny shrubs, it can be used as a barrier. It grows three to six feet high and equally wide and takes full sun.

American Beautyberry, French Mulberry *(Callicarpa americana).* This deciduous native owes its popularity to the extravagant profusion of purple berries growing in the leaf axils from August through November. Birds and animals are known to appreciate their taste as much as we enjoy their beauty. Its leaves are four to six inches long, and it can grow from three to six feet tall and three or four feet wide. It is an easy plant to establish from seed or cuttings. It does best as an understory plant and, therefore, can take some shade. Cut back the beautyberry close to the ground after it goes dormant to prevent it from becoming too rangy.

Aralia *(Aralia sieboldii)*. The tropical look of its large, maple-shaped leaves makes the evergreen aralia a good choice for a bold statement. It can be planted singly or in a group. Growing to six feet high and four to five feet wide, it prefers partial to full shade and rich soil.

Aucuba, Gold Dust *(Aucuba japonica)*. Gold specks or variegated leaf patterns make this tropical-looking plant an easy-to-spot specimen. A hardy evergreen that grows to ten feet tall and five feet wide, it needs partial shade to prevent sunburn. The female plants produce bright red berries in winter. A less common but very handsome solid green variety that produces red berries in autumn is also available. While aucuba is cold tolerant, its leaves turn limp and black during a hard freeze. Do not despair; it will snap back to life as soon as the temperature rises.

Azalea *(Rhododendron* spp.). Despite its inappropriateness for many of our Central Texas alkaline soils, legions of people are willing to go to great lengths to enjoy the spectacular beauty of these members of the *Rhododendron* genus. And understandably so, for the azalea is a flowering shrub of outstanding beauty. A woodland plant, its primary demand is cool, moist, acid soil. This means removing all soil from the hole in which the azalea is to be planted, and then backfilling with moistened sphagnum peat moss (avoid other peats that are less expensive but lack the water retention quality of sphagnum) or a mix of peat moss with some sand to ensure good drainage.

Moisture can be retained and the temperature kept down with two to three inches of mulch, preferably a medium or fine pine mulch or oak leaves. In our severe climate, the azalea must be planted in partial shade. A fertilizer formulated especially for azaleas should be applied after the blossoms have fallen and then every six weeks until August. During very hot and dry periods, azaleas may need to be watered several times a week because the feeding roots are close to the surface. Failure to maintain even moisture may result in poor blossom quality and/or quantity. Two evergreen species recommended for our area are the **Indica Azalea** *(R. indicum)* and the **Kurume Azalea** *(R. obtusum)*. Both are available in a wide color range with single or double blossoms. The indica is a larger plant, growing to six feet tall and five feet wide, with larger leaves and blossoms; flowers are two or three inches across. Hardier, the kurume has a more compact growth habit, reaching about three or four feet in height and width with flowers to one inch across. Azaleas need cold protection when the temperature falls below the upper twenties. Get out the spare sheets and blankets (no plastic sheets, please).

AZALEA (Rhododendron spp.)

Boxwood or **Japanese Littleleaf Box** *(Buxus microphylla* var. *japonica).* A three- to six-foot shrub introduced into the United States from Japan in 1860, this shrub is widely planted in the southern states, where it thrives. Its evergreen leaves are about an inch long. Its dense, compact growth—which does best in full or partial sun—and its low maintenance make it useful as a hedge. Some find its pungent odor objectionable, so check it out before buying.

Camellia *(Camellia* spp.). For the past 150 years, these beautiful specimen plants have been inspiring flower lovers and homeowners in America. Camellias can be large shrubs or styled as standards, which means pruned and trained to a single trunk. The soil for camellias should be well drained and rich in humus and acid. These plants are renowned not only for their flowers but also for their lustrous, leathery, evergreen leaves. The smaller of the two varieties, the **Sasankwa Camellia** *(C. sasankwa),* is considered by some the superior. It produces blossoms to three and a half inches across in a variety of rich colors,

CAMELLIA (Camellia japonica)

white and mostly the pinks to reds, from September to December. The **Common Camellia** *(C. japonica)* has large flowers up to five inches wide, single or double, and blooms from October to April. If you plant both species, you get a long blooming season. Although camellias like sun, partial shade is a must in our hot climate. If you decide you must have camellias, cultural practices for these acid lovers should be similar to those for azaleas, including cold protection.

Cenizo *(Leucophyllum frutescens)*. This is a local favorite for a number of reasons: silver-gray evergreen foliage with a soft appearance, bell-shaped violet flowers that bloom in high humidity (hence its alternate name, barometer plant), and good adaptation to sandy or clay soil. It must have full sun to show off its full glory. Shady conditions will result in leggy growth and few blooms. Its attractive, erect shape makes it an excellent choice for medium-sized (to four or five feet) hedges or as specimens. The green leaf varieties 'Green Cloud' and 'Green Leaf' are very handsome and increasingly popular. The 'Compacta' is an excellent choice if you desire a smaller, denser plant. All varieties are drought tolerant. This is excellent in a xeriscape setting.

Cherry Laurel *(Prunus caroliniana).* A handsome, fast-growing evergreen native to the southeastern United States, this shrub has a rich foliage with two- to four-inch green leaves, inconspicuous white flowers, and shiny black fruit. Left unpruned, the versatile cherry laurel can grow to twenty-five feet high and twelve to fifteen feet wide. However, it tolerates heavy pruning well and is an excellent hedge shrub. It grows well in full sun to partial shade.

Cleyera *(Cleyera japonica).* As one of the few shrubs that does best in shade, this medium-sized evergreen with simple, glossy leaves and inconspicuous, white spring flowers has special value. Variegated forms with attractive white leaf margins are also available. Cleyera is a specimen plant that can be easily shaped and pruned. It grows to seven feet tall and five feet wide and can take full sun but prefers partial shade.

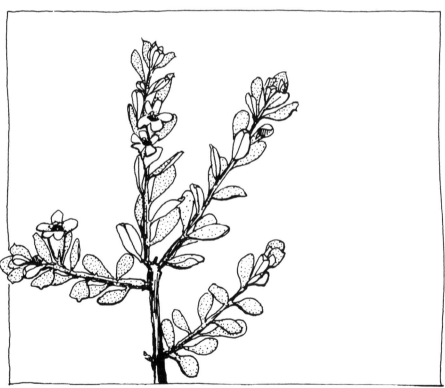

CENIZO (Leucophyllum frutescens)

Crimson Pigmy Barberry (*Berberis thunbergii* var. *atropurpurea* 'nana'). The red-purple foliage of this attractive, compact, deciduous plant punctuates the green landscape nicely. It is partial to full sun, attractive in rock gardens, and a good drought-tolerant plant. It grows to two feet tall and one or two feet wide. It does have thorns, which may be a consideration.

Dwarf Yaupon *(Ilex vomitoria).* The superb dwarf yaupon *I. vomitoria* 'nana' is the justly deserved workhorse of our urban and suburban landscapes. Trouble-free, thriving in sun or shade, and tolerating all manner of trimming, including topiary, it is a difficult plant to beat. Without regular trimming it will grow quite large. Try the very slow-growing, compact 'Stokes' variety for small spaces. Two recent cultivars are dramatic plants for special places: '**Will Fleming Yaupon**' is a very slender, almost columnar, tree of dense foliage, great for narrow entryways; and the '**Weeping Yaupon**' *(I. pendula)* has branches that cascade in a graceful droop. (See also chapter 8, "Trees.")

Elaeagnus *(Elaeagnus pungens).* This large evergreen shrub has dappled, gray-green leaves with rusty spots on the underside to add color interest to the landscape. It is a good, tough specimen or hedge shrub and will thrive in sun or partial shade. It has a tendency to "throw" (send out) lanky shoots, however, and requires regular trimming to maintain shape. It will reach fifteen feet high and six feet across.

Euonymus *(Euonymus* spp.). Susceptibility to scale and powdery mildew detracts somewhat from the many attributes of this Japanese import. It has handsome lustrous evergreen leaves, compact growth, and a liking for either sun or shade. **Evergreen Euonymus** *(E. japonicus)* is often used as a specimen. '**Silver King**' *(E. japonica)* is compact, growing to four feet in height and three feet in width. It tolerates heat and poor soil. The leaves are white and green. '**Manhattan Euonymus**' *(E. kiautschovica)* is a good hedge shrub. Tolerating severe pruning, it can be trimmed into formal geometric shapes. It will grow to nine feet tall and eight feet wide.

Fatshedera *(Fatshedera lizei).* A curious hybrid of fatsia and English ivy, fatshedera has oversized palmately lobed leaves (seven to eleven inches across) that give it a tropical appearance. Its high tolerance for shade makes it a valuable plant for dark courtyards, areas between buildings, and other deeply shaded nooks. Fatshedera is an evergreen that grows up to seven feet in height and five feet wide and makes an interesting specimen in the garden. It roots easily from softwood cuttings.

Gardenia *(Gardenia jasminoides).* Best known for that heady, romantic fra-

GARDENIA (Gardenia jasminoides)

grance that has filled so many school gymnasiums on prom night, this hand-some evergreen has dark green, waxy leaves. Depending on the variety, garde-nias grow from three to ten feet tall. They can suffer from chlorosis in this area, a problem that is compounded when gardenias are planted near a foundation line or other masonry. To correct this condition, the plants should be given regular applications of copperas or other forms of iron and acidifier. We have found that dwarf varieties require less care and are generally hardier. Garde-nias will do best in sun to partial shade. In Texas, two popular varieties of *G. jasminoides* are the 'August Beauty,' which produces more abundant but smaller blossoms, and 'Mystery,' in which both the foliage and flowers are larger. *Gardenia radicans* is an excellent dwarf variety.

Indian Hawthorn *(Raphiolepis indica).* Dark, evergreen, leathery leaves and charming pink-white flowers in early spring define this sun-loving native of China. It is a popular plant, susceptibility to fire blight and scale notwithstand-ing. The standard varieties can grow to five feet in height and width. Good choices for Central Texas include 'Majestic Beauty' and 'Pink Lady.' For smaller areas, try the compacts 'Ballerina' and 'Enchantress.' Their tight, dense growth habit is very pleasing.

Holly (*Ilex* spp.). Hollies are an enormously popular family due to their glossy, evergreen foliage, shade tolerance, and sturdy growth habits. All standard-sized species can grow to heights of twelve to fifteen feet but most are available in dwarf varieties. All do well in sun or partial shade. Of the numerous varieties, the handsome **Burford Holly** *(I. cornuta burfordii)* is a moderate grower, to ten feet, and up to five or six feet wide. It has dark green glossy oblong leaves and is heavily fruited when grown in sun. It takes well to pruning. For areas in which a smaller plant is desirable, the **Dwarf Burford Holly** *(I. cornuta burfordii compacta)* is a superbly dense and compact shrub. The richly green, impenetrable, and stiff foliage of the **Dwarf Chinese Holly** *(I. cornuta rotunda)* gives it a luxuriant texture. The leaves are spiny and will prick if touched, so be careful where you plant this handsome shrub. **Carissa Holly** *(I. cornuta* var. *carissa)* is a fairly recent addition to the family in dwarf

BURFORD HOLLY (Ilex cornuta burfordii)

size and has a most attractive dense, spreading foliage, although it does not produce berries. Hollies make fine hedge or specimen plants. The *Ilex x hybrida* **'Nellie R. Stevens'** will grow to fifteen feet tall and five feet wide. It has lovely dark green glossy leaves and is a rapid grower. With careful pruning it can be shaped into a small tree.

Hydrangea *(Hydrangea macrophylla)*. Hydrangea is a moderate-growing shrub that does best in well-composted, sandy soil. This is a deciduous plant with small flowers growing in large ten- to twelve-inch clusters that blossom in summer, good for cutting. Its flowers are blue if the soil is acid or pink in Central Texas alkaline soils. To produce blue blooms, add aluminum sulfate to the soil before the buds appear. Often called bigleaf hydrangea because of its four- to eight-inch leaves, it prefers partial shade. It grows to four or five feet tall and three or four feet wide. Prune the shrub after flowers fade. The **Oak-leaved Hydrangea** *(H. quercifolia)* is a native of the southeastern United States and is more tolerant of sun and drier soils than is the bigleaf. Bearing handsome foliage, oak-leaved hydrangeas seldom grow to their six-foot maximum height and four-foot width.

Japanese Flowering Quince *(Chaenomeles japonica)*. This deciduous plant belongs to a popular group of Asiatic shrubs grown mostly as specimens. The low-growing *C. japonica* (three feet high by two feet wide) has bright coral flowers. The variety 'Maulei' has orange flowers. Both bloom in late winter or very early spring, just when our yearning to see flowers again is strongest. Blooming before it leafs out, it is a very showy shrub when in flower; however, it is quite inconspicuous during the remainder of the year. Quince needs full sun to bloom well and is subject to scale.

Japanese Yew *(Podocarpus macrophyllus)*. Tall and narrow, with long, needle-like leaves, this bright evergreen adds variety of texture, color, and form to many landscape plans. Prized for its columnar shape, it is commonly used in narrow spaces and to soften the corners of buildings; however, creative pruning and training widens the possibilities of this excellent shrub. It is not fussy about soil, takes considerable shade or sun, and grows to ten to twelve feet tall and two or three feet wide.

Juniper *(Juniperus chinensis)*. New varieties ranging greatly in color, size, and growth habit are introduced continuously by the nursery trade. The juniper's popularity in Central Texas is well deserved. While it grows well in alkaline soils, tolerates intense sun, and is drought resistant, spider mites and bagworms can be problems. The plants have stiff, scaled leaves, which vary from a blue-gray to dark green to golden green. The 'Hollywood Juniper' has a dra-

JAPANESE YEW (Podocarpus macrophyllus)

matic twisted appearance that makes it a great specimen plant. It grows to twelve feet in height and five feet in width. 'Old Gold's' blue-gray foliage is golden with new growth. It has a softer, more informal appearance than other junipers, and grows to four feet in height by four feet in width. The 'Pfitzer' is a large spreading juniper, making it a good shrub for a screen. Its foliage is gray-green and it reaches six feet in height and fifteen feet in width. 'Robusta' is upright in habit with foliage that has a tufted appearance. It grows to fifteen feet high and four feet wide. 'Sea Green' has distinctive arching branches and gray-green foliage, growing to four feet in both height and width.

Leatherleaf Mahonia *(Mahonia bealii).* This rugged evergreen with large stiff, spiny leaves (up to sixteen inches long) brings a decidedly architectural look to the garden. Its clusters of small yellow flowers in January or February are followed by grapelike fruit that mockingbirds love. Plant it in partial to heavy shade and prune to keep it from getting too tall.

Ligustrum, Japanese Privet, Waxleaf Ligustrum *(Ligustrum japonicum).* Once ubiquitous in our urban landscape, the ligustrums were hard hit during the severe winters of 1983 and again in 1989–90. They are utilitarian shrubs that serve a number of functions well. These shade-tolerant shrubs are commonly used as hedges, border plants, or specimens, and grow from six to fifteen feet tall and to six or seven feet wide. Clusters of small, white flowers fill the air with a heady fragrance in spring. A topiary form known as 'Poodle Ligustrum' (spheres of foliage separated by segments of exposed trunk, suggesting the elaborate haircut of the French poodle) is popular to complement more formal architectural styles. **Glossy Privet** *(L. lucidum)* attains a height of fifteen feet. This slender and frequently multitrunked, treelike shrub is serviceable as a windbreak or screen. The bark is light gray to tan and the semievergreen leaves have a pale undersurface.

Nandina *(Nandina domestica).* Long a popular import from China, this medium-sized evergreen displays large clusters of bright red fruits in the fall and winter. It has white, inconspicuous flowers in the summer, and its compound, oval leaves turn red to scarlet in the fall. Nandina thrives in sun but tolerates semishade quite well. Its foliage begins to thin out and look straggly if shade is too dense. It makes a fine border plant or even hedge, and is reputed to be deer resistant. New varieties are being introduced regularly. 'Nana dwarf' is compact, growing to eighteen inches tall; its leaves turn scarlet in fall. 'Harbour

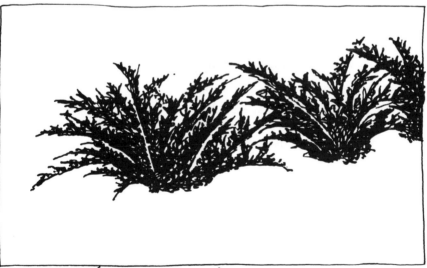

JUNIPER (Juniperus spp.)

WAXLEAF LIGUSTRUM (Ligustrum japonicum)

dwarf' is an extremely dense, compact version of common nandina, reaching two feet in height. The much acclaimed 'Gulf Stream' came onto the market in the 1980s. It grows to three or four feet and remains full and compact. 'San Gabriel' is an ethereal variety with feathery foliage. Growing to three feet, it adds visual interest in a perennial border.

Oleander *(Nerium oleander).* Thriving with little attention in hot, dry situations, the oleander boasts flowers of pink, red, white, or yellow and blooms throughout the summer. Its evergreen foliage is similar to that of the bamboo plant. While the standard oleander can grow to twenty feet, dwarf varieties are now available. This is a poisonous plant and should not be planted in yards where children play. Oleander likes a lot of sun and tolerates poor soil and drought, which is why we see it planted in the median of so many of our highways. Some varieties are hardier than others, so check with your nursery before buying.

Photinia (*Photinia* spp.). A strikingly handsome evergreen with large leathery, toothed leaves, the **Chinese Photinia** *(P. serrulata)* has long been a southern favorite. When it is used as a specimen, its dignity is fully appreciated. **Red-tip Photinia** *(P. fraseri)* replaced ligustrum as the workhorse of the Central Texas urban landscape after the freezes of 1983–84 and 1989–90. It is distinguished by its bright red new growth in spring. Tolerating severe trimming, it serves well as a hedge. Unfortunately, in recent years it has suffered from *Entomosporium maculatum,* a fatal fungal disease. Both varieties are capable of reaching to more than twenty feet unless trimmed and will grow in sun or partial shade. While requiring good drainage, neither species is particular about soil.

Pittosporum *(Pittosporum tobira).* Dense foliage and rapid growth characterize this evergreen native of China and Japan, which does well in sun or partial shade. Its foliage is dark green and leathery or light gray-green rimmed by white in the variegated form. In May, pittosporum produces small, sweetly scented blossoms. It tolerates pruning well and works in a variety of landscape plans. Left on its own, it will grow to a large size (six to eight feet high by four feet wide); dwarf varieties are available for more confined areas. Pittosporum,

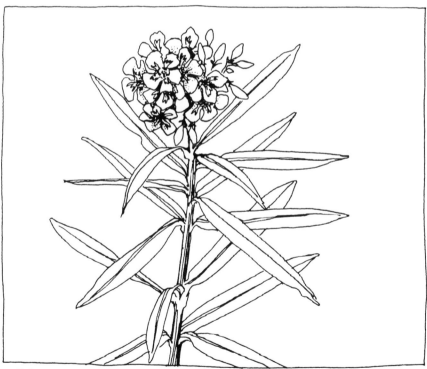

COMMON OLEANDER (Nerium oleander)

PITTOSPORUM (Pittosporum tobira)

however, did not survive the severe winter of 1989 and is considered vulnerable in very cold winters. Dwarf pittosporum (*P. tobira* 'Wheeler's Dwarf') growing to two feet tall and four feet wide is available.

Pomegranate *(Punica granatum)*. Large, showy, orange-red flowers all summer long account for the pomegranate's popularity in the South. A tough, deciduous plant with bright green leaves, it demands full sun. Attaining a height of up to ten to twelve feet, it is an excellent specimen plant. Its wide-spreading growth habit (to five feet) should be considered if you are planting it near the house or other structures. Dwarf varieties are available for confined areas. The pomegranate tolerates poor soils and is somewhat drought tolerant, although not for extended periods of time. Since pomegranates are available in fruiting and nonfruiting varieties, you need to decide if you want fruit or flowers before you buy.

Possumhaw *(Ilex decidua)*. With brilliant red berries dotting its naked, wide-spreading branches, this holly family member comes into its full glory in winter. A deciduous native with lustrous foliage, it is well adapted to our region's soil and climate conditions. Possumhaw likes sun but will tolerate some shade. It will grow to twenty-five feet high and eight feet wide. Its fruit attracts birds.

Primrose Jasmine *(Jasminum mesnyi).* Long, willowy branches bear large, golden flowers in late winter or early spring. Its mounding habit makes primrose jasmine ideal for banks and slopes, though it also looks good as a specimen or in groups as a hedgerow. Semievergreen foliage is composed of thick, shiny leaves. Blooming best in full sun, it will attain a height of five to seven feet and will spread to four or five feet. Similar in appearance and habit is the **Italian jasmine** *(J. humile),* its flowers are smaller and bloom later in the season. The evergreen foliage has three to seven dark green leaflets. It takes full sun to partial shade.

Pyracantha, Firethorn *(Pyracantha coccinea).* A vivid, attractive, woody plant, pyracantha is evergreen in Central Texas. It is often seen espaliered on walls or fences, showing off bright orange-red berries in fall and winter and clusters of small white flowers in spring. It has inch-long deep green leaves,

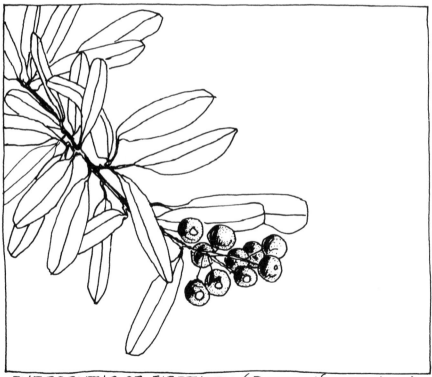

PYRACANTHA OR FIRETHORN (Pyracantha coccinea)

likes lots of sunshine, and will certainly produce more berries when grown in full sun. Although it is subject to fire blight, it usually thrives in our area. This is one of those shrubs that is often seen out of control, so prune regularly in winter after the robins and cedar waxwings have had their fill of berries. And wear gloves; its long sharp thorns demand respect. It grows to twenty feet high and can be espaliered to that width.

Rose of Sharon, Althea *(Hibiscus syriacus).* Dating from colonial times in this country and much earlier abroad, this hardy shrub has three-lobed leaves and colorful, two- to three-inch flowers (single or double) in white and rose to purple shades; flowers appear in late spring to summer. It can be pruned severely in spring to obtain large flowers. Deciduous, the Rose of Sharon is a handsome specimen or background shrub. It grows six to eight feet high and up to four feet wide and takes full sun.

Sago Palm *(Cycas revoluta).* Slow-growing, the sago palm may take fifty years to make a trunk five feet tall. Evergreen, sagos display long, dark, fernlike leaves growing from a shallow base. A good accent plant for a sheltered spot, it will require protection against the cold. The best way to do this is to mound leaves up over the crown of the plant and remove them after the last freeze date.

Spirea *(Spirea* spp.). With a soft spot in our hearts for this early spring bloomer, we recommend the **Bridal Wreath Spirea** *(S. reevesiana* or *S. cantoniensis)* for its graceful arching habit and profusion of blossoms. It is equally useful as a specimen or an informal, flowering hedge. The small white flowers are borne in flat clusters in early spring. Spirea grows to about six feet tall and four feet wide in sun or partial shade. While preferring moist soil, once established it does well on less if mulched. Although deciduous, it keeps its leaves for most of the year. **Anthony Waterer** *(S. bumalda* 'Anthony Waterer') bears flat-topped clusters of almost iridescent tiny rose-red flowers later in the season. It does best in sun and likes good soil and moisture. It will grow to three feet tall and two feet wide.

Sumac *(Rhus* spp.). Three of our native sumacs, **Fragrant** *(R. aromatica),* **Flameleaf** *(R. copallina),* and **Evergreen** *(R. sempervirens),* are unusually well suited to the suburban or urban landscape, adding color and texture. With a rangy shape, they reach a height of twelve to twenty-five feet and six to ten feet across. They all like sun but will tolerate partial shade. The flameleaf is the largest and most conspicuous of the three. It transplants easily and provides excellent red color in fall. It is deciduous and sun-loving. Older, treelike specimens can be found where contractors spared the bulldozer. The evergreen has glossy, leathery leaves that turn a purple-bronze hue in fall. It can be pruned to shape. The deciduous sumac called fragrant has a distinctive, delicate, three-lobed leaf that gives off a pleasant aroma when crushed.

Viburnum (*Viburnum* spp.). This handsome, versatile and vigorous family of flowering shrubs well deserves its position as a reliable southern landscape standard. All can grow to fifteen feet tall and five feet wide and are useful as hedge shrubs or specimen plants. **Laurestinus Viburnum** (*V. tinus*) is a shade-tolerant evergreen but its bountiful fragrant blossoms require sunshine. It is a very early spring bloomer and must be pruned immediately after spring blooms fade for the next season's blossoms to develop. With gently arching branches and lustrous, leathery leaves, the **Black Haw** (*V. rufidulum*) is a deciduous native well worth considering. It gives nice fall color and can be pruned into a graceful small tree of up to twenty feet. Possessing perhaps the best-looking green leaves in shrubdom, the **Sandankwa Viburnum** (*V. suspensum*) is an attractive evergreen shrub for partially sunny to quite shaded areas. Inconspicuous but fragrant small white blossoms occur late winter to very early spring.

❧ 10 ❦

Vines and Climbers

Along the ground from root to root;
or climbing, high with random maze . . .

EDITH HOLDEN,

THE COUNTRY DIARY OF AN EDWARDIAN LADY

Don't overlook vines and other climbers. They can play an important part in your landscaping plans because their climbing habits give a rich appeal to your yard, creating "rooms" as well as concealing features such as rocks, privacy fences, toolsheds, and work areas. Vines also can enhance, by either softening or emphasizing gateways and doorways, or by turning stark wood, masonry, or even an ordinary chain link fence into a green hanging blanket. A few vines that are noted for their tenacious growth also serve well as ground covers in areas where there is little or no foot traffic; the ivies and Asiatic jasmine are good examples of this category. Many vines have spectacular blossoms and/or colorful fruit, and vines come in both evergreen and deciduous varieties.

Climbing is achieved by three basic methods: twining, attaching by tendrils or leaf stalks, or clinging to a surface with small disks or rootlike projections. Vines that twine or attach themselves by means of tendrils or leaf stalks require wire or a trellis or other lattice work for support. Clingers need only a surface or a tree trunk to which to attach themselves. Knowledge of how vines climb is essential for selecting the proper plant for a given situation. For instance, to train a twining vine to cover a stone wall, a trellis would first have to be attached to the wall, otherwise the vine cannot hold on. A trellis will also prevent vine tendrils and disks from weakening mortar or stonework.

When planting, place the vine at least a foot from the surface it is intended to cover. But remember, soil near building foundations, a popular location for vines and other climbers, often is impoverished and requires enrichment with organic matter as well as frequent watering. As for any plant, make a generous-sized hole to allow roots to spread freely. Vines may be annually fertilized in early spring with a balanced fertilizer; however, if overgrowth threatens, withhold fertilizer.

Many people neglect pruning their vines until the situation is out of control. While many vines will survive severe treatment with the pruning shears, the gardener who regularly removes suckers, dead sections, and stems that have gone awry will be rewarded with a neater vine appearance. Vines that fall or are blown from their support require special attention because old growth will not reattach itself. In these cases, plants should be cut back drastically and the emergent new growth supported by means of ties or hooks until the vine has reestablished itself.

Listed below are desirable vines and climbers, both natives and introduced ornamentals, that are well adapted to the Central Texas environment.

Asiatic Jasmine *(Trachelospermum asiaticum).* Performing well in sun or shade, dry or moist conditions, heavy clay or thin soils, Asiatic jasmine is deservedly our premier ground cover, especially for large areas or steep slopes. A well-established Asiatic jasmine area can be kept looking neat if sheared with the lawnmower once a year or so. The glossy leaves have a handsome bronze cast. Smaller-leaved and variegated varieties are available.

Balsam Gourd *(Ibervillea lindheimeri).* A member of the cucumber family, this native vine produces oval leaves and a striped blossom of yellow and pale green. Its real glory, however, is the large (one- or two-inch) orange-red fruit. Farmers and ranchers like to plant this deciduous vine along barbed-wire fences. In the wild, it prefers full sun in open woods and thickets. Gourds climb by tendrils.

Bougainvillea *(Bougainvillea* spp.). It is not the small, white, inconspicuous flowers but the brilliant bracts (leaflike parts usually located just below the flower) that provide the intense shades of pink, red, orange, yellow, or purple of this tropical twining vine. A favorite patio pot plant, it requires a hot, sunny location sheltered from the wind. While bougainvillea will withstand mild winters in the southern part of Central Texas, north of Austin it is best to plant this deciduous vine in pots or hanging baskets for wintering indoors. Plant with care, because the root system is delicate, and mulch for winter protection. While applications of a 10-5-10 fertilizer in spring and again in summer will guarantee a long period of blossoms, be aware that the bougainvillea will not

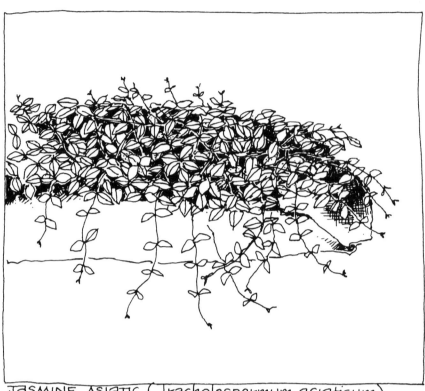

JaSMINE, ASIaTIC (Trachelospermum asiaticum)

bloom if given too much water and tender loving care. Withhold fertilizer and water until the plant droops—this will help to stress it into flowering. As soon as the plant droops, begin to water. Although vining varieties grow from sixty to a hundred feet in tropical environments, we can expect them to reach a length of twenty to thirty feet in Central Texas. Pruning keeps this vine vigorous. New plants can be started from softwood cuttings taken in late spring or early summer.

Carolina Jessamine *(Gelsemium sempervirens)*. An attractive evergreen vine producing delicate yellow flowers very early in the season if it gets full sun, this popular twining vine is a native of the Carolinas. It climbs ten to twenty-five feet at a moderate rate and has shiny, oblong leaves.

Chinese Wisteria *(Wisteria sinensis)*. This prime ornamental vine rapidly climbs by twining to twenty-five feet or more. Large clusters of fragrant, sun-loving flowers in violet-blue (the 'Alba' variety has white, very fragrant flowers) appear before the leaves in spring. Wisteria climbs from left to right and has light green foliage with seven to thirteen leaflets. It requires lots of humus.

Severe pruning may be necessary to keep it within bounds. Use of an arbor or trellis will impose some discipline. It's best to buy one in bloom to be sure it's a bloomer. Specimens trained to a tree, or standard, form are also available.

Clematis (*Clematis* spp.). Several native species of this delicately branching deciduous genus bear beautiful, conspicuous flowers, making them desirable for home garden cultivation. **Old Man's Beard** *(C. drummondii)* produces a white blossom with numerous long stamens, in March through September. It is partial to sun and well-drained soil. In the wild, the **Scarlet Clematis** *(C. texensis)* is most at home on the Edwards Plateau, preferring limestone out-croppings rather than rich soil. It has a striking red, bell-shaped flower. Smaller than other species of clematis, this variety grows to ten feet. Cultivars of the introduced *C. viticella* ('Comtesse de Bouchard,' 'Ramona,' and 'Ville de Lyon') should be planted in light, fertile soil that is well drained yet moist. A good rule of thumb: clematis like their heads in the sun and their feet in the shade. Mulch to protect the roots from exposure. Morning sun is preferred for these hybrids.

CHINESE WISTERIa (Wisteria sinensis)

VINES AND CLIMBERS

Climbing Fig *(Ficus pumila).* Its dense growing habit and adaptability to semishade conditions make this fast-growing evergreen vine popular for use on southern garden walls. A native to China, Japan, and Australia, it has small rootlets for clinging and grows to sixty feet. Older plants produce inedible figs. Pruning is needed to keep the small but numerous oval-shaped leaves healthy and attractive. Harsh winters cause this vine to die back, but it grows back from roots the following spring.

Coralvine, Queen's Wreath *(Antigonon leptopus).* Known in Mexico as the chain-of-love vine, this deciduous perennial displays masses of small, pink, heart-shaped blossoms from late summer to early fall. The leaves are also heart shaped. Attaching itself by tendrils, the coralvine grows rapidly to forty feet. It requires full sun to partial shade and thrives in our hot climate.

Honeysuckle *(Lonicera* spp.*).* Climbing vine or sprawling ground cover, the honeysuckle is one of our most versatile plants. If the weather cooperates with enough moisture, honeysuckle can fill the air with its familiar sweet fragrance several times a year. It is little wonder that so many people find a place for this vine in their gardens. **Purple Japanese Honeysuckle** *(L. japonica* var. *chinensis)* and **Hall's Japanese Honeysuckle** *(L. japonica* var. *halliana)* are two common species in Central Texas. Both are evergreen and fast-growing, preferring full to partial sun. Flowers usually appear from late spring through early summer. New blossoms of Hall's are white, gradually fading to a yellowing ivory shade as they age. Both varieties grow to thirty feet by twining. They may be left to sprawl over banks or trained to trellises. The beauty of our native evergreen **Coral Honeysuckle** *(L. sempervirens)* is more than adequate compensation for its lack of scent. Hummingbirds are attracted to the long (one- or two-inch) orange or scarlet blossoms, and cardinals and purple finches are fond of its fruit. Although drought tolerant, it flourishes with a bit of water.

Hyacinth Bean *(Dolichos lablab).* A spectacular late season bloomer, the hyacinth bean bears pink to purple pealike flowers followed by large hand-some deep purple beans. Supported on a trellis, the vine will give quick cover-age of attractive fan-shaped leaves to thirty feet. Usually treated as an annual, it reseeds easily.

Ivy *(Hedera* spp.*).* Clinging to walls, holding onto trees, or just filling in shady spots on the ground, ivies are among our most useful plants. When planning and planting, remember the gardener's old adage about ivy: "the first year it sleeps, the second year it creeps, and the third year it leaps." Two evergreen species popular in Central Texas are **Algerian Ivy** *(H. canariensis)* and **English Ivy** *(H. helix).* Algerian ivy has large, glossy leaves and is resistant to heat and drought. A rapid grower, it is an excellent ground cover for erosion control. Although its leaves are smaller and it grows more slowly, English ivy is extremely hardy, and given rich, moist soil, it will do better in full sun than will Algerian ivy. Much as we love the appearance of ivied walls, we must warn that ivy can be destructive to masonry. Both ivies grow to about forty feet.

Passionflower (*Passiflora* spp). Tropical natives that use tendrils to climb rapidly to great heights in our warm southern gardens, passionflowers have handsome lobed leaves and produce large glorious red to blue or purple to white flowers, three inches across, when planted in full sun. Although susceptible to frost, passionflower will grow back in the spring. To prevent it from becoming invasive, keep it in a container. Dwarf varieties are available.

Peppervine *(Ampelopsis arboreal).* This slender, rapid climber grows best in rich, moist soil and shade. Small dark purple flowers in June through July develop into shiny, black, inedible fruit in fall. The dark green, deciduous leaflets are deeply incised, giving the vine a delicate appearance. New leaves may have a reddish bronze cast. This vine climbs by tendrils.

Silver Fleecevine, Silverlace Vine *(Polygonum aubiertii).* This good-looking, vigorous vine may twine twenty to thirty feet in one season. Its small, white or greenish white flowers bloom in dense clusters during late summer. This deciduous vine does well in full sun or partial shade and looks good on a chain link fence, which it will cover in no time. It can withstand severe pruning.

Star Jasmine *(Trachelospermum jasminoides).* A staple in southern gardens so long that it is often affectionately called Confederate jasmine, this vine's dark, shiny, evergreen leaves provide an excellent background for clusters of fragrant white flowers. Growing well in a variety of conditions, it is better as a climber than as ground cover.

Trumpetvine, Trumpetcreeper *(Campsis radicans).* A native of the southeastern United States, this rapid-growing clinging vine is easily recognized by the orange to scarlet, trumpet-shaped flowers in summer. Most profuse in full sun, the flowers are well loved by hummingbirds. The trumpetvine's deciduous leaves are compound and have nine to eleven leaflets. It climbs twenty to thirty feet and becomes very heavy; without support, it may break away from the walls on which it grows.

Virginia Creeper *(Parthenocissus quinquefolia).* Growing wild throughout much of the United States, this deciduous creeper no doubt owes its popularity as a cultivated vine to the attractive leaves, which turn scarlet in autumn. For an area noticeably lacking red in its fall color scheme, the Virginia creeper is a welcome addition. Its small, blue berries are cherished by birds. It does

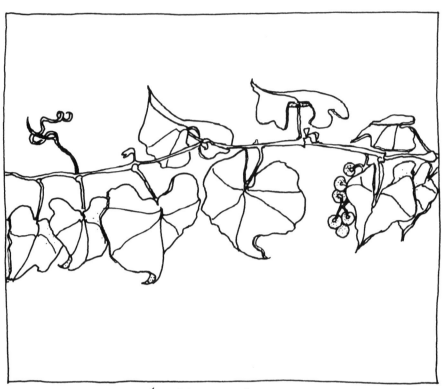

WILD GRAPES (vitis spp.)

equally well clinging to trees, walls, and fences or trailing on the ground, and it tolerates full sun to partial shade. Caution: The insecticide Sevin will defoliate the vine.

Wild Grapes (*Vitis* spp.). Several species of native grapes make attractive vines and provide good fruit for preserves or wildlife food. The broad, often toothed, deciduous leaves of wild grapes are of a pleasing shape, and their lush growth lends a southern look to the landscape. **Winter Grape** *(V. berlandieri)*, **Mustang Grape** *(V. candicans)*, and **Summer Grape** *(V. aestivalis)* are among the most commonly found in Central Texas. Rapid growers (to sixty feet), they are most productive in full sun to partial shade. Cuttings and layering are successful methods for propagating grapevines. Transplant grapes in January through February. All grapes climb by tendrils.

❧ 11 ❧

Flowers

In a thousand valleys far and wide,
Fresh flowers; while the sun shines warm.
WILLIAM WORDSWORTH,
"INTIMATIONS OF IMMORTALITY"

Flowers are the faces of the garden. They call to the visitor, "Here I am!—Have you ever seen such color? How about these reds? And just look at my blues!" And we do. In Central Texas we can look almost year-round. Although our summers can be sweltering and exhausting and winters generally bring a freeze, with judicious planning and planting Central Texas gardeners can grow an amazing variety of flowers. As for so many other garden elements, proper planning and plant location, careful selection of plants, good soil preparation, and appropriate tending during the season are the surest way to successful flower gardening.

The best flower beds are well planned. Become familiar with available species and their requirements through books, catalogs, and frequent visits throughout the season to area garden centers. Many cities and towns in Central Texas have garden clubs that sponsor tours of outstanding gardens. We can't think of a better way to see flowers at their best in local growing conditions. Because flower gardens are often secreted in backyards, tours afford the best opportunity to see these treasures. Sharing must be a garden club credo. Chat with a garden club member and you will come away with a bounty of information—and most likely flowers too.

You've seen the flowers and decided what you want. Now before purchasing or planting a single plant, plan your flower garden on graph paper. Drawing the plan to scale will help you calculate the number of plants and the amount of fertilizer you will need.

Be sure to note on your plan spacing requirements and flower heights. Taller flowers, while they should not necessarily be relegated to the back row, must not be allowed to interfere with the light requirements of smaller plants or to block your view of them. Remember, too, that gardening chores will be easier if you group together plants with similar watering needs.

Nowhere else in gardening are there greater opportunities for creative expression than in the flower garden. Color, texture, and size variables of flowers abound. Do you prefer the serenity of related colors to the energy created by planting color opposites side by side? Experience the change in emotional tone as the cool-colored spring flowers yield to the hot reds and oranges of summer. As you play with color schemes for your flower beds, there are a few helpful points to remember:

Gray foliage, such as dusty miller or artemisia, serves superbly to enhance the colors adjacent to them.

Very pale flowers will fade in our unrelenting summer sun.

White will illuminate dark corners and other shady locations.

White and other pale colors will make the garden come alive as the last evening light fades, while the deep shades of red and purple tend to go black. For appreciating the garden view under a full moon, white is essential.

You may want to consider using crayons or colored markers when drawing your plan. This way you will get an idea of the overall effect of your color scheme. Sometimes, although not always, it's best to have the surprises show up on paper first.

Your first consideration in planning a flower bed is location. Many flowers bloom best if they receive six to eight hours of sun. Others, such as impatiens and caladiums, prefer shade. In our climate, the cooler morning sun is preferable but not essential, especially for shallow-rooted plants.

Try to place your beds so that they do not interfere with your other garden uses, and avoid creating small, isolated beds scattered about the yard. Not only are they a nuisance in terms of mowing, edging, and watering, but as Daniel Burnham observed, "Make no small plans, they have not the strength to move mens' minds."

Second, think about the amount of time and care you wish to devote to garden work. While extra attention will be rewarded, an attractive flower bed can be simple and carefree. Flowers planted in pots provide color for small areas and reduce work. A trowel will do the job of the garden hoe and spade, a watering can replaces miles of hose, and smaller amounts of fertilizer are needed. It is important to remember that potted plants require smaller applications of fertilizer at slightly more frequent intervals. Also, containers must provide for drainage, and watering chores cannot be neglected.

Demanding more work and attention in the initial preparation, perennials, once established, go on for years with a little weeding, one or two annual applications of fertilizer, and division of overgrown plants every two to three years. Annuals must be planted each year and watered and fertilized more frequently. While some gardeners welcome the opportunity to start anew each year, others prefer to watch an established bed mature through the years. Because interest in a garden is provided by variety in color, texture, shape, and size, we prefer flower beds that contain both annuals and perennials. Small shrubs such as crimson pigmy barberry or dwarf cenizo planted in mixed borders or large island beds can provide character, texture, and year-round interest. Years ago, when the guiding philosophy for flower gardens was more formal, it was fashionable to have a yellow bed, a blue bed, and so forth. Today rules are less rigid, and creativity is encouraged; gardeners are free to make their own choices. Choose your flowers to provide seasonal color, and not only will you prolong your enjoyment but you will be practicing good gardening, too.

Finally, a flower garden with little in bloom does not give much pleasure, and flower beds that are neglected because nothing is blooming are quickly invaded by weeds and grass.

ANNUALS

Since their entire lives span only one season, annuals tirelessly produce an abundance of flowers in an effort to make seed and ensure another generation. This and the joy of planting a seed and watching it grow are among the reasons so many people grow annuals.

Annuals are grown from seed or purchased as bedding plants from garden centers. If you plant annuals from seeds, it is best to start them in flats indoors. Seed sown outside in late winter for spring blooms are at risk from frost; those sown outside in summer for fall color are vulnerable to intense heat after they germinate and are very fragile.

Before visiting a garden center for your selections, plan ahead and think about what would look best in your garden and how you want to use annuals—in a bed or border, to flood with color or to offset other plants. Next

Name	Spacing, Height (Inches)	Color	Exposure	Comments
Ageratum (*Ageratum* spp.)	6–9, 6–9	blue, white, pink	sun, part shade	Good border plant even though it does not grow uniformly. Does best in part shade because of summer heat. Start from bedding plants and try 'Blue Danube,' 'Pink Powderpuffs,' or 'Summer Snow.' Plant in spring.
Alyssum (*Lobularia maritima*)	6–8, 4–8	white, pink, violet, lavender	sun	Alyssum works well as a border plant. It is hardy enough to take a freeze. Deadhead regularly to encourage new blooms. Plant in early spring.
Alternanthera or Joseph's Coat (*Alternanthera* spp.)	8–10, 4–8	flowers are inconspicuous, but leaves are bright and have many colors	sun	Brilliant, variegated foliage. Likes dry conditions. Grow from nursery stock or cuttings as seed will not come true. Plant in late spring.
Begonia (*Begonia* spp.)	6–8, 6–12	red, pink, white	sun, part shade	There are over one thousand species of this plant. While generally used in pots, it does well as a border plant when massed. If they are to be in full sun all summer, select bronze-leaved plants. Plant in spring.
Bluebonnet (*Lupinus* spp.)	6, 8	blue	sun	Our state flower. It likes well-drained soil, without too much organic matter. If bedding plants are used, don't bury the crown. If you use seeds, make sure they are scarified (scratched) and barely cover them with soil. Seed in the fall.
Cleome or Spider Flower (*Cleome hasslerana*)	24, 36–48	pink, white	sun	Likes hot, dry location. Not fussy about soil. Works best (because of height) as a back-of-the-bed plant. Plant in late spring.

Plant	Size	Color	Light	Notes
Cockscomb (*Celosia cristata*)	9–12, 6–24	purple, pink, yellow, white	sun	Likes dry soil. Flowers are long lasting and can be dried readily. Plant in spring.
Coleus (*Coleus* spp.)	8–12, 8–24	leaves are pink, white, red, green	sun, part shade	Grown for foliage; pinch flower buds as they appear. Don't overfertilize. Try new varieties of coleus that can grow, indeed must grow, in full sun. Plant in late spring.
Copper Plant (*Acalypha wilkesiana*)	18–24, 36	copper leaves	sun	Heat tolerant; heavy feeders. Grown for the leaves and not the flowers. Plant in late spring.
Cosmos (*Cosmos* spp.)	9–24, 12–24	white, red, purple	sun	Long blooming season. Don't overfertilize or overwater. They make excellent cut flowers. They are hardy annuals and will survive mild winters. Plant in late spring.
Dusty Miller (*Centaurea cineraria*)	12, 12–36	purple	sun	Gray-white foliage is more predominant than its flowers. Makes a perfect foil for other flowers. Plant in spring.
Gomphrena or Bachelor's Button Globe Amaranth (*Gomphrena globosa*)	12, 10–15	white, blue, red, pink, coral	sun	Requires little care but likes well-drained soil. Start from bedding plants or seed started indoors. Plant in spring.
Gazania (*Gazania rigens*)	8–10, 8–10	multiple, with stripes	sun	These are tender perennials that can be indoors for continuing bloom. They can take heat. Deadhead to encourage blooming. Plant in spring.
Impatiens (*Impatiens wallerana*)	12, 6–15	pink, red, white, purple	shade	Pinch back main stem to encourage vigor and more blooms. Cuttings can be rooted. Needs frequent watering. Plant in late spring.
Larkspur (*Delphinium grandiflorum*)	12–36, 12	white, blue, pink, purple	sun	A reseeding annual that, once planted, will have to be thinned each year. Transplanting is difficult and seeding works better.

Name	Spacing, Height (Inches)	Color	Exposure	Comments
Marigold (*Tagetes* spp.)	6–18, 6–36	yellow, rust, orange, white	sun	A constant favorite because it is almost foolproof. But, as a gardening friend observes, each marigold seed comes with a spider mite couple intent on having a large family. Plant in spring.
Nierembergia (*Nierembergia* spp.)	6–9, 6–15	purple	sun, part shade	Produces violet blooms on a fernlike mass of leaves. Use bedding plants. Likes well-drained soil and monthly feedings. It blooms throughout the summer. Plant in late spring.
Periwinkle or Vinca (*Vinca rosea*)	8–10, 10–18	white, pink, lavender	sun	Loves heat. Blooms all summer. Plant no earlier than mid-April to avoid fungi that will kill the plant.
Penta (*Pentas lanceolata*)	18, 12–18	pink, red	sun, part shade	Good color. Grows well in almost any environment. Fertilize regularly (each month) during growing season. Butterflies love this plant. Plant in late spring.
Petunia (*Petunis* spp.)	8–12, 6–12	red, blue, pink, purple, orange, white, mixed	sun	Hybrids are introduced continually. The plant also can take winter weather to below freezing. Seeds are difficult to germinate and it is easier to buy started plants. Plant in spring.
Phlox (*Phlox drummondii*)	6–10, 15–18	white, yellow, pink, red	sun	Heat tolerant. Good cut flower. This is a Texas native. Plant in spring.

Plant		Color	Light	Notes
Poppy (*Papaver* spp.)	12–18, 18–36	red, orange, purple, white	sun	Poppies like to be in sun and good organic matter. They reseed, but do not like to be disturbed after germinating. Seed in the fall.
Portulaca or Moss Rose (*Portulaca grandiflora*)	12–15, 4–6	yellow, rose, orange, pink, white, salmon	sun	Takes poor soil; likes heat. Good self-sower. Works well along borders and also in hanging baskets. Water lightly. Plant in late spring.
Purslane (*Purslane oleracea*)	6–12, 4–8	pink, white, yellow, orange	sun	Plant in masses. The flowers last one day but are followed by continuous blooms through the summer. Plant in late spring.
Sunflower (*Helianthus* spp.)	24–48, 12–144	yellow, white, bronze	sun	Varieties range from one to twelve feet tall. Start seeds indoors or sow after the soil has warmed. They like it hot and sunny and do not need a lot of water. Good for drying. Plant in spring.
Swan River Daisy (*Brachycome iberidifolia*)	6, 12–18	blue, red, rose, white	sun	Plant after soil is warm, in organic conditions. While it makes a good cut flower it is not a long-blooming plant, so make successive plantings to ensure continued bloom. Plant in spring.
Tithonia or Mexican Sunflower (*Tithonia rotundifolia*)	24–36, 48–60	orange, gold	sun	Heat and drought resistant. Fast growing but takes three to four months to flower. Fertilize lightly each month. Plant in late spring.
Zinnia (*Zinnia* spp.)	6–12, 8–36	yellow, rose, cream, red, orange, white	sun	Heat tolerant. Good cutting flower. New varieties are introduced regularly. Susceptible to mildew. One notable introduction is the species angustifolia (*Z. linearis*). It produces masses of small daisylike flowers. Plant in summer.

ANNUALS (FALL–WINTER BLOOMING)

Name	Spacing, Height	Color	Exposure	Comments
Calendula (*Calendula officinalis*)	12–15, 10–24	yellow, white	sun, part shade	This is an excellent winter bloomer. It rarely blooms after May. Plant in the fall.
Carnations or Pinks (*Dianthus* spp.)	6–12, 6–18	pink, red, purple, white	sun, part shade	There are numerous varieties of this genus. Some are perennial, some biennial, and some are spring bloomers. Plant in summer.
Cyclamen (*Cyclamen persicum*)	12, 8	pink, white	part shade	Bright, iridescent flowers. Does well in a cool, humid environment in rich, organic soil. Will rot from too much water. Plant in fall.
Ornamental Cabbage and Kale (*Brassica oleracea*)	12–15, 10–12	green, red, white	sun	Handles frost well. Colors turn when temperature drops below fifty degrees and are intensified by frost. Plant in the fall.
Pansy (*Viola* spp.)	6–12, 6–12	multiple	sun, part shade	Likes rich, organic soil. Fertilize monthly. Keep moist and deadhead plants. Start with plants, as seeds are very small and hard to germinate. Flowers are edible. Plant in the fall.
Snapdragon (*Antirrhinum* spp.)	6–15, 12–30	multiple	sun	Numerous cultivars of this fall and spring favorite have been developed. If starting from seed, do not cover; they need sunlight to germinate. They like well-drained soil and regular deadheading. Plant in the fall.
Stock (*Matthiola incana*)	12–15, 12–18	white, pink, lavender	sun	Fertilize monthly and water regularly, so that plant will not bloom prematurely. It is easiest to buy started nursery plants. Good cut flower and very fragrant. Plant in the fall.
Viola or Johnny-jump-up (*Viola tricolor*)	6–8, 6	purple, white, yellow	sun, part shade	Flowers are small, so violas have their greatest impact as a mass planting. Fertilize monthly. Will take temperatures down to twenty degrees. Plant in the fall.

ANNuaLs: PoRTuLaca, maRIGOLD, PETuNIa

consider the plants' light, soil, and spacing needs and whether you can meet them. While general rules are broken as quickly in gardening as anywhere else, one can say that most annuals like sun, moisture, and good drainage.

With selections improving each year, we find it difficult to restrain ourselves from purchasing one of each kind. However, one petunia, one marigold and one cosmos does not make for a coherent garden design. Grouped plantings are far more effective for annuals.

If you are creating a flower bed for the first time, dig the soil at least a month in advance and add organic matter—lots of it, two to four inches. Just before planting, cultivate again and add more organic matter and the proper amount of 5-10-5 fertilizer for the size of your garden.

Now you are ready to plant. Be sure to transplant container-started plants or seedlings from flats into holes large enough to allow the entire root system to extend downward. You may want to shade the tender seedlings for a day or two

FLOWERS

to reduce heat stress. Gently firm the soil around the plants and water well. After planting, pinch off the growing tip to just above a set of leaves to encourage bushier growth. Mulch the plants well with compost, shredded bark, or other organic material. Annuals are not in the soil long and do not have time to develop strong root systems. Mulch protects roots from heat or cold, aids in moisture retention, and reduces weeds.

Fertilize annuals regularly throughout the season with an all-purpose fertilizer. To prolong blooming, "deadhead" them, or remove the spent blossoms. This will prevent plant energy from going to seed production. If you wish to produce larger, single blossoms, "disbud," or remove all but the terminal bud.

Watering, and pest control are the remaining maintenance procedures. When the soil is dry, water to a depth of an inch or two. As many annuals are susceptible to mildew, watering by soaker hose is better than using an overhead sprinkler.

PERENNIALS

A long blooming season, lower maintenance, and seemingly infinite variety leave little reason to wonder why interest in perennials has been burgeoning in recent years.

Because perennials (broadly defined as herbaceous plants that live three or more years but not necessarily forever) are around for a while, careful planning and bed preparation are more important than they are with annuals, where a mistake can be resolved by not repeating it the following year. While fertilizer can be applied periodically to restore nutrients, improving soil is more difficult once a flower bed has been established. Clay soils in particular tend to get compacted over the years, denying root systems air circulation. If poor drainage is likely to be a problem because of clay soil and flat terrain, consider planting your perennials in raised beds. Very sandy soils drain too rapidly for many moisture-loving perennials.

Soil preparation should be done several months in advance. Begin by incorporating a two- to four-inch layer of compost, peat moss, or well-rotted manure. The bed should be dug deeply (twelve to fifteen inches, ideally), and a light dressing of low-nitrogen fertilizer should be added and worked well into the soil (abundant nitrogen at this time would burn the tender, young plants). Other essential considerations when planning for perennials are height, color, blooming season, and exposure.

Although some perennials can be started from seed, many varieties that have

PERENNIALS: CHRYSANTHEMUM, SHASTA DAISY, DAY LILY

been developed to produce very colorful blossoms only propagate asexually. Therefore, it makes sense to purchase container-grown or dormant bare-root plants at nurseries. (Dormant bare-root plants also can be purchased by mail order.) Since most are easily propagated by division, the gardener has an excellent opportunity to increase his or her supply within a few years.

While container-raised plants can be planted almost any time but midsummer, if you buy bare-root perennials, they should be planted in the fall. When you plant, it's important that the hole be large enough to allow the roots to spread down and out. Container-grown plants should be planted at the same depth as they were in their pots. It is easy to determine how deeply to plant dormant plants by finding the soil mark from the previous season's growth. It's a good idea to insert support stakes for the taller perennials at planting time to avoid disturbing the roots systems later in the season.

After planting, water thoroughly and gently firm the soil, making certain there are no air pockets. Mulch to conserve moisture, hold down weeds, and moderate soil temperature.

Perennials will "naturalize," or grow new plants each year. Periodically you'll need to divide clumps of multiple plants to maintain vigorous, reliable bloomers. In the long growing season of Central Texas, perennials may require more frequent dividing than they do in other areas of the country.

It's best to divide early-blooming perennials in fall and late bloomers in early spring. While there is some latitude in the timing, never divide plants in the heat of summer.

To divide, dig and lift out the plant or clump with a fork or sharp spade. This may be a formidable task if the plant has been in the same location undivided for several years. If the clump has a small root system, gently pull apart the plants. This may be made easier by washing the soil from the plants. You may need to pry apart heavier, matted clumps by driving two forks back to back into the root ball and easing them apart. Finally, there may be times when a hatchet or pruning saw is totally appropriate to cut through the plant mass. Now you have vigorous new plants for your garden with extras to share.

Trim off any damaged or dead roots. If dividing bearded iris, discard the old center. Before replanting, rework the soil, adding organic matter and fertilizer.

Care for perennials in successive years includes cultivation to aerate the soil and an application of 5-10-5 fertilizer in early spring and then again about six weeks later. Use a spading fork when cultivating, as it is less likely to damage roots and rhizomes than is a hoe or spade.

As with annuals, deadhead to prolong blooming and remove unsightly spent blossoms. Large blossoms can be encouraged by disbudding, or removing all but the terminal buds.

BULBS

Bulb, tuber, corm, rhizome, whatever. We consider them together here because they all begin as underground stems containing nutrients stored to create and/ or nurture a plant.

Bulbs, so the myth goes, have one overriding need: good drainage. While this is usually true of bulbs proper, some similar plants—Louisiana iris, for one—thrive in wet conditions. So be sure you know each variety's requirements before purchasing any plants that start from underground stems.

When preparing beds for bulbs, cultivate to a minimum depth of six to twelve

BULBS: RANUNCULUS, ANEMONE, HYACINTH, CROCUS

inches. Dig in a good amount of organic material in the form of compost, well-rotted manure, or peat to make a good bottom layer, as bulbs will send out roots to twice the depth at which they were planted. At this time, work in a high-phosphate fertilizer such as superphosphate or bone meal to ensure good root development. Since the former is quick-acting and the latter slower-acting, we make a fifty-fifty mix and add it when we plant. A good rule of thumb for planting is that bulbs are planted at a depth roughly three times their di-ameter. In heavy soils, they can be planted slightly less deep. Generally bulbs should be planted with the broader base at the bottom and the tip pointing up. Most bulbs are planted from mid-October through December. The popular caladium, an exception, is planted in spring. Water thoroughly after planting, and mulch. If the winter is a dry one, don't forget to water the beds.

After the flowers have faded, the bulbs will benefit from an application of 5-10-5 fertilizer. Do not remove the foliage, which is producing nourishment

FLOWERS

PERENNIALS

Name	Spacing, Height (Inches)	Color	Exposure	Blooming Season	Comments
Artemisia (*Artemisia* spp.)	9–24, 6–36	gray leaves; small, yellow flowers	sun	spring	Most artemisias are grown for their gray leaves, although some are green. They need good drainage. Varieties to consider include *A. vulgaris*, *A. schmidtiana* 'nana,' and *A. ludoviciana*.
Autumn Sage (*Salvia gregii*)	12–18, 12–24	red, white, pink, salmon	sun	spring–fall	This plant takes hard use: modest drainage, low water. Its name is misleading; it will bloom from spring until frost. It needs to be pruned back hard after each bloom cycle. This is a native. Also consider other salvias, such as *S. elegans* and *S. guaranitica*. Any salvia will make a contribution in the garden.
Blackfoot Daisy (*Melampodium leucanthum*)	12, 6–12	white	sun	summer	Well-behaved, sweet in appearance, and tough as nails if given the proper environment, which is excellent drainage (amend with sand) and little fertilization. They will die back in winter but will return in spring. This is a native.
Blue Sage (*Salvia farinacea*)	14–18, 18–24	violet, white, blue-purple	sun, part shade	summer–fall	Blue sage will work in almost any soil. It will grow most compactly in sun, but will tolerate some shade. It may freeze but will come back from the roots. Prune hard in late summer. It is a native.
Brazos Penstemon (*Penstemon tenuis*)	12, 18–24	lavender, pink	sun, part shade	spring	Originally from coastal Texas, it likes moist conditions. After flowering, cut plants back to near ground and they may bloom again, but not as vigorously. It is a native.

Plant	Size	Color	Light	Bloom	Notes
Candytuft (*Iberis sempervirens*)	12–24, 6–8	white	sun	spring	Candytuft makes a good border plant. White flowers cover the plant in spring. There are also several annual varieties: *I. umbellata, I. amara* and *I. pinnata*.
Carnations or Pinks (*Dianthus* spp.)	8–12, 6–18	white, cream, orange, red, pink, lavender	sun, part shade	summer–fall	The new cultivars are treated as annuals biennials since they can't take the heat. Some older varieties are truly perennial. They like well-drained soil and regular fertilization.
Chrysanthemum (*Chrysanthemum* spp.)	8–12, 12–48	white, cream, rust, yellow, maroon, pink	sun, part shade	late summer–fall	Sensitive to day length, chrysanthemums bloom as the days get shorter. They are easy to propagate, but need good organic soil. Excellent as cut flowers.
Columbine (*Aquilegia* spp.)	36, 18–24	yellow, red-yellow	part–full shade	spring	Columbines like high organic matter. Divide them in the fall. Good varieties to grow: 'Hinkley's' and a new introduction, 'Texas Gold.' *A. canadensis* is a native and also a good addition to the garden.
Coneflower or Black-eyed Susan (*Rudbeckia maxima*)	18–24, 24–36	yellow	sun, part shade	summer–fall	Coneflowers do well in this area. They can be propagated by division. 'Goldsturm' is a compact variety that blooms profusely. *R. maxima* is a native.
Coreopsis (*Coreopsis lanceolata*)	18, 12–36	yellow	sun, part shade	summer	*C. lanceolata* is a native, but tends to flop over when in bloom. New species that are more compact: 'Sunray,' 'Threadleaf.'
Daylily (*Hemerocallis* spp.)	18–24, 12–36	multiple	sun, part shade	spring	It is *not* a lily. But it *is* tough, reliable, capable of thriving on neglect. Divide the tubers every couple of years and plant in well-amended soil. Fertilize spring and fall with low-nitrogen fertilizer (1-4-4 ratio).
Fall Aster (*Aster x*)	one plant, 18–48	blue, lavender, purple	sun	fall	You will need to plant only one fall aster. This hardy plant thrives in any well-drained soil. Its profusion of flowers are good for cutting. It is a native.

PERENNIALS *(continued)*

Name	Spacing, Height (Inches)	Color	Exposure	Blooming Season	Comments
Firebush (*Hamelia patens*)	24–36, 18–30	red	sun	summer	A good Texas summer plant. Takes the heat and doesn't need a lot of water. It can take some shade. Dies back in winter, but will come back the next spring.
Four Nerve Daisy (*Hymenoxys scaposa*)	9, 12	yellow	sun	spring–fall	The four nerve is compact, elegant, and tough. It likes full sun and good drainage. The flowers bloom atop long stems that undulate in the breeze. It is a naturalizing native.
Four O'Clock (*Mirabilis jalapa*)	24, 24–36	red, lavender, yellow, white	sun, part shade	summer–fall	Four o'clocks are tough. They like well-drained soil, but can survive almost anywhere. They are invasive, so remove most new growth in the spring.
Gaillardia (*Gaillardia pulchella*)	10–24, 10–24	red, bronze, maroon with yellow tips	sun	summer–fall	A native of Central Texas, gaillardia likes sun, heat and dry soil. They make good cutting flowers. Fertilize little and deadhead spent flowers.
Gerbera Daisy (*Gerbera jamesonii*)	12–18, 12–18	multiple	sun, part shade	spring–fall	Good in the garden or as cut flowers. Clumps are divided in early spring and planted so that crowns are not covered. Fertilize regularly during bloom season.
Havard Penstemon (*Penstemon havardii*)	12–24, 24–72	red	sun	spring	Start from seed as it does not transplant well. Do not overwater or the plant may reach to six feet tall. Cut back the stalks after bloom and it may rebloom in the fall. It is a native.
Indigo Spires (*Salvia* 'Indigo Spires')	18–24, 36–48	blue-purple	sun, part shade	spring–fall	This is a new introduction. It has intense blue-purple color on flower spikes that go to fifteen inches. Good cut flowers. It takes heat well.

Plant	Size	Color	Light	Season	Notes
Lantana (*Lantana* spp.)	12–18, 12–30	yellow, red, orange, white, bicolored	sun	summer	This plant loves sun and heat. Varieties that do well here are *L. horrida* (a native), *L. camara*, and *L. montevidensis*. It will take drought but likes some water and well-drained soil. Fertilize lightly once in the spring.
Liatris or Gayfeather (*Liatris elegans*)	12–24, 24–36	purple, white	sun	fall	Plant in early spring. Do not fertilize or overwater or the plants will get too leggy. Excellent cut flower, which will last for months and dry well. It is a native.
Mexican Bush Sage (*Salvia leucantha*)	36–48, 36–60	white, purple	sun, part shade	fall	Sends up long, rose-purple spikes throughout the fall. The flowers are good for cutting. It is drought and heat tolerant and a native.
Mexican Hat (*Ratibida columnaris*)	3–4, 8–12	yellow	sun	summer	Mexican hat likes well-drained soil; beyond that it is not fussy about soil. It will bloom all summer. Do not feed. This is a native.
Mexican Heather (*Cuphea hyssopifolia*)	10–12, 12	purple	sun, part shade	summer–fall	The Mexican heather is a "tender" perennial: it will generally survive all but the most severe winters. In the summer and fall it is covered with small bright purple flowers. Fertilize every six to eight weeks.
Mexican Honeysuckle (*Justicia spicigera*)	36, 36–48	orange, red	sun	spring–summer	This native from Mexico will naturalize and form clumps up to five feet wide. Though it wilts when dry, it is drought tolerant and will easily revive when watered.
Mexican Marigold Mint (*Tagetes lucida*)	12, 12	yellow	sun	fall	Blooms from midfall until frost. Will naturalize; divide clumps in spring. Will freeze back and return, vigorously, in spring.
Mexican Oregano (*Poliomintha longiflora*)	24, 24–36	pink	sun, part shade	summer	Likes well-drained soil and is drought tolerant. Forms compact mounds, but prune to *shape* in fall after blooms fade.

Name	Spacing, Height (Inches)	Color	Exposure	Blooming Season	Comments
Mexican Petunia (*Ruellia brittoniana*)	12–18, 48–60	purple	sun	summer–fall	*R. brittoniana* is an aggressive grower that will take over a small garden. It is good for large areas. The cultivar 'Katie' is more compact and well-behaved for small gardens. 'Blue Shade' is a ground cover variety that does well in dappled sun. It is a native.
Moss Phlox (*Phlox subulata*)	6, 6	pink	sun	spring	An early bloomer with an abundance of bright pink flowers. Good drainage is a must. Also consider blue phlox (*P. divaricata*).
Obedient Plant (*Physostegia virginiana*)	12–18, 15–24	lavender, pink, white	sun, part shade	summer–fall	This plant likes water and good organic soil. It will bloom late summer through fall. It makes a good cut flower, but it can be aggressive. It is a native.
Oxalis (*Oxalis crassipes*)	6, 12	pink	part shade	spring–fall	Blooms most heavily in spring, takes a summer break, then will return, although diminished, in the fall. Likes rich soil and lots of water.
Persian Centaurea (*Centaurea dealbata*)	18, 12	rose with white fringe	sun, part shade	spring	Centaurea needs humusy soil. Its deeply fringed silvery foliage make this an exceptionally handsome plant even when not in bloom. Blooms throughout spring.
Plumbago (*Plumbago ariculata*)	24, 36–48	blue	sun	spring–fall	Plumbago likes it dry, hot, and sunny, like our summers. It will survive all but the most brutal winter, particularly if planted early. It likes well-drained soil and will bloom prolifically through the heat of the summer.

Plant	Size	Color	Light	Bloom	Notes
Purple Coneflower (*Echinacea purpurea*)	12–18, 24–36	purple, white	sun	spring–fall	Tough, prolific bloomers that do well in alkaline soil. They reseed easily, but divide clumps every two to three years. Good cut flower, but cut the stems; pulling them may uproot the entire plant. It is a native.
Red Husker (*Penstemon* 'Red Husker')	18–24, 18	red	sun	spring	Bright red flowers are borne on eighteen-inch spikes. It will naturalize well and spread. It does not seem particular about soil conditions.
Rock Rose (*Pavonia lasiopetala*)	24–36, 24–36	pink-rose	sun, part shade	spring–fall	Drought tolerant, but likes good drainage. Use as a border plant or in mass plantings. Shear the plant back periodically to keep it compact and flowering. It is a native.
Scarlet Sage (*Salvia coccinea*)	24–30, 14–24	red, pink	sun, part shade	spring–fall	Scarlet sage adapts well to most soil conditions. A native, it will bloom spring to first frost.
Shasta Daisy (*Chrysanthemum superbum*)	12, 12–24	white	sun, part shade	spring	Shastas like organic soil and moist conditions. They make good cut flowers. Divide annually. Doubles and big-flowered types do not do well here. We have had good success with 'Alaska.'
Stokes Aster (*Stokesia laevis*)	6–12, 12–24	pink, white, blue	sun	spring–fall	Likes moist but well-drained soil. Will bloom best in spring, then may take a break until the fall. Will take some filtered sun.
Summer Phlox (*Phlox paniculata*)	15–18, 18–30	red, pink, white	sun	summer–fall	Summer phlox likes organic soil and good watering. The flowers are fragrant and are butterfly favorites. Mulch and protect from afternoon sun.
Turk's Cap (*Malaviscus arboreus* var. *drummondii*)	24, 36–60	red	sun	spring–fall	Turk's cap has small delightful blossoms and lush foliage. Cut back after two years. It is very aggressive and needs to be controlled by thinning. It is a native.

Name	Spacing, Height (Inches)	Color	Exposure	Blooming Season	Comments
Verbena (*Verbena hybrida*)	12–18, 12–20	pink, purple, white, red, lavender	sun	late spring–fall	Often treated as an annual, they can work as perennials if cut back and/or divided. They work best as trailing plants, hanging over pots or walls.
Winecup (*Callirhoe involvucrata*)	3–4, 4–8	purple	sun	spring–summer	With its low-growing foliage, this is a desirable cultivated plant. Sow seeds in fall. Nursery stock is available. This native has intense color.
Yarrow (*Achillea* spp.)	12–15, 24–36	red, pink, white, yellow	sun, part shade	summer	Flat-topped flowers float above fernlike foliage. In spite of its delicate look, it is drought tolerant. Flowers are good for cutting, even though they will turn brown. They like good soil and little competition, especially from trees.

BULBS

Name	Spacing, Height (Inches)	Color	Exposure	Blooming Season	Comments
Amaryllis (*Hippeastrum* spp.)	12–36, 12–36	red, pink, striped	sun, part shade	April–May	Naturalizes. Produces large flowers. Most garden varieties are hybrids of Dutch, English, and African strains.
Anemone (*Anemone* spp.)	4, 12	multiple	part shade	early spring	Treat as annuals. Plant with points down, preferably in humusy soil.
Caladium (*Caladium* spp.)	1–2, up to 12	leaves come in multiple colors	shade	blooms are insignificant	Plant in spring after soil has warmed (cool soil will cause them to rot). Remove flower heads when they develop. When plants wilt in the fall, dig and store in a warm location until the next spring. Plant two to three inches deep.
Canna (*Canna* spp.)	6–24, 18–60	red, coral, yellow	sun, part shade	summer	Plant in well-composted soil. Deadhead old flowers before seed heads form. After the first freeze, cut to the ground and mulch; divide in the spring.
Crinum (*Crinum* spp.)	18–24, 12–18	white, pink, red	sun, part shade	spring–fall	Crinums will grow under a variety of conditions. They prefer, however, to be deep set in well-prepared soil. They will bloom off and on from spring until first frost. They will naturalize and grow to large clumps.
Daffodil (*Narcissus* spp.)	4–12, 6–12	yellow, white	sun, part shade	spring	Make sure you purchase bulbs that will naturalize in Central Texas. Otherwise you will get one, maybe two, years of bloom, then only leaves. Plant six inches deep in fall.
Gladiolus (*Gladioulus* spp.)	8–12, 6–18	multiple	sun	summer	Glads make excellent cut flowers. Dig up and store after the leaves die back. They like organic, well-drained soil. Plant corms six inches deep biweekly beginning in mid-January.

BULBS (*continued*)

Name	Spacing, Height (*Inches*)	Color	Exposure	Blooming Season	Comments
Hyacinth (*Hyacinthus* spp.)	4–5, 4–5	blue, purple, lavender	sun, part shade	spring	Plant four to six inches deep in the fall. They will naturalize easily.
Iris, Bearded (*Iris* spp.)	6, 8–48	various	sun, part shade	spring–summer	Plant very shallow (tops of rhizomes at soil level). Divide every three to four years to maintain healthy rhizomes and good blooms. They like well-drained soil. Divide in September and feed with bone meal at that time.
Iris, Louisiana (*Iris* spp.)	12, 12–24	various	sun, part shade	spring	Plant three or four inches deep in the fall. They like boggy conditions. Some gardeners grow them in plastic wading ponds. Keep well watered, particularly in the summer. Fertilize with fertilizer designed for acid-loving plants and divide in the fall.
Lily (*Lilium* spp.)	6–10, 36–48	various	sun	spring–summer	Lilies need particular care in our hot environment. They need loose soil and a good layer of mulch for moisture retention. Varieties that do well include *L. candidum* (Madonna), *L. tigridum* (Tiger), and *L. regale* ('Regal').
Lycoris or Spider Lily (*Lycoris radiata*)	6–8, 18–24	red, pink	sun, part shade	fall	Foliage dies down in spring, then in fall bloom spikes will shoot up. Can be interplanted with nonaggressive ground covers. Makes a good cut flower.
Oxalis or Wood Sorrel (*Oxalis crassipes*)	4–10, 8–12	rose, white	sun, part shade	fall–spring	Oxalis is a hardy little bulb that will do well in three seasons. They fade in the heat of summer and need shade then. Divide every four years. *O. regnelli* has purple leaves and a small, white flower. It needs shade.

Plant	Height/Spacing	Color	Light	Season	Notes
Spider Lily (*Hymenocallis* spp.)	23–36, 18–24	white	sun, part shade	spring–summer	There are numerous species of this plant. The most common, however, has eluded classification. These bulbs can be treated like crinums.
Ranunculus (*Ranunculus asiaticus*)	6–8, 12–18	red, pink, yellow, white	sun, part shade	spring	Plant two or three inches deep in organically rich soil in the fall. They do not naturalize well and should be treated as annuals.
Tulip (*Tulipa clusiana*)	4–6, 4–6	various	sun	spring	Traditional tulips do not do well in Central Texas. Try the *T. clusiana*, which naturalizes. It produces a small but bright flower. Plant three or four inches deep in well-drained soil. Another species that naturalizes is *T. saxatilis*.

for the next season's growth, until it has yellowed and dried. Some bulbs should be replaced every year, while others may be left in the ground to naturalize. Then there are those that should be dug up, properly stored, and replanted the next fall (see the chart that follows). Before you store them, you should allow bulbs to dry for a week in a dark, well-ventilated area. Residual soil should be removed, and the bulbs then stored in a paper bag or unsealed box filled with dry peat moss or vermiculite. Bulbs should be stored in a cool, dark location.

WILDFLOWERS

One does not have to be too sensitive a soul to be aware that Texas is a veritable flower basket. More than four thousand species of flowering plants have been identified in its varied regions, "where they smile in secret, looking over wasted lands," as Alfred Lord Tennyson put it in "Song of the Lotus-Eaters." Wildflower societies, the Texas Department of Transportation, and commercial wildflower seed purveyors do their best to help Texans enjoy this renewable resource.

It wasn't too long ago that those of us who wanted to grow wildflowers were limited to collecting our own seed or seeking out the few seed houses that carried them. How things have changed! Now collections of wildflower mixes are found everywhere—from discount outlets to gift boutiques. Many, including the venerable Texas bluebonnet, are container-grown. Others have been tamed, hybridized, miniaturized, or colorized, further blurring the distinction between wildflower and "garden variety."

We have included in the flower tables many wildflowers that are commonly used in gardens. We have noted their "native" origin under Comments.

The Wildflower Meadow
Since many species of wildflowers look their best when planted in masses, we think the "meadow look" created by wildflowers interplanted with native grasses can be an excellent low-water-use alternative to the traditional turf lawn. Before you choose to go this route and broadcast bluebonnets across the front yard, there are major considerations. It is easy to be seduced by the seemingly indestructible appearance of wildflowers, especially when we see them growing through the asphalt at the edges of a road or in cracks in the sidewalks. Yet for many species, that crack in the sidewalk is the perfect environment—and a difficult one for the gardener to duplicate. We confess to having done in an embarrassing number of the very charming blackfoot daisy *(Melampodium leucanthum)* with kindness. Rich, fertile garden soil is not for everyone.

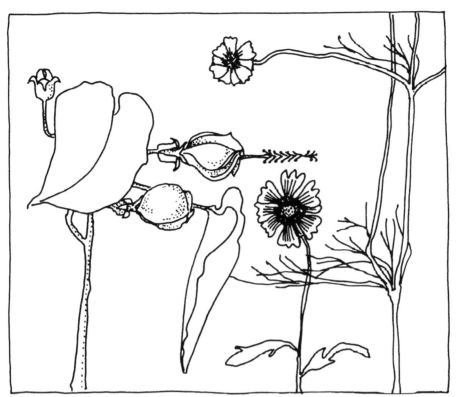

WILDFLOWERS: TURK'S CAP, FIREWHEEL, COREOPSIS

While so beautiful and striking when in bloom, many a wildflower looks like an unwanted weed a good part of the year. The dazzling display of spring flowers will be short-lived if the meadow or garden has not been sown or planted for a succession of flowers.

If interplanting wildflowers with grass, use native grasses. Their water needs are likely to be similar to those of the wildflowers and their growth habits tend to be less invasive than those of turfgrass. The common turf varieties, St. Augustine and bermuda, will quickly outcompete any wildflower.

Knowing wildflower needs, strengths, and weaknesses is essential. A successful wildflower meadow requires planning, soil preparation, and time. Annuals will be up and blooming in a year, but it will be two years before the biennials and many perennials flower.

The Lady Bird Johnson Wildflower Center in Austin is an excellent resource for all kinds of native plant information. It has an excellent website and research library as well as superb fact sheets available for a fee. Fact sheet topics include recommended species lists by geographic region, seed source lists, and wildlife and wildflower gardening.

Bluebonnet (*Lupinus* spp.), **Coreopsis** (*Coreopsis* spp.), **Indian Blanket** (*Gaillardia pulchella*), **Mexican Hat** (*Ratibida columnaris*), and **Purple Horsemint** (*Monarda citriodora*) are excellent choices for a wildflower meadow.

Directions for Planting Wildflower Seeds

(We prefer using container-started plants when planting only a few plants in pots, a mixed border, or other garden setting. Seeds should be reserved for large planting areas.)

1. Plant at the correct time (when the flowers are sowing their seeds) and in soil and light conditions similar to those in which the flower is ordinarily found.

2. Cultivate the soil surface to allow the seedlings to get a foothold.

3. If broadcasting several varieties of seed, you will get a more even distribution if you spread each species separately. It is difficult to spread evenly a mix containing seeds of different sizes and weights. It is sometimes useful to mix very fine seeds with damp sand before spreading.

3. Cover seedlings lightly with soil, and firm gently. *Good contact with the soil is key to successful wildflower germination.*

4. Water lightly. All seeds need moisture to germinate.

Remember that the germination rate for wildflowers is below that of the packet of marigold seeds you buy at the nursery.

Finally, a word about our state flower, the bluebonnet (*Lupinus* spp.). It is interesting to note that only in 1971 did the state legislature deem all six *Lupinus* species growing in Texas the state flower. Traditionally heralding spring with its spikes of blue-and-white blossoms, the bluebonnet is now available in white, pink, and maroon. In 1994 at a Texas A&M naming ceremony, a lavender cultivar, 'Barbara Bush,' was introduced. Besides their value in wildflower plantings, container-started bluebonnets make handsome potted plants.

Bluebonnet seed should be planted in September (September 15 is the latest date to plant in Dallas; Thanksgiving in San Antonio). Transplants should be in the ground by the end of October in Dallas; by mid-February in San Antonio. Use only chemically scarified seed for a good germination rate.

Aggie Horticulture, Texas A&M University's website, recommends the following procedure to ensure a bumper crop of bluebonnets.

1. Plant in full sun, in soil which drains well and doesn't stay wet for long periods.

2. Use transplants or chemically scarified seed. Barely cover seeds with soil. If you use transplants, don't bury the crown.
3. Water seeds only on the day of planting and transplants only when the top inch of soil dries. No applications of fertilizer are required, but they are helpful and will cause more abundant bloom.
4. Don't overwater.

ROSES

Immortalized in poetry and celebrated in song, roses, to so many, are the essence of flowers. Extolled by many cultures throughout history, the rose was named the national flower of the United States by Congress in 1986. There are roses that are native to Asia, Europe, and our continent. There are climbing roses, trailing roses, shrub roses, tree roses, and miniature roses. Subject to endless hybridization in pursuit of the perfection of specific attributes, roses are now available for almost any taste and Central Texas garden. Volumes have been written on roses and new roses are introduced continuously. Our discussion of rose classes is designed to assist you in selecting the right rose for your garden.

Old Roses. The newest and most exciting development in roses is the rediscovery and subsequent cultivation of old roses. Roses were brought to Texas by pioneers to grace their gardens. As time went by and interest focused on hybrids that emphasized color and size of bloom, old roses with their charming but less spectacular flowers were overshadowed; they fell from grace and declined in use in the garden. But in the late 1980s they were "rediscovered" growing in old cemeteries, at abandoned homesteads, and along roadsides. These hardy survivors of generations past gained the respect and attention of today's rose growers for their unfussy simplicity, fragrance, and toughness. Here were roses that, unlike the many demanding modern hybrids, had come through neglect and our capricious climate "smelling like a rose."

Happily, we are now reaping the benefits created by those who set to work to cultivate these roses anew. New/old vigorous varieties have taken a well-earned place in the rose section at many garden centers. Old roses, an imprecise category, fall into a variety of rose classes. They can be teas, Chinas, Noisettes, or Bourbons, for instance. Think of an old rose as any rose that was introduced seventy-five years ago or earlier. A few of our favorites are the delicate pink 'Old Blush' and climbing 'Old Blush,' the fragrant, creamy-yellow 'Céline Forestier,' the petite pink 'The Fairy,' and the prolific rose-colored tea, 'Mrs. B. R. Cant.'

HYBRID TEA ROSE

Hybrid teas are what many of us "see" when we think of a rose. The bush is generally upright in habit; a single, pointed bud is produced on the stem. Blooms are usually double and come in an extraordinary range of colors. Well cared for, they can be a spectacular and sensuous experience. Although fragrance has often lost out to bloom size and color in many of the hybridization efforts, the pink 'Tiffany' and dark red 'Mirandy' are gloriously fragrant exceptions. In our climate they bloom in spring and fall and intermittently in summer. They are hardy but require care to prevent disease and insect damage. Hybrid teas make wonderful cut flowers.

The old favorites, the red 'Chrysler Imperial' and yellow blend 'Peace' are excellent examples of hybrid teas. Other desirable varieties are 'Alabama' (pink blend), 'Double Delight' (red blend), 'Pristine' (white), 'Honor' (white) and 'Helen Traubel' (pink blend).

Floribundas. Although they generally produce smaller flowers than the hybrid teas, the floribundas feature clusters of blossoms and color in the garden beginning in the spring and continuing through late fall, a longer time than hybrid tea roses. They are also apt to be hardier and more disease resistant. They may be upright or spreading in habit.

Some of the varieties popular in Central Texas are 'Angel Face' (mauve), 'Europeana' (dark red), 'Fire King' (orange-red), Gene Boerner' (medium pink), 'Ginger' (orange-red), 'First Prize' (pink blend), 'Handel' (red blend), 'Lawrence Pink Rosette' (pink), 'Sarabande' (orange-red), and 'Vogue' (pink blend).

Grandifloras. A cross between the hybrid tea and the floribunda, the grandiflora is a tall, imposing bush that produces large blooms in the cluster of the floribunda and is as hardy as the hybrid tea.

Some recommended varieties are 'Aquarius' (pink blend), 'Apricot Nectar' (apricot blend), 'Camelot' (medium pink), 'Granada' (red blend), 'Golden Girl' (medium yellow), 'Montezuma' (orange-red), 'Queen Elizabeth' (medium pink), and 'Sundowner' (apricot blend).

Polyanthas. Bountiful and hardy, this class produces large clusters of small flowers. Generally the bushes themselves are smaller and more compact than those in other classes, making polyanthas particularly suitable for small spaces and even containers. Some varieties are more fragrant than others. Good polyantha varieties for Central Texas are 'Cécile Brünner' (light pink) and the very fragrant 'Marie Pavie' (white).

Climbing Roses. Although climbing roses have no special climbing equipment, such as tendrils, they vigorously produce long shoots or canes that can be trained over fences and trellises and that make a perfect screen while providing a profusion of blossoms. The flowers of today's climbers can resemble those of hybrid teas or floribundas. If you have a small yard, bear in mind that all climbers require space, and some have a limited blooming season. Attention to pruning is essential to their control.

The more popular are 'Don Juan' (dark red), climbing 'Cécile Brünner' (light pink), 'Golden Showers' (medium yellow), 'New Dawn' (light pink), and the tough 'Lady Banksia' (most often seen in the thornless yellow variety but available in a white, which does have thorns).

Miniature Roses. The delicate buds, stems, and foliage of miniature roses have made them popular with certain rose enthusiasts. Miniatures come in a great variety of colors, grow from three to twelve inches tall, and, for continuous blooming, can be grown indoors as potted plants and then put outside when warm weather arrives. Some popular miniature roses are 'Beauty Secret' (medium red), 'Chipper' (light pink), 'Cinderella' (white), 'Judy Fischer' (medium pink), 'Magic Carrousel' (red blend), 'Mary Marshall' (orange-pink), and 'Over-the-Rainbow' (red blend).

Site selection is key to success with roses. No amount of loving care can compensate for an inadequate location. Roses need sun and lots of it. Six to eight hours daily will do nicely. And while most roses, especially the modern hybrids, appreciate regular watering, good drainage is essential. Because many rose varieties are prone to the fungal disease black spot and to mildew, roses should be given plenty of space for air circulation.

Bare-root roses arrive at garden centers from December through February. They should be planted immediately or covered with moist peat moss or soil until you can plant them properly. They will benefit from an overnight soak before planting. Container roses can be planted any time, but spring and fall are preferable. Roses like slight acidity—a pH of 6.0 to 6.5—so chances are you will have to add bone meal or superphosphate as well as a large amount of humus to the soil. Dig your hole about twelve inches deep and at least a foot and a half to three feet wide, depending on variety. Consider a raised bed if you do not have sufficient depth in your yard. Raised beds also facilitate drainage, an additional advantage. A local rosarian suggests substituting for the original soil a mixture of one-third coarse sand, one-third good soil, and one-third peat moss or compost. Preferably this bed should be prepared at least a week before planting time. Also, many garden centers carry premixed rose soil.

Roses should be planted about eight to ten inches deep and two feet apart. Trim out any dead or damaged roots or canes and cut the healthy canes back to about a quarter-inch above the first healthy-looking bud. Follow the general rules for planting (see chapter 7, "Tree and Shrub Planting and Care"). Be sure to eliminate any residual air pockets by tamping lightly but firmly on the soil. Mulch loosely with pine needles or bark, leaves, or compost to help retain moisture and control weeds.

Fertilizing and Watering. Your roses should be fed about every six weeks beginning in spring and ending in September, for a total of four feedings. Use a good commercial rose fertilizer or an 8-8-8 formulation. Your soil type will dictate how frequently you will need to water. Remember that roses do not like to dry out completely. If you have sandy soil, you may want to water as often as every three to four days in the summer months. More clayey soils should be watered about once a week. Soaker hose or drip irrigation methods are preferred, as overhead sprinkling will wet the leaves, leaving them prone to fungal disease.

Disease and Pests. The most troublesome part of raising roses comes under the heading of pest and disease control. Black spot and powdery mildew are the major diseases that threaten roses in Central Texas. The leaves of plants suffering black spot display (no surprise) large black spots. The leaves yellow and drop. Applications of a fungicide such as Benomyl or Funginex can control this condition. Frequent inspection will catch the disease in the early stages. Powdery mildew is evident by the presence and spread of irregularly shaped grayish fungal spores. The same fungicides are recommended for this condition.

Pruning. Rose bushes are pruned to produce more and better blossoms, and for that reason their pruning needs are more demanding than those of other shrubs. Pruning begins with cutting back dead and diseased canes to the live wood, removing canes that conflict, and snipping off suckers coming up from the roots. Next, prune to shape. The rigid rose-pruning orthodoxy of years ago has been replaced by greater latitude in letting the gardener exercise judgment. Roses can be pruned high, medium, or low. While there are many opinions on what the optimal cut is, it is safe to remove one-third to one-half of the previous year's growth. The cane should be cut about a quarter-inch above an outward-pointing bud at a thirty-degree angle. When you direct the growth outward, the plant will have good sunshine and air circulation.

Hybrid teas, floribundas, and grandifloras should be pruned in the spring. Large-flowered climbers are also pruned lightly in the spring. Climbers that bloom only in the spring should be pruned after they blossom. Old roses, which often tend naturally toward a graceful shape, may need less frequent pruning than do hybrid teas.

If flowers are cut, late-summer pruning often is unnecessary. Otherwise, it is advisable to prune in a similar manner, although somewhat less severely.

Remember always to make your cut with a sharp tool. Ragged cuts may fail to heal, making them vulnerable to insect and disease invasion.

Despite the demanding regimen, most gardeners are tempted to try roses at one time or another. And as one knowledgeable rosarian said to us, "No flowering plant is as gratifying." In our area you can actually have roses in bloom for nine months of the year. For many, that's reason enough to grow the "queen of flowers."

❧ 12 ❧

Vegetables

Earth in her heart laughs, looking at the heaven,
Thinking of the harvest, I look and think of mine.
G. MEREDITH, "LOVE IN THE VALLEY"

Vegetable gardening is so much more than planting and harvesting. To us, it is a microcosm of life, representing its joys, frustrations, failures, and successes. The appeal of nurturing something to the finished product is so basic that even gardeners who (by their own reckoning) fail can seldom resist the temptation to try again.

The temptation arises because to gardeners, growing vegetables is fun. If you don't find it fun, don't bother. Our numerous grocery and specialty stores carry enormous varieties of fresh produce, including some that is organically grown. The urge to grow vegetables does not arise from need; it emanates from the joy of working the garden, watching plants grow, and harvesting your own produce.

FOUR ELEMENTS

If you do enjoy vegetable gardening—or think you might—there are four main ingredients you must have to make the "veggie garden" work: good soil, nutrients, a sustaining climate, and adequate water.

Soil

First, and always, there is the soil. It is the foundation of all gardening, especially vegetable gardening. In Central Texas we have two basic choices of soil:

poor and worse. Poor soil is what one of our gardening friends calls "ten o'clock dirt": at 9:55 A.M. it is too wet and heavy to plow; at 10:05 A.M. it is dry and concrete-hard. The only time you can till it is at 10:00 A.M. It is, in short, thick black clay.

The "worse" (and these terms are relative) is caliche, which anyone but a Central Texan would call rock. Actually, much of it *is* rock—limestone—mixed with expansive clay. While it is only a few inches deep in some parts of the area, many gardeners find that it goes down about a half-mile in their yards. Generally, Central Texas east of Interstate 35 has ten o'clock dirt, and the caliche lies to the west.

The only way to garden in these soils is to amend them by adding organic matter to the soil. Organic matter is anything that used to grow: grass clippings, leaves, kitchen waste, and manure (remember, it used to be green material before the cows or horses took care of it).

Overwhelmingly, the amendment of choice is compost. This "gardener's gold" is easy to make from readily available, cheap products, and it will provide the substance to make your soil productive (more on that later in this chapter). Other suitable amendments include composted manure from horses or cows. Make sure that the manure is composted and not fresh or "hot" (too fresh from the farm or stable), in which case it will burn plants. If the manure is hot, it can be made suitable for planting simply by working it into the soil and leaving it to age for several weeks before planting anything in it.

There are also commercial amendments available from local nurseries, such as bagged manure, composted sewage sludge, and potting soils. Just make sure that the product is suitable for vegetable gardening. There are products that are perfectly suitable for horticulture or lawns but not for application on soil that will grow produce because they may contain elements (such as heavy metals) not suitable for human consumption.

Other amendments will also aid in soil improvement. Gypsum can be added to loosen the ten o'clock dirt. Sand opens up the soil and allows for better drainage. Peat moss adds humus for water retention (note: in ten o'clock dirt, peat moss is not desirable).

What the gardener is looking for is soil that is friable. The condition of "friability" can be tested with a handful of soil. Simply scoop up some soil in your hand and squeeze it into a ball. Then open up your clenched fist and test your handiwork. If it does not stay balled but easily falls apart, the soil is too loose and will not retain sufficient water. If the soil stays balled and won't fall apart even when you poke it with a free finger, it has too much clay and will retain water too long. If, however, it is balled when you open your hand but falls apart when poked, you have friable soil. This is soil that is loose enough for roots to grow and expand in, yet is sufficiently dense to hold water and release it slowly enough for your plants' use.

If your garden plot consists only of caliche or barren rock, or if you want something different or more tidy, it makes sense to create a raised bed garden. Raised bed gardens simply elevate soil above grade. You can accomplish this quite easily in a variety of ways.

The most common practice is to till the entire garden area, then dig out paths within the space, piling the soil that is dug out onto the beds, thus raising them above normal elevation. And you can border your raised beds in pressured-treated lumber, stone, brick, or other solid material to give your garden a more finished look.

The purpose of raising beds is to raise the soil level, facilitating drainage, creating beds that will warm earlier in the season, and isolating them for the specific purpose of growing vegetables. Once created, raised beds should never be walked upon; that will compact the soil, making it more difficult for plants to grow. For this reason it is best to create beds about four feet wide. That way the gardener can reach in from either side of the bed to plant, tend, and harvest without stepping on the soil.

Once the soil is prepared, you still don't know if it will sustain plant life. You need to know which vital elements are in the soil and which are missing and need to be added. A soil test is in order. Send a sample of soil from your garden to be tested (see chapter 2, "Soil and Its Conditioning.")

Nutrients

Three nutrients need to be in all soil: nitrogen, phosphate, and potassium, expressed by the letters N, P, and K. Fertilizer packages always contain this formula and always express it in numbers in the order N (nitrogen), P (phosphate), and K (potassium). Thus, a fertilizer with a listing of 20-10-10 is composed of 20 percent nitrogen, 10 percent phosphate, and 10 percent potassium (the remaining 60 percent is filler material). The numbers are important depending upon the type of plant you are growing (your grass, vegetables, shrubs, or flowers) and upon the quality of soil.

Other nutrients, called trace elements, also need to be present. These include but are not limited to iron, zinc, and boron.

Once you have determined what is missing or needs boosting, there are two fundamental ways to obtain the nutrients: organically or chemically. The de-

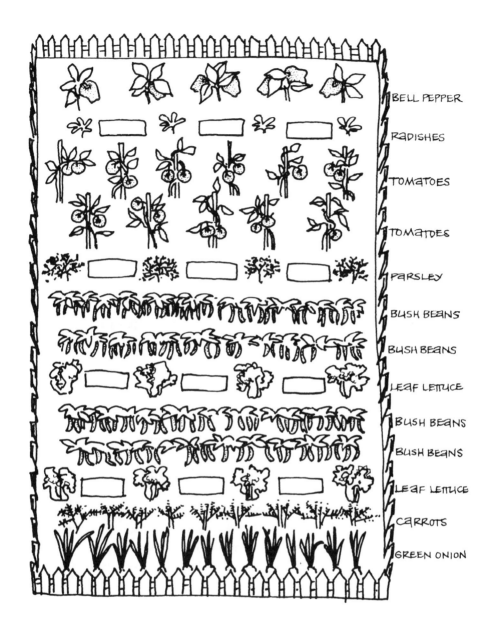

BELL PEPPER

RADISHES

TOMATOES

TOMATOES

PARSLEY

BUSH BEANS

BUSH BEANS

LEAF LETTUCE

BUSH BEANS

BUSH BEANS

LEAF LETTUCE

CARROTS

GREEN ONION

SAMPLE VEGETABLE GARDEN

WITH CHANNELS

bate over which to use has ranged and raged for decades. It is not our intent to enter that debate in this book. Rather, we suggest that you visit your local nursery and discuss what is available from which sources. The supply of fertilizers, both organic and chemical, is extensive, so choose one that appeals to you, apply it according to the instructions, and prepare to garden veggies. The two most important considerations when applying fertilizer are the ratio (NPK) and the amount. Don't think that if your garden needs 10 percent nitrogen you will do better with 20 percent, or that if directions call for a rate of one pound per hundred square feet, you'll get better results applying two pounds per hundred square feet. The ratios and rates have been thoroughly tested before they are recommended. Applying too much can burn plants and kill rather than nourish them.

Climate

Temperature is the only condition over which a gardener has little control. Temperature in Central Texas ranges from subfreezing in deep winter to searing hundred-degree-plus temperatures—sometimes lasting for days—during the summer.

This is why vegetable gardeners in Central Texas don't have one long growing season as do their fellow gardeners farther north. Rather, we have two growing seasons, and both of them are relatively short. The spring season begins in the deep of winter when the beds are tilled, some plants are planted in the garden, and some are started indoors to be transplanted later. The objective of the spring garden is to grow and harvest before the searing summer heat halts production.

The fall season begins in the blistering heat of the summer, and the soil is again tilled. Some plants are planted directly in the garden and some are started in pots to be transplanted later. The objective of this season's gardening is to realize harvest before the first frost. Each season has its "cheating" techniques—practices that can be employed to overcome the vicissitudes of the season. These are discussed in the section listing vegetables at the end of this chapter.

Regardless of the time of year you plant, your garden should receive between six and eight hours of sunlight. Vegetables are not very shade tolerant, so consider the amount of sunlight the garden will receive when you plan your layout.

Water

Consider how rapidly veggies grow. A tomato, for example, will be a seed in January and should be producing literally pounds of tomatoes in June—five to six months from seed to production. Vegetable plants need a lot of food (fertilizer), a lot of sun, and a lot of water. They should be "turgid"—full of water—throughout their productive cycle.

While this does not mean vegetable gardens *must* be irrigated, it does help, particularly if you use the new drip irrigation, which puts water right at a plant's root zone. This technique delivers water only where it is needed and reduces water squandering, not to mention utility bills. Hand watering and sprinkling can certainly get the job done but are more time consuming and less efficient.

Vegetables should also be heavily mulched. This promotes water efficiency and moderates temperatures around the root zone. Dry grass clippings (don't use wet, freshly cut clippings because when they dry they will form a crusty surface and actually keep water away from the plants), compost, straw, and bark chips are only a few examples of types of mulch that may be used.

GROW UP!

We aren't talking about your maturity but about taking advantage of space. Most urban homes, particularly new ones, are on small lots. But that shouldn't prevent a gardener from growing vegetables. Cages and trellises can be used to help plants grow vertically, thus saving space. Cucumbers are a good example. Left to their natural tendencies, they will sprawl over the garden hogging valuable space. But grown inside a cage, they can be trained vertically to save space. Cages can be purchased from nurseries or made from a variety of products. We use concrete reinforcing wire to make cages two feet in diameter and anchor them to the ground with stakes.

Trellises can be used in the same manner for any crops that can be grown in cages. Pole beans and melons are particularly adapted to this environment.

Don't forget pots. Any plant that can be grown in the garden can be grown in a container. Apartment or townhome dwellers can create vegetable gardens in pots. Consider tomatoes, for example: several varieties on the market have been bred specifically for containers.

GARDEN PREPARATION

Vegetable garden soil should be turned before each planting. Some gardeners use power tillers, others hand dig. Regardless, it is an opportunity to aerate the soil, remove weeds and rocks, add amendments and fertilizers, and get ready for growing.

Soil should be worked when it is damp (remember the ten o'clock dirt?). But don't work wet and waterlogged soil. Not only is wet soil difficult to work in; the work is also counterproductive. Wet soil is easily compacted, producing an environment hostile to vegetables. At the other extreme, don't try to work dry soil. It is difficult to turn and frustrating to the gardener.

Some gardeners "double dig." This is an intensive process in which the top level of soil is turned, removed, and set aside. Then the second, lower level of soil is turned, and the first level is returned to the bed. Doing this provides turned soil to a depth of two to three feet. While you are turning the soil, add fertilizer, compost, and other amendments.

After turning, water so that the soil is moist to a depth of eighteen to twenty-four inches. Let the garden settle for about a week. This allows hot spots made by fresh manure to cool and will provide time for soil microorganisms to go to work. (Remember, if you add hot manure, to let it sit for several weeks, and turn it lightly a couple of times.) You should now have soil that is ready for planting. The soil should be moist at planting time, not soggy or dry.

PLANTING

Now it is time to plant—our favorite part of gardening. Ah, the air of expectation! Years ago, toward the end of winter gardeners set out cold frames and started seeds indoors in flats. These methods are just as good today as they were then and are still the most economical for large gardens. But gardening has changed, and so has the typical gardener. Lots are smaller now, and gardeners have less time. Nurseries carry young plants of endless varieties at low prices. It doesn't seem to make sense to set out a flat, buy a package of seed, and take careful, tender care of seedlings if you need only three or four pepper plants.

When you buy young vegetable plants from a nursery, it is important to make sure they are strong and vigorous. Bargains may not always be bargains. Some plants clearly look shopworn: they are wilted, bottom leaves are yellowing, and roots extend far beyond the limits of the container. Spring and fall are busy times at nurseries, and often some chores just get neglected. A common problem with such plants is that they have been allowed to dry out. The containers are small, and unless watered regularly, they dry out rapidly. Beware of plants with soil that looks hard and has withdrawn from the container walls. When selecting plants from a nursery, gently pull one from its container and look at the root system. It should look vigorous (generally numerous white roots growing outward) but should not be root bound (roots filling the container and growing in a circular pattern). Look carefully for signs of bug infestation (leaves chewed, for example), and check out the general health of the plant (no yellow leaves). If they pass your selection test, odds are that they will have a better than average chance to survive and thrive in your garden.

Some plants, however, are best grown from seed. The discussion later in this chapter of each type of vegetable plant indicates whether it should be grown from seed or from started plants.

Plant according to the planting guide developed for your county by the Texas A&M Agriculture Extension Service. But remember, these planting times are based upon average temperatures. And in Central Texas you should not be surprised by an early or late frost and can lose your tender plant. Such are the vagaries of vegetable gardening.

When planting, remember to stay out of the bed. You have already spent time and energy getting it ready for the plants. Don't spoil it by walking in it and compacting the loose, friable soil your veggie plants need.

TENDING

After your plants are up and growing in the garden you can't rest on your laurels. You must take an active role in getting your plants into production. When the plants are well on their way, it's time to mulch. In our hot, dry, and windy climate, this practice cannot be overemphasized. Mulching with clean straw, bark mulch, dried grass clippings, or compost will conserve moisture, and when you turn the mulch under at the end of the season, it will add organic material back to the soil. Black plastic is a useful mulch for strawberries, squash, and other fruits and vegetables that tend to rot when they sit on wet soil. Mulching is also an effective weed control. How much mulch to add is an individual decision. Smaller plants, obviously, don't need inches of mulch. Plants that grow all season (tomatoes and peppers, for example) should be mulched several times during the growth cycle. You can test the effectiveness of mulch by pulling some aside a couple of days after a rain or after you water. If the soil under the mulch is still damp, you have a sufficient layer. If it's dry, add more mulch.

Throughout the growing seasons—remember we have two of them—your vegetables will need new applications of fertilizer. Side dressings of small amounts at more frequent intervals are better than larger, less frequent applications. This is particularly true in sandy soils, where moisture retention is poor. Follow the directions on your fertilizer label.

Side dressing simply means scattering small amounts of fertilizer alongside the plant, then scratching it in with a garden cultivator (generally a three-pronged fork). The purpose of side dressing is to provide additional nutrients to fast-growing plants.

From time to time, you will need to cope with insect invaders and/or diseases (see chapter 13, "Trouble in the Garden"). Again, the first line of defense is a well-kept garden, one free of debris. More active measures that work to varying degrees are putting collars made from plastic or cardboard around young plants; sprays concocted from foul-smelling ingredients such as garlic, hot peppers, onions, and marigolds; importing natural predators; and companion planting with naturally repellent flowers and herbs. When you resort to applying pesticides, never exceed label instructions, which will tell you the number of days before harvest you may apply the chemical. For our part, we should note that we do not use pesticides in our vegetable gardens. Our approach is to try any other means to save the plant, and if that doesn't work, to admit that we were overpowered by the bugs and to move on, either replanting or waiting until the next season.

After your vegetables have been planted, mulched, fertilized, and watered, don't forget the most important duty: visit them—daily. Take time out of your schedule each day to walk among the vegetables, check on how they are progressing, and look for signs of trouble. Remember, you are interested in the produce of the vegetable garden. So are many critters. You will find, as most of us do, that time spent in the garden is relaxing. Visit your plants often. Someone once said, "The best fertilizer is from the gardener's shadow."

VEGETABLES

Asparagus. This delicately flavored and expensive vegetable is a true perennial. Plant three-year-old crowns in January. The first year take no harvest; take a small amount the following year; and then harvest what you need thereafter.

Planting and Tending: Plant the crowns (purchased at a local nursery in January or early February) twelve inches deep in a well-prepared and organically rich bed. Dig a trench and plant the crowns on a small mound so that the roots fan out. Cover with about three inches of soil and add additional soil as the plant begins to grow. Shop carefully for roots; a survey of local nurseries revealed great differences in quality. Fertilize in the fall.

Beets. Beets are not only an easy crop—they are entirely edible. Young leaves are great in salads and more mature roots provide the traditional beet: boiled, pickled, or whatever. But since they are easy growers, many gardeners plant too many beets and end up with a harvest they can neither eat nor give away. Rather than one large crop, try sowing small areas several weeks apart. Except for humans, not much else eats beets. Nematodes can be a problem, as can grubworms and wireworms. Look for whitish or blackish worms that look like pieces of wire as you prepare the soil. Consult your local nursery for control products.

Planting and Tending: Plant seeds half an inch deep in rows about one foot apart. Thin to three inches apart if harvesting the root and two inches if harvesting the leaves. Alternately, scatter seed in a small area and thin to a two- to three-inch distance after they emerge. Forget about the rows. Plant in loose, enriched soil and side dress with fertilizer at least once during the growing season.

Beans. There's a World War II song that goes "The Navy's got the gravy, but the Army's got the beans, beans, beans." Well, so do Central Texans. A plethora of them grow here—bush and pole varieties. The former are planted in rows, and as the name implies, have an upright, shaggy appearance. The latter grow right up any convenient pole, hence the name. Beans like to be planted in warm, loose soil. So don't rush to plant in the spring, but do amend the soil to lighten it. Since beans are legumes, they manufacture their own nitrogen, so fertilizer applications are minimal. Beans need regular watering, preferably by the drip method. Rust and powdery mildew are two major problems. Although they can be controlled with a fungicide, by the time they generally appear we've already had several harvests of beans. We pull up the plants; there'll be time to plant another crop.

Planting and Tending: Plant bush bean seeds one to one and a half inches deep about one inch apart. When they emerge, thin to three inches. Rows should be two to three feet apart. Pole beans are best grown up teepees of three or four poles. Two to three seeds should be planted at the base of each pole. They can also be grown up trellises or walls.

Broccoli. We generally consider broccoli a fall crop, though we do know Central Texas gardeners who get a good spring harvest. Regardless of planting time, begin with young plants, not seed. If you start from seed, they can take up to five months to mature. Prepare the soil with organic matter and add some fertilizer to get the young plants off to a good start. Spring planting should occur about two to three weeks before the last killing frost. Fall planting should begin in late summer. Remember, the plants are cold hardy and do well in cool conditions. Harvest when the heads are about six to seven inches in diameter but before they begin to flower. When cutting the head, be careful not to damage smaller heads emerging near the main stem. These small heads can be harvested as they mature for cooking or for use in salads. If we have a mild winter, you may be able to harvest until spring. If you have never seen a broccoli plant in flower, it might be fun to let one go to seed.

Planting and Tending: Space young plants eighteen to twenty-four inches apart in rows thirty-six inches apart. Mulch well, particularly when planting for the fall. Side dress with fertilizer twice during the growing season.

Carrots. The prime directive for growing carrots is to remember that the root (actually a storehouse of food) goes down, then it fills out. It does not push its way down into the soil. Therefore, loose friable soil is an absolute necessity if you want long, tapered carrots. Any rocks, dirt clods, or other impediments will cause the carrot to be misshapen. Carrot seeds are also small and persnickety. Like most root crops, carrots are an excellent fall crop.

Planting and Tending: Plant seeds about an eighth of an inch deep in rows twelve inches apart, or scatter seed in a small area. For best germination results, cover the planted area with a board and begin checking for germination in about seven days. When the plants are about four to eight weeks old, thin to about two inches apart. Side dress with fertilizer after thinning.

Corn. Don't plan on planting a few stalks of corn—plant a block of it rather than a few rows. Corn depends on wind for pollination, and without enough plants to fill the air with pollen, corn will be a hit-or-miss affair. Corn earworms are almost as much a part of corn as the tassel. Sevin sprayed on the silks soon after they appear and then again in about a week is a good control. Those who wish to take an organic approach can use baby oil on the tassels. The sugar in corn begins to turn into starch immediately after the corn has been picked. This means older varieties should go directly from the corn patch to the pot. The newer, sweeter varieties, however, can be harvested up to a week before serving. Because corn takes up a lot of space, gardeners should consider carefully whether they can grow a large enough block to make it worth their while.

Planting and Tending: Plant two seeds about an inch deep, about one foot apart in rows three feet apart, after the soil has warmed. If both seeds germinate, snip off the weaker one at ground level when they are a couple inches tall. Plant at least six feet of rows and at least four rows to ensure adequate pollination. Corn is a heavy feeder, so till in organic matter and a pound of garden fertilizer per hundred square feet. Side dress twice during the growing season.

Cucumbers. Cucumbers are good candidates for vertical or container gardening. They tend to sprawl unless trained vertically. They need loose soil rich in organic matter and plenty of water. Other than that, they are not particularly difficult plants to grow.

Planting and Tending: Plant about six seeds in mounded-up soil. When plants emerge, thin to three. A side dressing once during the growing season is helpful but not necessary. Cucumbers are heavy drinkers so ensure that they receive adequate water.

Lettuce. This salad favorite is so easy and quick to grow that one can sow seed in flower beds. Pill bugs love the new leaves, so watch out. Recommended varieties are essential to avoid untimely bolting (the plant begins to form a seed head and the lettuce turns bitter). For color and leaf texture, mix and sow together several types of seed (e.g., Red Sails and Black Seeded Simpson) in a container (we use empty herb jars that have plastic caps with dispensing holes on the top).

Planting and Tending: Rake the area to be planted and broadcast (scatter) the seed. Cover the seed with a light sprinkling of soil or sifted compost and water in. When plants emerge, thin them by gently drawing a garden rake through the lettuce patch in intersecting directions. This will thin the plot and provide some early, tender lettuce. Fertilize lightly and water.

Melons. The best melons are space gobblers, and are therefore good candidates for vertical gardening (watermelons excluded). The vines can be tied up in cages or other structures and slings (made from cloth or old pantyhose) can be tied to the frame to hold the fruit to maturity. Alternatively, there are bushing varieties of many melons, though their quality generally doesn't match that of the standard varieties.

Planting and Tending: Melons like loose soil, so add organic matter and sand as you till. Plant five or so seeds in a hill (soil mounded up about three feet in diameter) and thin to three when mature leaves appear; hills should be at least five feet apart. Ripe melons have a high water content, meaning they must be kept thoroughly watered during their growing period. The plants should be fertilized a couple of times with a balanced product. Melons are subject to powdery mildew, which can be handled with sulfur or other products recommended by your local nursery.

Onions. Onions in Central Texas are best as spring vegetables. This means that onion transplants, about the size of a pencil, should be set out in later winter. Those who want to start from seed should do so between mid-September and mid-October. Transplants, however, are the surer method. The soil should be rich in organic matter, so add compost, manure, and a balanced fertilizer a couple of weeks before planting if possible. Here is a tip for storing your bumper crop of onions once you have harvested them (which is done after the tops die down). Cut the legs off a pair of pantyhose. Drop one onion down into the toe and make a knot above it. Repeat this process until you have a string of onions separated by knots. Hang the result in your cupboard. When you need an onion, simply cut the pantyhose below the lowest knot. Your string of onions remains until another is needed.

Planting and Tending: Plant onions three to four inches apart in holes one inch deep and press the soil in around the transplant. Fertilize about a month after planting. Use a cultivator to keep the soil loose around the top of the plant. Plants should be well watered during the growing period. Mulch with organic matter to conserve water. Pull the mulch aside to apply additional fertilizer when the plant begins to bulb (swell at the soil line). We have no major insect or disease problems with onions in Central Texas, but onions are subject to powdery mildew (which can be controlled by a fungicide) and they can be attacked by thrips, which cause the leaves to turn brown. Thrips can be controlled with a pesticide, but they generally reduce yield without destroying the crop, so the use of pesticide is the gardener's call.

Peas. Peas are not an easy crop for Central Texas. We've had our best luck planting them in late January or early February for an early spring harvest. We prefer sugar snaps to the other two varieties: garden, or English, peas and pod peas. Choice, however, is a matter of success and preference. Sugar snaps also take up less room in the garden and the entire pea can be eaten, straight off the vine if you wish. Peas like enriched, well-drained soil, so add compost or other organic matter a few weeks before planting. Being legumes, they are able to fix nitrogen and need little fertilizing, though a bit added before planting can help. And peas are climbers, regardless of their mature height. So even the dwarf varieties need something to climb on. Chicken wire strung between stakes works. And for dwarf varieties, small tree limbs can be used. Gather a bundle of small limbs (harvested from winter pruning, perhaps) and stick them into the soil so that they support one another and, in turn, support the peas.

Planting and Tending: If you plant peas to grow up trellises, seeds should go in about one inch deep in rows one foot apart. When we plant with branches, we remove some soil (putting it in a cart for later use), put in the branches, scatter the seed, and put the soil back. Peas are so hardy, though, that we've seen them germinate on top of the ground. Keep them well watered until harvest. They are relatively problem-free and need little tending.

Peppers. Whether hot jalapeños or sweet bells, peppers like our heat and our sun—they love sun. So make sure that they are planted where they receive a maximum of it: six to eight hours a day. Also make sure they do not get "wet feet" (stay in damp soil). Peppers, like all vegetables, like water, but they don't like to sit in it. Raised beds and well-tilled, compost-amended soil are ways to ensure good drainage. Since peppers set fruit in temperatures up to about ninety degrees, it is best to use started plants rather than seeds. If you plant seeds late enough to avoid a freeze, that will bring plants into blossom after temperatures have climbed above the ninety-degree mark and your plants will not produce. At the other end of the thermometer, peppers will be damaged if the soil temperature drops below the mid-fifties. If you are uncertain, use a soil thermometer. Do not use air temperature—it does not necessarily correlate with soil temperature. Peppers will do best in soil amended with organic matter. Garden fertilizer (a 1-2-1 ratio) added a few weeks before planting will also get pepper plants off to a good start. Peppers are subject to mosaic virus, the symptoms of which are stunted growth, yellowing, and hard, shriveled leaves. The best control is to remove the affected plant (do not put it in the compost pile). Peppers are also prey to spider mites, which can be controlled with insecticidal soap. (See chapter 13, "Trouble in the Garden.") Fruit may also display whitish spots on the surface. This is sun scald and not much can be done (peppers are notoriously resistant to wearing "shades"). The condition does not affect the quality or taste of the rest of the pepper.

Planting and Tending: Set out started plants about eighteen to twenty-four inches apart in rows two feet apart. Plant after all danger of frost has passed and as soon as the soil is warm enough. Side dress with a general purpose vegetable fertilizer every month. Keep plants well watered but not soggy. After they bloom begin applying mulch regularly throughout the growing cycle.

Potatoes. Potatoes are a good spring or fall crop for all but the smallest garden. They do require space but are worth the effort. Potato tubers are formed underground and need loose soil to grow. The best soil preparation is to add compost and till in leaves. This increases the soil's friability. Potatoes grow from—well, potatoes. Be sure to purchase seed potatoes from a local nursery. Those sold in grocery stores often are treated to inhibit sprouting, which is exactly what you do not want in a seed potato. We prefer to select small seed potatoes and plant them whole. You may, however, select larger potatoes and cut them into large pieces, making sure that each piece has at least one eye (or bud). After cutting each piece, cover the cut portion with sulfur to prevent fungal problems after planting, and let the pieces season, or dry, for several days before planting. About a month after planting (plus or minus a week), potatoes will break ground and begin to grow, eventually flowering. This signifies nothing, particularly as regards the size of the tubers. The crop will be ready for harvesting about three to four months after planting. Spring-planted potatoes will begin to yellow. That is the sign they are ready. Fall-planted potatoes will continue to grow up to the first hard freeze. Harvest them before that freeze arrives.

Potatoes may be harvested while they are still growing. A few months after the plants have broken ground, carefully pull away the soil from around the plants. If there are new potatoes, you may harvest a few. Replace the soil and the plant will continue to produce potatoes. You will then have new potatoes during the growing season and mature ones at the end of the season.

Planting and Tending: There are several ways to plant potatoes. Here's how we do it. In well-composted and turned-in soil, dig a trench about eight inches deep, piling the soil alongside. Press the potatoes into the soil about one foot apart in rows two feet apart. Cover them with soil, but do not fill the trench. When the plants are about six inches tall, begin filling in the trench, pulling the soil in from the sides. This is called "dirting" the potatoes. It keeps the plants cool and promotes healthier development. Dirt the potatoes a couple of times; once the soil is level, put a couple inches of mulch on the bed (grass clippings and leaves do well). Diseases will attack potatoes. In the Central Texas area, scab is one of the more prevalent. It causes a rough, scablike (hence the name) area on the potato's surface. The best way to avoid this is by crop rotation, avoidance of hot manures, and using certified seed potatoes that you treat with sulfur (if you cut them up).

Radish. Tough and quick, the radish comes as close to being a "bulletproof" vegetable as anything we can think of. Sow the seed in late winter or late summer, making successive sowings at two- to three-week intervals for a long harvest. Radishes "make" (set their growth pattern) in about three or so days. Since they mature so quickly, they are ideal for planting between slower-growing crops such as lettuce and broccoli.

Planting and Tending: Sow seeds about one-half inch deep in rows one foot apart; thin to two inches apart in rows as soon as the seeds germinate (since they grow so fast, early thinning is needed so that selected plants can develop). Radishes have few insect or disease problems as long as good cultural practices are followed.

Spinach. This a tough one in our region, where summer can begin without warning. Spinach is definitely a cool-season crop. It grows well as a spring crop when it can be planted in late winter, but it tends to bolt in early summer. As a fall crop, it does quite well, its hardiness taking it into winter. It is quite possible to have a lettuce and spinach salad from your garden for Thanksgiving. But how to beat the summer heat, since spinach will not germinate in hot weather? Make the seed think it is going to grow in cool weather. Soak the spinach seeds for twenty-four to forty-eight hours in water stored in your home refrigerator. The seed will think winter has come and get with it.

Planting and Tending: Plant spinach one-half inch deep and about two inches apart in rows eighteen inches apart. After they start growing, thin to eight or nine inches apart. Seeds can also be broadcast and then covered with soil. Whether you opt for row or broadcast, tamp the soil down after sowing to ensure soil contact. Spinach, particularly when fall-grown, is attractive to aphids—very attractive. Remove affected leaves or treat with an insecticide. But make sure that you monitor the crop regularly. Today's amorous aphid couple with a longing for a family are next week's parents of millions. White rust and blue mold are common foliage diseases. Remove affected leaves or treat with a fungicide.

Squash. Those who have seen the movie *Forrest Gump* will remember the protracted conversation about the many ways to use shrimp. The same lengthy list applies to squash, be they summer or winter varieties. Why the two types are called that is a puzzle. The former can be grown in the fall, the latter in the spring. And winter squash cannot take a freeze. The two do have different planting and cultural practices, however. Summer squash is a bush variety, although the plants are large. They mature in about two months and are harvested when the fruit is young and tender. Winter squash is vining and takes up to four months to mature. The fruit is harvested when mature and once the skin has hardened.

Planting and Tending: Plant summer squash in hills three feet in diameter, in rows four feet apart. Plant five seeds in each hill and after they germinate, thin to three plants (snip off the rejects, rather than pulling them up, so as not to damage the roots of the chosen ones). Winter squash should be planted in hills and given about a six- by eight-foot area to grow in. Both varieties are heavy feeders, so work compost, manure, and/or a general purpose vegetable fertilizer into the soil a couple of weeks before planting. Both types are also sensitive to cold weather, so make sure all frost has passed and the soil is warm. The most prevalent threat to squash is the vine borer. Eggs are laid on the stem after the plant blooms. The borer emerges from the egg and chews into the plant's stem. It will do substantial damage and kill the plant. Remedies include slitting open the stem and removing the borer. Once this is done, cover the opened stem with soil. Another method is to inject *Bacillus thuringiensis* into the stem with a syringe. Still another approach is to harvest what you can, admit you have been foiled by the critter, pull up the plant, and start over. This reminds us of still another method: covering stems with kitchen foil to prevent the borers from chewing into them.

Tomatoes. Tomatoes are the centerpiece in most vegetable gardens. Everyone wants to grow them, and for good reason. They are relatively easy to grow, are a focal point in the garden, and can produce pounds of great-tasting tomatoes per plant, which can be the main ingredient of salads and are used in a multitude of dishes, hot, cold, steamed, or grilled.

Tomatoes come in an unimaginable variety of sizes shapes and colors: cherry (small) or large or in between, round or oblong, smooth or knobby, single-colored, striped, red, yellow, or even black. While the number of varieties is large, make sure to select seeds or plants that do best in Central Texas. Our short seasons require tomato plants that reach maturity and produce quickly.

When selecting, also check to ensure that the plant is listed as "VFNTM" resistant. This means that they are not susceptible to verticillium wilt, fusarium wilt, nematodes, or tobacco mosaic, all of which are deadly to the plants.

Tomatoes require lots of sun, good drainage, and a uniform supply of water. Too much or too little watering can result in blossom end rot, a dark discoloration at the tip of the tomato.

The numbers of varieties of tomatoes is exceeded only by the planting and maintenance practices of those who grow them; here is how we do it. As soon as possible (according to the Texas A&M planting guide for the county where you live), set out started plants. Ideally these should have been growing in pots in a sunny window so that they are somewhat root bound (the roots are beginning to grow around the inner walls of the pots they are in) and are getting "leggy" (the stems are elongated).

Plant tomatoes in holes dug out and backfilled with compost. Set in plants as deeply as possible. This means removing lower leaves, leaving a tomato plant with at least three branches coming out at or near the top of the stem. Tomatoes are unique in that the portion of the stem buried in the ground will generate roots, so you can set tomato plants deeper in your garden soil than they were in their nursery pots. This results in a larger root structure, which helps the plant during the searing heat of early summer.

After planting, shape the soil into a basin so that water collects around the plant. Place a wire cage over the plant (see Grow Up! earlier in this chapter). Secure the cage to the ground by tying it to wooden stakes or pieces of rebar (concrete reinforcing rods) sunk into the soil. Next, wrap the cage in clear plastic (get rolls of it at your local hardware store). Secure the plastic by encircling the cage with twine or by rolling the two ends of the plastic together and stapling them.

You have now created an individual tomato greenhouse. This structure will do three things. First, it will allow temperatures inside the cage to heat up during the day but to dissipate gradually during the night. The added heat will encourage the plant to grow. Second, you will protect the plant from airborne mites that carry the leaf curl virus (a deadly one). Third, you will protect young plants from buffeting by early spring winds.

When daytime temperatures begin to stay in the eighties, remove the plastic. You will have plants that are substantially larger and further along than those planted later or planted without the benefit of the plastic wrap. After removing the plastic, prune away the plant to three leaders (main branches) and trim off any other small side shoots. Make sure the three leaders are about three inches above the soil line. This will provide adequate air circulation around the plant and give you space for adding mulch later.

And remember to secure the cages to the ground. You are not only making a small greenhouse; you are also making a potentially excellent kite. If you don't secure them (and this is the voice of experience speaking), some windy night you will hear tomato cages bumping the house as they sail skyward.

Planting and Tending: Plant tomatoes about three feet apart in rows similarly spaced. They can be allowed to trail on the ground or trained to stakes, but we prefer to grow them in cages. When plants begin to set fruit, fertilize them every ten days to two weeks. Try the "Texas pot" method: place a one-gallon plastic nursery pot with holes in the bottom between each pair of plants. Fill it with fertilizer and then add water several times until the soil is soaked. Maintain soil moisture throughout the growing season. Add a couple of inches of mulch when you fertilize and add a little more mulch each time you fertilize thereafter.

Vegetable Varieties for Central Texas

Asparagus: Jersey Giant, UC 157, Jersey Gem.

Beans: bush—Contender, Blue Lake, Tendercrop, Topcrop, Greencrop; **pinto**—Luna, Pinto 111; **pole**—Stringless Blue Lake, Kentucky Wonder, Dade; **lima bush**—Jackson Wonder, Henderson Bush, Florida Butter.

Beets: Detroit Dark Red, Pacemaker, Asgrow Wonder.

Broccoli: Waltham 29, Topper 43, Green Comet, Premium Crop, Emperor, Baccus Hybrid, Packman.

Brussels sprouts: Jade Cross, Catskill, Valiant.

Cabbage: Globe, Drumhead (savoy), Early Jersey Wakefield, Early Round Dutch, Golden Acre, Red Rock (red); **hybrids**—Rio Verde, Market Prize, Gourmet, Ruby Ball, Bravo, Red Rookie.

Cantaloupe: Perlita, Smith's Perfect, Uvalde, Ambrosia, Magnum 45, Mission, Caravelle.

Carrot: Danvers 126, Imperator, Nantes, Red Core, Texas Gold Spike, Orlando Gold.

Cauliflower: Snowball, Snow Crown, Snow King.

Corn: Calumet, Merit, Golden Security, Bonanza, Silver Queen (white), Country Gentlemen (white), Kandu Korn, Sweet G-90, Summer Sweet.

Cucumbers: pickling—Piccadilly, National Pickling, Salty, Liberty, Sweet Success, Multipik, Calypso, Carolina; **slicers**—Palomar, Ashley, Poinsett, Straight 8, Victory Hybrid, Sweet Success, County Fair, Sweet Slice, Spacemaster, Patio Pick, Dasher II.

Lettuce: head—Great Lakes Strains, Valverde, Buttercrunch; **leaf**—Salad Bowl, Oakleaf, Ruby, Butter Crunch, Mission, Red Sails, Prizehead, Black-seeded Simpson; **butterhead**—Summer Bibb, Tendercrisp; **romaine**—Valmaine.

Onion: 1015Y, Eclipse, Granex (yellow and white), Grano 502.

Peas: edible pod—Sugar Snap, Sugar Bon, Sugar Ann; **southern**—Blackeye No. 5, Burgundy (purple hull), Champion (cream), Cream 40, Mississippi Silver.

Peppers: sweet—Yolo Wonder, Keystone Giant, Emerald Giant, Big Bertha, Shamrock, Bell Tower, Rio Grand Gold; **hot**—Hungarian Wax, Jalapeño, Long Red or Thin Cayenne, Texas Serrano, TAMU Mild Jalapeño.

Potato: Kennebec (white), Red Lasoda (red).

Radish: Black Spanish, Cherry Belle, Early Scarlet Globe (short top), White Chinese, White Icicle (winter), Red Prince, Champion, Sparkler.

Spinach: Dixie Savoy, Early Hybrid 7, Melody.

Sweet potato: Centennial, Porto Rico, Jewel.

Squash: acorn (winter), butternut (winter), Dixie Hybrid Crookneck, Early Prolific Straightneck, White Bush Scallop, Zucco, Multipik, Hyrific, Goldie, President.

Tomato: standard—Celebrity, Bonus, Better Boy, Terrific, Jackpot, Spring Giant, Homestead, Early Girl, Whirlaway, Merced, Heatwave, Surefire; **cherry type**—Small Fry, Red Cherry, Sweet 100.

A Central Texas spring garden: four nerve daisy, blue-eyed grass, penstemon, agave, and evergreen sumac mulched in a bed of decomposed granite

Xeriscape shrubs: cenizo, dwarf yaupon, and crimson pigmy barberry

Shade garden: bridal wreath spirea, asiatic jasmine, river fern, hydrangea, and Texas mountain laurel

Shade shrub: leatherleaf mahonia

Pond: Louisiana iris

Small-space garden: impatiens, rose, dusty miller, and ageratum

Creating a view: clematis and rose on an arbor

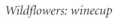
Wildflowers: winecup

Raised-bed vegetable garden: onions, lettuce, and radishes in a raised bed with drip irrigation

Garden retreat: bridal wreath spirea, Louisiana phlox, ranunculus, gaillardia, zinnia linearis, eleagnus, and virburnum

Sunny border: verbena, iris, rosemary, Japanese black pine, and ligustrum

Any place can be a garden. Here, petunia, marigold, ageratum, and begonia hang in half-baskets on a fence.

*Novel combinations:
prickly pear, larkspur,
and salvia*

Classic mixed border: petunia, ageratum, Gerbera daisy, rose, marigold, dusty miller, and alyssum

Textures in green: agarito, dwarf yaupon, and fountain grass in a well-mulched bed next to a decomposed granite walk

Classic spring border: alyssum, ranunculus, dianthus, salvia indigo spires, tulip, and artemisia

Sweet smelling, diverse in texture, adaptable, and often delicately blooming, herbs should not be overlooked as an addition to the vegetable garden. These fast-growing plants are very successful where their undemanding requirements of well-drained soil, good drainage, and lots of sun are met.

Basil. There is a plethora of basil types, shapes, and flavors, including sweet, holy, lemon, purple, and opal. Like most herbs, basil does best when pruned regularly to prevent the plant from flowering.

Planting and Tending: Plant basil in full sun about a foot apart. Fertilize very modestly throughout the growing season. Basil can manage well on a minimum amount of water.

Chives. Every garden should have chives, otherwise why would you want to bake potatoes? Chives grow from bulblets and are in the allium family, as are onions. There is also a garlic variety, which smells like it sounds.

Planting and Tending: Plant in any acceptable soil in clumps a couple of inches apart. Divide clumps to propagate. They take full sun but will tolerate partial shade. Chives will actually deter many harmful insects, so they can be interspersed in the garden to maximize this attribute.

Dill. This is a hardy annual with sparse feathery leaves. If you see caterpillars striped in black, white, and yellow chomping away voraciously on your dill, try not to destroy them. The dill will survive, and the caterpillars will turn into Monarch butterflies.

Planting and Tending: Plant in full sun a foot or so apart. Dill grows best in well-drained soil. When it matures and the seeds turn brown, harvest, otherwise dill will seed randomly in your garden (which may or may not be what you intended).

Fennel. Fennel is a tall, bright green herb similar in appearance to dill. It is somewhat taller than dill and can reach five feet.

Planting and Tending: Plant seed in full sun a few feet apart. Fennel takes average soil with good drainage. It needs moderate water.

Mint. There are several varieties and flavors of mint: peppermint and spearmint are the most commonly recognized. But also available are pineapple, apple, and orange mint. Mints take full sun and prefer frequent watering.

Planting and Tending: Mint is very aggressive! We recommend that you purchase started plants and then grow them in containers. If let loose in the garden, mint will take over. Regularly harvest cuttings from the plants whether you use them or not, to encourage new, more tender growth.

ROSEMARY (Rosmarinus officinalis)

Oregano. Popularly associated with Mediterranean dishes, oregano is easily started from seed after the soil has warmed.

Planting and Tending: Plant in full sun in average, well-drained garden soil. The mature plant can sprawl out over six feet, so one should suffice. Harvest as needed for cooking.

Parsley. Curled is the most popular parsley variety. It can be planted and harvested year-round. Parsley is a true biennial. It will flower and die in its second year, so plan ahead and have at least one replacement plant started each year.

Planting and Tending: Parsley can be planted from seed, but it's easier to pick up plants from your local nursery. Plant in well-drained soil. Plants can go in about one foot apart. They prefer some shade and do well planted close to larger plants.

Rosemary. Dark green, needlelike foliage, a pungent fragrance, and an attractive growth habit make this herb, which grows in the shrub form, extremely desirable in a rock garden or as a patio border. While it is possible to start rosemary from seed, it is best to select specimens started at a nursery. Rosemary withstands heavy trimming, and its branches can also be rooted by pegging them to the soil with bent wire pins. Although semihardy, it can suffer frost damage.

Planting and Tending: Plant in dry, well-drained soil, and water minimally. While rosemary does best in full sun, it can take some shade.

Thyme. Delicate, woody stems covered by minute, fragrant leaves form a rapidly spreading lacework mat over the ground. Tiny lavender flowers appear in spring. Thyme seeds germinate quickly. New plants may also be started by stem cuttings.

Planting and Tending: Plant a foot apart in any well-drained soil. It does best in full sun and takes a minimal amount of water.

FRUIT

Backyard gardens are generally not the place for extensive fruit gardening. Most gardens are small, and most fruits take a lot of room. We've listed several, however, that gardeners may want to try. This is the eternal tradeoff in gardening: blackberries or tomatoes? Ultimately it is the gardener's preference—or perhaps what the kids will eat—that determines what is planted.

Blackberries. Although blackberries require a fair amount of space, they adapt to a wide variety of soil and climatic conditions and are low maintenance plants. Blackberries are biennial, which means that they put on vegetative growth the first year and produce fruit the following year. Plant two to three feet apart and in rows at least ten feet apart. Prune out only producing canes after the harvest. New canes should be pinched back during the summer to encourage branching. Be sure to fertilize with a complete fertilizer and water well immediately after pruning. No particularly vicious pests attack blackberries. New varieties have an upright disposition and need no trellising.

Recommended varieties: Brazos, Comanche, Arapaho, Arkansas, Humble, Navaho, Shawnee, Rosborough.

Grapes. New developments in grape culture have increased this fruit's potential in Texas. Although well adapted to many climates, successful grapes will depend on the gardener's selection of varieties suitable to our region. The varieties recommended for Central Texas are resistant to cotton root rot, a deadly disease prevalent in alkaline soils such as ours.

While grapes like heat and sandy loam, they will not tolerate sitting in wet soil. We caution against overfertilizing, which will result in lush foliage at the expense of fruit production. Because grapes grow only on new growth, substantial pruning is essential before the new growing season begins.

Recommended varieties: Champanel, Barbera, Beacon, Ellen Scott, Favorite, Fredonia, Herbemont, Petit Sirah.

Strawberries. Strawberries can be grown as perennials, although they will only last a few years, not several decades. Because of our devastating summers, however, they are best grown as annuals. Plant spring-bearing strawberries in the fall for late spring harvest. They should be planted eighteen inches apart in soil well prepared with compost and additional fertilizer. Strawberry plants must not be allowed to dry out; therefore a polyethylene or straw mulch is absolutely necessary.

Recommended varieties: Allstar, Gem, Cardinal, Ozark Beauty, Gem, Ogallala, Sunrise.

❦ 13 ❦

Trouble in the Garden

Come forth into the light of things
Let Nature be your teacher.
WILLIAM WORDSWORTH, "THE TABLES TURNED"

Environmental awareness and a broader appreciation of gardening have dramatically altered how we deal with the less-welcomed aspects of gardening—pests and disease. No longer is our first impulse to grab for the chemical insect spray upon seeing an aphid. We are more conscious of and knowledgeable about the chemicals designed to rid our gardens of problems, and many of us have expanded our definition of gardening to include wildlife such as butterflies and birds. Frogs, toads, lizards, and beneficial insects (e.g., praying mantis and ladybugs) are invited to participate and enrich the garden environment. Our gardens, then, become more than just locations where plants grow. We appreciate them as settings in nature, full of the richness and variety of life.

These attitudes compel us to reconsider the effects of chemicals on everything that lives in our garden. You can't spray for caterpillars if you want butterflies. If you attack the voracious pest, you will destroy the desired beauty. Reflecting this outlook, a commonsense approach known as Integrated Pest Management (IPM) has gained recognition and acceptance. Safe and effective, it's an excellent method for our home gardens.

PREVENTION

With emphasis on prevention, IPM reinforces the first key to successful gardening: appropriate plant selection. You're a step ahead when you choose plants, natives or well-adapted non-natives, that thrive in our soils, heat, and humidity. Healthy, flourishing plants are more resistant to disease and able to withstand a few chewed leaves without significant damage. Conversely, plants that are forced to accommodate are often stressed and vulnerable to an array of troubles. Many new cultivars of old favorites (the crape myrtle is an example) are now available in disease-resistant varieties. Your nursery staff can provide guidance. After selecting the species, the next step is to purchase the hardiest members of the group. Even the best gardener needs to have good stock to be successful.

Variety also serves to prevent trouble, whether you're selecting vegetables, fruits, shrubs, trees, or flowers. This is why crop rotation is as important to the home gardener as the commercial grower. A good rule to follow is to avoid growing crops with common diseases in the same location season after season. This applies only to vegetables and flowering annuals.

Also consider companion planting, choosing plants for their compatibility and the mutual benefits they offer each other. This includes using plants with different root depths near one another so that they don't compete for nutrients and staggering the heights of plants so that they can all get sunshine. Another aspect of companion planting is the selection of plants with features other plants need. For instance, you can use marigolds in a vegetable garden to repel the nematodes in nearby plants, or you can make sure you have annuals that attract bees, which are needed for cross-pollination.

PROPER PLANTING AND MAINTENANCE

Remember to plant that five-dollar plant in a ten-dollar hole and keep plants healthy through appropriate and consistent watering and fertilizing. Many opportunistic diseases get started when plants are weakened by drought, heat stress, and nutrient depletion. Overcrowded conditions are inviting to many fungal and bacterial diseases. Provide good air circulation by giving your plants plenty of space. Always follow the manufacturer's label to ensure correct fertilizer application and to avoid fertilizer burn. Don't forget to weed, prune dead and damaged branches that harbor insects, and mulch to discourage weeds and retain moisture.

SANITATION

Cleaning up the garden is seldom done with the plants' well-being in mind, but it can prevent much trouble down the road. Get rid of old wood and other debris that collects so easily, providing great habitat for insects. Make sure watering cans, pots, any items that can collect water in the yard don't become containers for stagnant water, a magnet for breeding mosquitoes. And because compost can fail to heat up sufficiently to kill off disease organisms or seeds of weeds, it is best to discard diseased plants and weeds bearing seed in the garbage rather than in the compost. In any case, it is always a good practice to turn the compost pile regularly to keep the processes going and to generate heat.

OBSERVATION

Be sharp-eyed as you enjoy your garden. Leaves that are chewed, punctured, spotted, wilted, and distorted indicate the presence of insects or disease. In addition to chewing and sucking damage, insects are frequent carriers of disease. Be especially vigilant in rainy periods during moderate temperature. These are great conditions for diseases to take hold.

We always carry small pruning scissors during a garden tour to clip off diseased or invaded portions of plants to nip problems before they even get to bud. Be sure to tour your garden frequently. Opportunistic bugs and diseases can wreak havoc on a plant in the blink of an eye.

EARLY INTERVENTION

First, use what we call manual control methods. This means hand-picking weeds early in the season before they become rampant, larger, and well established; removing critters such as snails and slugs; and plucking out diseased flowers or vegetable plants before others are affected. A sharp jet of water in the direction of an aphid-infested vine can be sufficient if the population has not gotten out of control. Insecticidal soap (available at garden centers) can be used to control insects on shrubs, flowers, or vegetables. Insecticidal soaps work by smothering insects. Before using it, test on a small area. Some plants will not tolerate it. The soapy solution should be rinsed off as soon as the insects are gone.

There are times when the problems are too widespread or severe to eliminate with cultural and manual methods, and chemical controls are needed. You may want to first try products that are less persistent before using the heavy-duty pesticides. Diatomaceous earth is a nontoxic, fine powder made from diatoms. It is very effective on many ground crawlers (e.g., pillbugs, slugs), piercing their shells or soft bodies with its fine particles, resulting in their desiccation.

Sulfur is effective on powdery mildew and spider mites, but will stain buildings and walls and should not be used in temperatures over eighty-five degrees. It will burn the leaves and damage the plant.

Rotenone and pyrethrum are nonpersistent insecticides made from toxic plant products. They are useful against whitefly, aphids, and small caterpillars. They deteriorate more quickly in storage than other chemicals and should be used within a year. Both are toxic to fish.

If you are gardening to attract butterflies or have a pond with fish or other aquatic life, take great care not to use chemicals such as *Bacillus thuringiensis* (a microbial insecticide) that are toxic to insects in the larval stage. Fish are particularly vulnerable to many chemicals, so check the pesticide label carefully for this information before using a product.

While we are not qualified to enter the scientific debate over pesticides, we can provide general information about frequently used pesticides for common problems to help you make your decision on which chemical to use, if any. All chemicals—fertilizers or pesticides—should be used according to label instructions *only*. A quick way to determine a pesticide's toxicity is to look for the words "caution," "warning," or "danger" on the label. "Caution" denotes the lowest level; "warning" means moderate toxicity; and "danger" signals the highest toxicity. (See Extoxnet website, chapter 3, "Tools of the Trade" for more information.)

Pesticides come in many forms: dusts, sprays, granules, and baits. Dusts, granules, and baits can be applied directly to the problem; sprays are sold as wettable powders, flowable formulations, oil, or emulsifiable concentrates and need to be mixed with water before use. Sometimes pesticides occur in multipurpose combinations (e.g., fungicide, insecticide, and miticide in one). Most common insecticides are broad-spectrum, effective against many different kinds of pests; a few are selectively aimed at specific insects or insect families. Some insecticides kill on contact; others, referred to as systemics, are absorbed by roots, stems, or leaves and carried by sap throughout the plant to kill pests that feed on the treated plants. Systemic insecticides tend to be longer lasting than those that kill on contact. These are especially effective for sucking insects. *Never* use systemic pesticides on plants that you intend to eat.

When mixing pesticides, use measuring utensils dedicated only to that use. Don't grab the measuring spoons from the kitchen. Mix up only the needed amount. Always clean the utensils after use. This is especially important if you use the same utensil for insecticides, fungicides, and herbicides, since some chemicals are not compatible.

Store pesticides in their original containers in a dry, well-ventilated space away from children and food. Never remove the labels, and keep the containers securely closed. Liquid pesticides must not be allowed to freeze. Since many pesticides lose their potency over time, sometimes in as little as six months, it is best for the home gardener to buy small quantities.

Before applying, remove from the area that is to be sprayed toys, pet dishes, and other items that the family or pets will touch. Choose a calm morning, without rain in the forecast, to apply pesticides. Should the breeze pick up, be sure to be upwind to avoid inhaling the pesticide. Because some pesticides can irritate skin and/or eyes, it's a good idea to wear long-sleeved and legged clothing and goggles. It is best to apply pesticide when the temperature is lower than eighty-five degrees. It is extremely important that you get complete coverage of the plants you are treating. Be sure to apply to both tops and undersides of leaves.

Pests and diseases are not the only problems you will face in the garden. Pets and visiting wildlife can also take their toll. Armadillos looking for grubs and worms can tear up a lawn and uproot a flower or vegetable garden overnight. Deer may be choosy about what they eat in good times when their selection is broad, but when conditions are bad nothing is safe. The list of sworn by and/or discredited repellents is long; the list for deer-proof plants is short. Repellents are said to include blood meal, human hair, and coyote urine spray. They work best when plant life is flourishing and abundant. When not, no repellent will work. Texas sage or cenizo, Mexican oregano, pampas grass, crimson barberry, red yucca, cast-iron plant and the salvia species known as 'Indigo Spires' are reputed to be deer-proof. Strong-smelling plants (e.g., rosemary, lantana, and juniper) are considered to be more deer-resistant than others. But gardeners are better off using fences or polyurethane mesh that is made for that specific purpose and is nearly invisible when installed in the landscape.

Damage due to construction is a common threat to trees. Efforts to protect trees above ground can be defeated if there has been a significant change in the ground level. Unfortunately, the effects may not be obvious for several months or even years. When fill is placed over the root system of a tree, it may become difficult for sufficient water to reach the roots. There is also a reduction in the oxygen supply to roots, which may cause the accumulation of gases and chemicals detrimental to good growth. When this happens, feeder roots don't develop, roots die, and the tree above the ground begins to deteriorate. To remedy the situation, it is necessary to provide aeration through the construction of a tree well.

Furthermore, if the grade is lowered near tree roots, there can be drought damage resulting from the loss of roots. In reality, infill problems, as well as the other troubles mentioned, may not always be preventable. Nonetheless, being aware of them can allow you at least to minimize the damage.

Premature tree leaf loss often occurs in late summer if the season has been very hot and dry. Frequently owners mistake this for a disease symptom, when actually the tree is only shedding luxuriant greenery it can no longer support. No permanent damage is caused, and the tree will leaf out normally the following spring.

COMMON DISEASES

Diseases can be difficult for the home gardener to diagnose and treat because many symptoms appear similar. A well-trained eye is often necessary to distinguish a bacterial problem from a fungal problem, for instance. Many disease troubles can be avoided with appropriate plant selection and good cultural practices. Because many diseases thrive in humid conditions, it's important to provide space for good air circulation. These problems are best treated by pruning out and properly discarding the excess from affected areas or, in the case of flowers or vegetables, by simply removing the diseased plant. The following list gives some of the more common disease problems encountered in the garden.

Anthracnose. These fungi cause leaf edges of diseased plants to have V-shaped spots, while spots in the centers may be angular or circular. Twigs may die back, and cankers may occur on limbs. Applications of a foliar fungicide can be an effective control.

Botrytis Blight. Present in most soils and thriving in moist, cool conditions, the fungi causing this disease infect many flowers, shrubs, trees, and vegetables, causing spotting and decay on leaves, flowers, and fruit of affected plants. Cut out affected plant parts in trees and shrubs; remove entire flower and vegetable plants.

Cankers. Caused by fungi, these black or brown irregular dead areas may encircle stems, branches, or trunks. This causes dieback, where the whole top of the tree may appear brown and dead. The condition is common in Lombardy poplars, cottonwoods, willows, and mulberries, as well as in gardenias and roses. A tree care professional should be called when this condition is suspected.

Cotton Root Rot. This rot is a soil-borne disease that suddenly kills seemingly healthy plants. It is most likely to occur from June to frost, and plants suffering from heat and drought are most vulnerable. Because of the deteriorating root systems, leaves on trees (and other plants) turn yellow. But yellow leaves can also be a symptom of other problems, such as improper watering. Plants with cotton root rot are easily removed from the soil, revealing roots covered with a yellow or brown growth. Unfortunately, no current fungicide has proven effective in controlling the disease. The best prevention is to buy plants that are moderately to highly resistant to the disease. These include bald cypress, boxwood, cedar elm, crape myrtle, holly, honeysuckle, juniper, live oak, pecan, pyracantha, redbud, red cedar, red oak, and sycamore. Trees and plants that are most susceptible are apple, chinaberry, Chinese tallow, cottonwood, elm (not cedar elm), fruitless mulberry, ligustrum, loquat, roses, silver maple, and willow.

Chlorosis. This condition is most commonly caused by an iron deficiency in the soil or by the alkaline nature of the soil, which prevents plants from using what iron is available. This is the demon of many beloved acid-loving plants, such as azaleas and camellias. The leaves turn yellow but the veins remain green. Chlorosis can be prevented by incorporating plenty of peat moss when planting acid-loving plants, and it can be corrected with applications of iron chelate. Chlorosis can also occur in lawns. Many lawn fertilizers formulated for Central Texas contain iron to prevent this condition.

Damping Off. This root disease affects seedlings or young plants and may cause them to die. The roots and the stems at the soil surface show symptoms of rotting. For prevention, the best control, use a sterilized potting mix.

Fire Blight. Symptoms of fire blight are easily identified: branch tips die back, giving the affected limbs a scorched, burned appearance. The chemical Kocide is effective as a preventive if applied when the tree is in full bloom. Once the symptoms appear, pruning out affected branches can help prevent the spread of the disease. There is, however, no guaranteed cure. Tools must be cleaned with a chlorine solution between cuts to avoid spreading the disease. Apples, pears, and the rose family are very susceptible to these bacteria, as are cotoneaster, Indian hawthorn, loquat, pyracantha, photinia, and quince.

Leaf Spot (bacterial and fungal). Many leaf-spotting fungi and bacteria cause only cosmetic damage and are no cause for alarm or treatment. You will notice that leaf spots are most severe in mild, wet weather. One fungal leaf spot disease, *Entomosporium maculatum,* is a serious disease of redtip photinia. The long-term prognosis for affected plants, even with fungicide applications, is not good. Practice good hygiene to prevent spreading the disease to other plants.

Collect and discard all fallen leaves. Be careful when watering lawns or beds in the vicinity of photinia to avoid prolonged periods when leaves are wet. It may be best to remove the plant and replace it with another species.

Powdery Mildew. One of the most common fungal diseases, powdery mildew appears as white or gray mold on the leaves, eventually turning them yellow. Unlike many other fungi, powdery mildew affects dry as well as wet leaves. Crape myrtles (especially the older varieties) and euonymous commonly fall victim. A foliar fungicide can be used to control this.

Oak Wilt. This fungal disease is a major problem for live oaks, Shumard oaks, Spanish oaks, and blackjack oaks in some Central Texas neighborhoods. Species of red oaks are especially hard hit, often dying within weeks. The symptoms vary according to species. In live oaks, the leaf veins remain green as the area between veins turns light green to yellow. On red oaks and the blackjack oak, leaves turn reddish brown and wilting proceeds inward from the tips; leaves remain on the tree for a brief time after tree death. The disease is transmitted through root spread and sap-feeding beetles that carry the fungal spores. Because firewood from infected trees can spread the disease, cover any questionable firewood pile with clear plastic, tucking the edges of the plastic cover into the ground to prevent insect infestation. Avoid pruning oaks between mid-January and mid-June, when the fungus-spreading beetle is most active. We recommended that pruning cuts and wounds on oaks in the vicinity of an oak wilt outbreak be painted with a wound paint. Trenching to separate root systems should be dealt with on a neighborhood level. Many neighborhood associations and municipal governments are prepared to assist you should there be an oak wilt outbreak in your area. Your county extension agent is an excellent source of information.

Root and Stem Rot. The foliage of affected plants will turn yellow and appear stunted. Brown or black spots of different shapes and sizes occur on the stem at or near the soil surface and on roots. The tips of small roots decay, and eventually there is complete rotting of the roots. Treat them with Terraclor.

INSECTS

Aphids. Many species of aphids in an array of colors attack our flowers, vegetables, and landscape plants. They injure by sucking plant juices. Often they can be controlled with repeated hose spray or a number of insecticides. It is our choice not to use pesticides on food crops, but if you choose to use these products, apply them according to manufacturers' directions.

Caterpillars. Remember that many caterpillars grow into butterflies, so you may want to identify the culprit or consider tolerating minor damage before taking steps to control them. We actually plant lots of parsley and dill to encourage the black swallowtail.

Tent caterpillars or webworms can engulf entire limbs in massive webs. Pruning out affected areas before caterpillars hatch is often most effective. A biological control called *Bacillus thuringiensis* can be used. It kills many kinds of caterpillars but is harmless to other living things. It is necessary to penetrate the web with a pole pruner or other sharp object before applying the chemical. Although tent caterpillars infest a variety of hosts, the pecan and mulberry are particularly susceptible.

Fire ants. Imported from South America, these pests with their stinging venomous bite are at the top of the Most Unwanted list. Decades of broad-

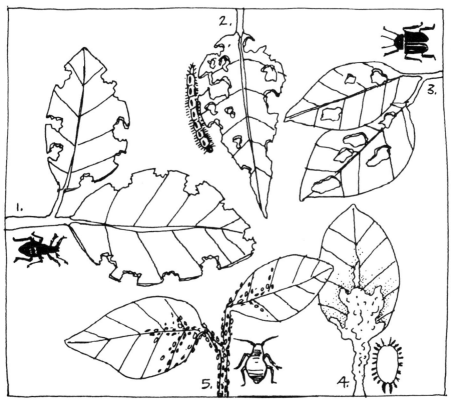

INSECTS: 1. WEEVILS 2. CaTERPILLaRS 3. BEETLES 4. SPIDER MITES 5. APHIDS

spectrum pesticide use to control them have yielded little success. Less harmful to the environment, baits such as Amdro, Ascend, Award, and Logic, which either kill the queen or act as a birth control, are currently recommended. Everyone hopes current university research on fire ant control by predator insects will yield a safer, effective solution.

Mealybugs. White, cottony webs appear on leaves and stems when mealybugs are present. The plants are weakened and will die if they are not treated. These pests attack many ornamentals, including azaleas and coleus. Remove mealybugs by swabbing the leaves with a cotton ball dipped in alcohol. If this doesn't work, consider treating with Malathion.

Nematodes. Leaf and root nematodes are microscopic worms. There are many, many species, and not all are troublesome. Some that grow in hot, dry soil, called root-knot nematodes, are bad. Most ornamentals are susceptible, especially boxwood, fig, gardenia, and passionflower, as are chrysanthemums and other annuals. In the vegetable garden, tomatoes and okra are major victims. Affected plants lose color, appear stunted, and may gradually die. Diseased plants have swollen and irregular roots or brown or black spots or streaks on the roots. Because many nematicides also kill all other insects, earthworms, and plants, be sure to read the manufacturer's instructions before applying the chemical. An alternative in the vegetable garden would be to plant a crop of Elbon rye in winter. Trapped in the roots of the rye, the nematodes will die. In the spring, turn the rye into the soil as a "green manure."

Red Spider Mites. Fine webs on plants tell you that spider mites are at work. You can just barely see these small invaders on the undersides of leaves of practically any kind of plant, especially junipers, marigolds, and roses, mostly during the hotter, drier months. They can be controlled with Kelthane, but in the vegetable garden we use insecticidal soap.

Scale. Masses of green, brown, or purple dots, usually found on the underside of leaves but sometimes on stems and fruits, indicate the presence of scale. These insects have protective shells; they suck the juices of a plant and destroy it. Common susceptible host plants are camellia and hibiscus (both of which have scale that is white), gardenia, jasmine, and schefflera. To control scale, spray with a garden-type oil emulsion in the spring or fall, when the temperature is between forty-five and eighty-five degrees for at least a week.

Sowbugs, also called Pillbugs. These dark gray, fat, hard-shelled bugs are rampant invaders of vegetable gardens and flower beds. When disturbed, they roll up into a ball. Preferring dark, moist places, they can be discouraged by the removal of garden debris. They love grapefruit rinds, so set out an overturned rind in the evening, collect your pillbug harvest in the morning, and discard. Diatomaceous earth or Sevin dust will also work.

Snails and Slugs. These being easy to see, we always try to hand pick them or give beer traps (shallow pans or jar tops filled with stale beer and sunk into the soil at ground level) a try before going to chemical controls.

Thrips. These tiny, winged, sucking insects cause streaked foliage, only partial opening of flowers, or brown edges on petals. A problem on roses, they are difficult to control and are best prevented by spraying with Malathion.

Whitefly. It's the wingless larvae that are the culprits here. They weaken plants by sucking the juices of many of our annuals and flowering plants. A good shot with the hose should get rid of them. Control of adults may require a pesticide.

As anyone who gardens knows, even the best attempts to keep plants healthy can fail. Determining what is wrong and curing the problem are not simple matters. Even nursery staff and plant experts sometimes disagree, and you may not be able to get a prescription in time to save the patient. Gardeners, always good at seeing the bright side of things, try to view the loss of a plant as an opportunity to plant something new.

❧ 14 ❦

Gardening Calendar for Central Texas

Shed no tear—O shed no tear
The flowers will bloom another year.
JOHN KEATS, "FAERY SONGS, I"

How fortunate that our climate makes it possible to be a year-round gardener. As with any undertaking, preparation and planning increase the dividends. This calendar is designed to serve as a guide in organizing monthly tasks and projects.

JANUARY

1. Plan your garden by gathering ideas and preparing a sketch of what goes where. Check out garden design books from the local library or purchase from local bookstores. Subscribe to at least one good garden magazine.

2. Plant bare-root roses and fruit trees. Container-grown roses may be planted whenever available, but if possible avoid hottest summer months. Transplant established trees and shrubs while they are dormant.

3. Remove fall garden debris and keep the lawn free of dead leaves. Pick up camellia blossoms from the ground to help prevent camellia petal blight.

4. Prepare gardens for spring and summer annuals and vegetables. In the vegetable garden turn in annual (Elbon) rye planted in the fall. Work the soil, adding sand, peat moss or compost to all beds. Fertilize fruit trees. Avoid working wet soil.

5. Purchase cabbage, broccoli, and cauliflower plants and plant late this month and into late February.

6. If necessary, spray dormant oil to control scale on shrubs and fruit and landscape trees on days when the temperatures will be above forty degrees Fahrenheit for twelve hours.

7. Begin seeding pepper and tomato plants. Put new plants under grow lights or in a sunny window. Sow annual and perennial flower seeds in pots and place them under the lights with the tomatoes and peppers.

8. Be sure to water trees, shrubs and lawns during dry periods. They may be dormant, but they still need water.

9. Begin to look for bagworms on junipers and other narrow-leafed evergreens. Remove the bags by hand and destroy.

10. In late January begin planting asparagus crowns, onion sets, and seeds for lettuce, peas, kale, radishes, and carrots.

FEBRUARY

1. Continue planting deciduous and evergreen trees and shrubs. Plant bareroot roses until the middle of the month.

2. Aphids begin to appear on ornamentals (daylilies are particularly susceptible) and should be controlled with a strong spray of water or insecticide.

3. Plant potatoes, beets, and parsley.

4. Begin a spraying program for fruit trees; check with your county extension horticulturalist.

5. Prune fruit and nut trees, landscape trees, evergreens, and summer-flowering shrubs.

6. Begin planting gladiolus corms six inches deep in well-drained soil in a sunny location.

7. Check ash and sycamore trees for tent caterpillars and anthracnose and treat if necessary.

8. Begin to harden tomatoes and peppers in cold frames or by putting out in the sun during the day and bringing them in on cold nights (below forty degrees).

9. Pear varieties such as Orient, Kieffer, and Maxine planted now will produce delicious fruit later. For a bountiful crop, follow spray schedule recommended by the county extension agent.

10. St. Valentine's Day is the "official" day to prune rose bushes, but not the climbing variety.

11. Fertilize cool-season flowers such as pansies, stocks, and cyclamens.

MARCH

1. Complete all dormant pruning of evergreens and summer-flowering shrubs by early March.

2. Don't plant fruit and nut trees or any bare-root plants after the first part of March. Balled-and-burlapped and container-grown plants may be planted throughout the summer season.

3. Fertilize all landscape plants and trees; they need nourishment after the winter.

4. Garden center activity begins to pick up with new arrivals of annuals. For early spring color, set out annuals such as ageratum, dianthus, coreopsis, cleomes, marigolds, petunia, phlox, portulaca, salvias, and zinnias after the last frost.

5. After midmonth plant cucumbers, squash, watermelons, tomatoes, sweet corn, and peppers.

6. Resod or replant turfgrasses, including bermuda, zoysia, St. Augustine, and buffalo.

7. It's a good time to turn the compost pile and add organic matter from your yard cleanup.

8. Start some hanging baskets to add to those you've kept inside during the winter. Some popular candidates are begonias, geraniums, and petunias.

9. Fertilize roses with a complete fertilizer as new growth begins. Start an appropriate spraying regimen to prevent black spot on roses.

10. Divide summer- and fall-blooming perennials, such as obedient plant, chrysanthemums, fall asters, and Mexican marigold mint.

11. Check tender new growth on susceptible plants such as daylilies for aphids. Control with insecticidal soap or Sevin.

12. Live oaks begin their annual shedding to be followed immediately by flowering and pollen release, increasing spring cleanup chores.

13. Late in the month aerate and fertilize lawns; use fertilizer with a ratio of 3-1-2 or 4-1-2.

14. Caterpillars will begin to emerge and gorge on plants; control with *Bacillus thuringiensis,* but make sure you are not controlling for caterpillars that will become butterflies you'd like to have.

15. Don't prune oak trees from now until July.

APRIL

1. Continue setting out bedding plants as more and more varieties become available at the garden centers. Bed ageratum, copper plants, cosmos, portulaca, daisies, daylilies, and shade-loving impatiens.

2. Put out hot-weather potted plants such as mandevilla, bougainvillea, hibiscus, and plumeria.

3. Fertilize azaleas after they finish blooming with azalea fertilizer such as 8-12-4, and mulch.

4. Fertilize vegetables lightly around bases of plants.

5. Select caladium bulbs and keep them warm and dry until ready to plant at the end of the month. Caladiums require warm soil.

6. Plant okra and sweet potatoes. Apply mulch around tomatoes, peppers, and other producing vegetables.

7. Prune spring-flowering shrubs immediately after blooming: climbing roses, flowering quince, and Indian hawthorn.

8. Seed bermudagrass and water frequently and lightly to keep soil moist.

9. Check plants for insects and take appropriate measures to control infestations.

10. Use fungicide to control mildew on roses.

11. It is natural for some old leaves on evergreens to turn yellow and fall at this time of year, so don't worry if this happens to your magnolia, gardenia, photinia, abelia, ligustrum, and pittosporum.

12. Remove old blackberry canes and pinch back new canes to encourage branching. Water and fertilize throughout the summer.

13. Thin peaches by removing some from the tree for a good harvest of large fruit.

MAY

1. Continue planting annuals.

2. Look for chinch bugs in your St. Augustine lawn later this month and treat appropriately if necessary.

3. Plant bedding plants of coleus, cockscomb, copper plant, marigold, portulaca, and zinnia.

4. Fertilize roses with balanced fertilizer every four to six weeks and continue treating for black spot if necessary.

5. Check vegetables, especially tomatoes, for spider mites on undersides of leaves and use insecticidal soap to control insects.

6. Do not remove the foliage of spring-flowering bulbs until the foliage browns and dies back.

7. Fertilize lightly producing vegetables such as beans, cucumbers, and squash.

8. Caladiums bulbs can continue to be planted.

9. Complete pruning of climbing roses after they have bloomed.

10. Pinch back spent blossoms on spring-flowering annuals to keep them blooming.

11. Fertilize bedding plants and hanging baskets, particularly if there have been heavy spring rains.

12. Clean water garden or pond.

JUNE

1. Plant bedding plants of ageratum, celosia, coleus, marigold, portulaca, purslane, salvia, and zinnia.

2. Summer has arrived and watering lawns and gardens requires more attention. Mulch flower and vegetable beds to conserve water and lower soil temperature. Give special attention to plants like azaleas and camellias, which are easily damaged by hot, dry weather. Don't forget to water and fertilize hanging baskets.

3. Pinch back chrysanthemums to encourage branching. Remove gladiolus bulbs after leaves turn brown and store in a dry place.

4. Fertilize annuals with a balanced fertilizer to assure continued bloom and vigor.

5. Check lawns for grubworms through July. Use appropriate control if necessary.

6. Turn compost pile and moisten.

7. Continue to pinch tips of blackberry bushes to encourage branching. This year's growth will produce next year's berries. Add iron chelate or sulfate to the soil to correct yellowing foliage.

8. Pinch back annuals such as petunias if they become tall and leggy. Then fertilize and water them to encourage growth.

9. Watch for powdery mildew on crape myrtle, zinnias, photinias, and euonymus. Use appropriate control.

10. Apply mulch such as compost or wood chips to flower beds to conserve moisture, lower soil temperature, and reduce weeding.

11. Cut back reblooming salvias *(Salvia greggii* and *S. farinacea)* to within a couple inches of their spent flower spikes. Pinch back lightly fall-blooming perennials such as *S. leucantha* and Mexican marigold mint to prevent them from becoming leggy and requiring staking. Do not pinch back after September 1, or you risk removing flower buds.

12. Fertilize lawn lightly with a complete fertilizer.

13. Start fall tomatoes from seed.

14. Be on the lookout for chlorosis (yellow leaves with green veins) and treat affected plants with iron sulfate or iron chelate.

15. Webworms begin to show at this time of year. Pierce or tear the web and wait a week or so to see if predator wasps eliminate the population; if not, spray with *Bacillus thuringiensis.*

JULY

1. Now's the time to think about your fall garden and prepare an area for it. Till, compost, and fertilize.

2. Plant the same flowering plants recommended for June.

3. Make first seeding of fall squash, okra, beans, and cucumbers. Start seeds for fall transplants of broccoli, cauliflower, and cabbage.

4. If you're going on vacation for more than four or five days, arrange for someone to tend your lawn and garden. Water thoroughly every five to seven days if there is no rain. Newly sown plants need special attention.

5. Make final cutting of blackberry canes to promote secondary shoot growth.

6. Fill in low areas of the lawn and garden with small applications of compost.

7. Check azaleas and camellias for iron chlorosis. If this condition appears, use copperas or iron chelate to correct.

8. By the middle of the month make the last pinch on early-blooming mums. Those that bloom in late fall can be given one more pinch the last of the month. Be sure to keep them watered.

9. If you missed lawn fertilizing in June, do so as early in the month as possible.

10. If you didn't start tomatoes for the fall last month, try pruning existing plants back to about eighteen inches. While drastic, it is likely to result in a new fall crop.

11. Fertilize azaleas for the last time this year before August 1.

AUGUST

1. Be sure to water frequently and thoroughly during the intense heat. Don't forget young vegetable plants.

2. Early in the month plant fall potatoes and later, radishes, carrots, and lettuce. Plant fall transplants of broccoli, cabbage and cauliflower.

3. Water the compost pile to aid decomposition. With your compost pile mostly depleted after preparing beds for the fall season, prepare a new compost pile to receive fall leaves and other garden refuse.

4. Begin to plant bluebonnet and other spring wildflower seeds late in the month. Prepare soil and plant half an inch deep.

5. Prune rosebushes to reinvigorate for fall blooming. Fertilize and water well.

6. Revive flower bed appearance by replacing spent and faded annuals with new ones from the garden center. They'll bloom until frost.

SEPTEMBER

1. Although it is September, it is still hot. Make sure everything is watered and continue to apply mulch.

2. Fertilize vegetables.

3. Divide and plant spring-blooming perennials and ground covers such as daylilies, bearded irises, shasta daisies, violets, liriope, and ajuga.

4. Brown patch is apt to appear on St. Augustine lawns; treat appropriately.

5. It is time for fall lawn fertilizing, perhaps the most important fertilization of the year. Use a complete fertilizer (which should include some iron) at a ratio of 3-1-2.

6. Prepare beds for spring-blooming bulbs that will be available at garden centers soon. Add lots of organic matter and be sure to provide good drainage.

7. Winter annuals begin arriving at garden centers late this month. Plant alyssum, calendula, candytuft, hollyhock, petunia, and stock for fall and winter gardens.

OCTOBER

1. For winter color in the garden try started plants of pansies, snapdragons, dianthus, flowering cabbage, and kale.

2. Plant container-grown landscape shrubs; they will have a growth advantage when spring arrives.

3. Make additional plantings of carrots, radishes, lettuce; plant spinach, greens, and parsley.

4. Select quality tulip bulbs. Chill Dutch varieties in the vegetable tray of refrigerator four to six weeks before planting. Naturalizing varieties such as *Tulipa clusiana* and *T. saxatilis* do not require chilling.

5. Dig and store caladium tubers in dry peat moss or perlite in an area where the temperature will stay above sixty degrees.

6. Plant onion seeds for transplanting in the vegetable garden in January. You can plant fall peas. Try the sugar snap variety.

NOVEMBER

1. Plant spring-flowering bulbs such as daffodils, Dutch irises, anemones, ranunculus, and tulips.

2. Harvest large green tomatoes before the first frost. Store at room temperature until red and ripe.

3. Prepare beds for new roses to be planted in December and January.

4. Clean flower beds and rework to prepare them for spring planting. Be sure to remove debris from flower beds and gardens to control diseases and insects.

5. Plant trees and shrubs.

6. Plant Elbon (annual) rye in unused garden beds to control root-knot nematodes; rotate crops annually.

DECEMBER

1. Begin planting bare-root roses, and try some new varieties (see chapter 11, "Flowers").

2. Although our climate is not ideal for Dutch tulips, if you have chilled the bulbs in the refrigerator, now is the time to plant them.

3. Use dormant oil spray to control scale on camellias, hollies, and euonymus.

4. Begin seeding broccoli, cabbage, lettuce, and impatiens in cold frames for later transplants.

5. Fertilize pansies and spring-flowering perennials with a 5-10-5 fertilizer.

6. Start your garden planning for next year. If ordering seeds for spring annuals, do it now.

7. Order as many seed catalogs as you can stand and settle back during cold winter evenings to think of what will happen in a few short months.

Bibliography

For a more detailed description of books and other resources we found to be particularly helpful to the home gardener, see chapter 3, "Tools of the Trade."

Aggie Horticulture. http://aggie-horticulture.tamu.edu

Ajilvsgi, Geyata. *Butterfly Gardening for the South*. Dallas: Taylor Publishing Company, 1990.

Appleton, Bonnie Lee. *Landscape Rejuvenation*. Pownal, Vt.: Storey Communications, 1988.

Austin Pond Society. http://www.ccsi.com/~sgray/austin.pond.society/apshome.html

Bender, Steve, and Felder Rushing. *Passalong Plants*. Chapel Hill: University of North Carolina Press, 1993.

Better Homes and Gardens. *Step by Step Landscaping*. Des Moines: Meredith Corp., 1991.

Brookes, John. *The Garden Book*. New York: Crown Publishers, 1984.

Catton, Chris, and James Gray. *The Incredible Heap: A Guide to Compost Gardening*. London: Pelham Books, 1983.

Climate of the States. Washington, D.C.: U.S. Government Printing Office, 1969.

"A Climatological Summary of Austin, Texas, during the Past 50 Years." Prepared by Weather Modification and Development Division, Texas Water Development Board. Austin, 1976.

Cottner, Sam. *The Vegetable Book*. Waco: TG Press, 1985.

Duble, Richard C. *Southern Turfgrasses: Their Management and Use*. College Station: TexScape, 1989.

Eck, Joe. *Elements of Garden Design*. New York: Henry Holt and Co., 1996.

Extoxnet. http://ace.ace.orst.edu/info/extoxnet/

Fisher, Ted. "Recommended Vegetable Varieties for Travis County." College Station: Texas Agricultural Extension Service, 1996.

Frank W. Gould. *Texas Plants: A Checklist and Ecological Summary*. MP-585/Revised. College Station: Texas Agricultural Experiment Station, 1975.

Hobhouse, Penelope. *Color in Your Garden*. Boston: Little, Brown, 1984.

Hortus Third: A Concise Dictionary of Plants Cultivated in the United States and Canada. Prepared by staff of the L. H. Bailey Hortorium, Cornell University. New York: MacMillan, 1976.

Knoop, William E. *The Complete Guide to Texas Lawn Care*. Waco: TG Press, 1986.

Kress, Steven W. *The Bird Garden* (The National Audubon Society). London: Dorling Kindersley Publishing Co., 1995.

"Master Composter Training Manual." GI-58. Austin: Texas Natural Resource Conservation Commission, 1994.

Miles, Bebe. *Bulbs for the Home Gardener*. New York: Grosset & Dunlap, 1976.

National Weather Service, Austin/San Antonio. http://www.srh.noaa.gov/ewx/

Ogden, Scott. *Garden Bulbs for the South.* Dallas: Taylor Publishing Co., 1994.

————. *Gardening Success with Difficult Soils.* Dallas: Taylor Publishing Co., 1992.

Paul, Anthony, and Yvonne Rees. *The Water Garden.* New York: Viking Penguin, 1986.

"Recommended Species for Central Texas." Austin: National Wildflower Research Center.

Shigo, Alex. *100 Tree Myths.* Durham, N.H.: Shigo and Trees, Associates, 1993.

Sperry, Neil. *Complete Guide to Texas Gardening,* 2nd edition. Dallas: Taylor Publishing Co., 1996.

————. *1001 Most Asked Texas Gardening Questions.* Arlington, Tex.: Summit Publishing Group, 1997.

Stell, Elizabeth. *Secrets to Great Soils.* Pownal, Vt.: Storey Communications, 1998.

Time-Life Gardeners Guide: Annuals. Richmond, Va.: Time-Life Books, 1988.

Texas Association of Nurserymen. "Outstanding Texas Landscape Color." Austin: Texas Association of Nurserymen, undated.

U.S. Department of Agriculture, Soil Conservation Service. "Soil Survey of Travis County, Texas." Washington, D.C.: Government Printing Office, 1975.

Vines, Robert A. *Trees, Shrubs, and Woody Vines of the Southwest.* Austin: University of Texas Press, 1960.

Wasowski, Sally, with Andy Wasowski. *Native Texas Plants: Landscaping Region by Region.* Houston: Gulf Publishing Co., 1991.

Watson, Gary W., and E. B. Himelick. *Principles and Practice of Planting Trees and Shrubs.* Savoy, Ill.: International Society of Arboriculture, 1997.

Welch, William C. *Perennial Garden Color.* Dallas: Taylor Publishing Co., 1989.

Wyman, Donald. *Wyman's Gardening Encyclopedia.* New York: Macmillan, 1971.

Index

Scientific names appear in italics and are cross-referenced to the most common name. Pages containing illustrations appear in bold type.

abelia, 88, **89,** 181; and hummingbirds, 35; and pruning, 65
Abelia grandiflora. See abelia
acacia. *See* huisache
Acacia farnesiana. See huisache
Acalypha wilkesiana. See copper plant
Acer saccharinum. See silver maple
Achillea. See yarrow
acidity. *See* soil: acid
Adiantum Capillus-verneris. See southern maidenhair fern
aeration: and compost, 18–20; and disease, 168; and lawn, 12, 42, 171, 180; and perennials, 124; and roses, 142; and vegetables, 149
aeration machine, 42, 43
afghan pine, 69
agarito, 88–89
Agave americana. See century plant
Agave victoria-reginae. See century plant
ageratum, 116, 180, 181, 182
Aggie Horticulture, 27, 138
Ajilvsgi, Geyata, 24
ajuga, **51,** 53, 184
Ajuga reptans. See ajuga
'Alabama.' *See* hybrid tea roses
Albizia julibrissin. See mimosa
Algerian ivy. *See* ivy
alkaline soil. *See* soil: alkaline
Allred. *See* plum trees
aloe yucca. *See* yucca
alternanthera, 116
alternatives. *See* lawn(s): alternatives

althea. *See* Rose of Sharon
alyssum, 116, 184
amaryllis, 133
Amdro, 176
American beautyberry, 89; and xeriscaping, 34
American plane tree. *See* sycamore
Ampelopsis arboreal. See peppervine
anemones, 4, **125,** 133, 185
'Angel Face.' *See* floribunda
annuals, 115, **121,** 178–84; properties of various kinds, 116–20
Anthony Waterer. *See* spirea
anthracnose, 172, 179
Antigonon leptopus. See coralvine
Antirrhinum. See snapdragon
aphids, 159, **175,** 169–80 passim
apple trees, 84, 173
'Apricot Nectar.' *See* grandiflora
'Aquarius.' *See* grandiflora
Aquilegia. See columbine
Aquilegia canadensis. See columbine
aralia, 90
Aralia sieboldii. See aralia
Arizona ash, 69
Arizona cypress, 69
arsenic, 20
artemisia, 126
Artemisia ludoviciana. See artemisia
Artemisia schmidtiana 'nana.' *See* artemisia
Artemisia vulgaris. See artemisia
Ascend, 176

ash, 179
ashe juniper, 68
Asiatic jasmine, 53, 107, **108**
asparagus, 7, 152, 161, 179
aspidistra, 34
Aspidistra elatior. See cast iron plant
aster, 7
Aster x. See fall aster
Athyrium Goeringianum japonicum. See Japanese painted fern
aucuba, 90
Aucuba japonica. See aucuba
'August Beauty.' *See* gardenias
Austin Pond Society, 27, 36
automatic sprinkler systems: and ground cover, 49; and landscaping, 30; and xeriscaping, 34
autumn fern, 50
autumn sage, 126
Ayres. *See* pear trees
azaleas, 61, 90, **91,** 173–83 passim

bachelor's button. *See* gomphrena
Bacillus thuringiensis, 34, 159, 170–83 passim
bacteria, 18, 19, 69, 173
bagworms, 97, 179
Balcones (region), 9–12, 69, 77
bald cypress, 69, 173
balled root tree, 32, **59,** 57–59
'Ballerina.' *See* Indian hawthorn
balsam gourd, 107
'Barbara Bush,' 138
bare root roses, 142, 178–79, 185
barometer plant, 92
basil, 163
beans, 153, 161, 182–83
bearded iris. *See* iris
'Beauty Secret.' *See* miniature roses
bedding plants, 181–82
beebalm, 35
beetles, **175**
beets, 152, 161
begonia, 116, 180
Benomyl, 143

Berberis thunbergii var. *atropurpurea* 'nana.' *See* crimson pigmy barberry
Berberis trifoliolate. See agarito
bermudagrass, 23, 37, **38,** 39, 47, 137, 180–81
bermuda mite, 46
Better Homes and Gardens, 24, 48
Big Thicket, 69
Bird Garden, The, 25
Blachly, Doug, 14
blackberries, 165, 181–83
black-eyed Susan. *See* coneflower
blackfoot daisy, 126, 136
black haw. *See* viburnum
blackjack oak, 69, 174
Blackland Prairies, 12
black locust, 69
black spot, 142–43, 180–81
blades, mower, 45
bleach, 62
bleeding, 63
blowers, 21
bluebonnets, 116, 138, 184
'Blue Danube.' *See* ageratum
blue mold, 159
blue phlox. *See* moss phlox
blue sage, 126
'Blue Shade.' *See* Mexican petunia
bolting, 155
bone meal, 125, 142
books, recommended, 24–26
border plants, 81, 87, 99, 116, 127, 131
Boron, 16, 46
botrytis blight, 172
bougainvillea, 107–108, 181
Bourbons. *See* old roses
boxwood, 91, 173, 176
Brachycome iberidifolia. See swan river daisy
bracts, 107
Bradford pear, 69
Braeburn. *See* apple trees
Brassica oleracea. See ornamental cabbage
Brazos penstemon, 126
bridal wreath spirea. *See* spirea

broccoli, 153–54, 162, 179–85 passim
brown patch, 47, 184
Bruce. *See* plum trees
brussels sprouts, 162
Buchloe dactyloides. See buffalograss
buffalograss, 23, 37, 40, 180
bulbs, 17, **125,** 124–25, 181–85 passim; prop-
    erties of various kinds, 133–36. *See also*
    specific kinds
burford holly. *See* holly
bur oak, 70
butterflies, 24, 34–35, 118, 131, 163, 170, 175,
    180
butterfly bush, 35
Butterfly Gardening for the South, 24
Buxus microphylla var. *japonica. See* box-
    wood

cabbage, 162, 179–85 passim
cacti, 49
Caddo. *See* pecan trees
cages, 149
caladiums, 114, 125, 133, 181–85 passim
calcareous soil, 12
calcium, 12, 16
calendula, 120, 184
Calendula officinalis. See calendula
caliche, 12, 145–46
Callicarpa americana. See American
    beautyberry
Callirhoe involvucrata. See winecup
Camellia japonica. See camellias
camellias, 61, 91, **92,** 173, 178–85 passim
Camellia sasankwa. See camellias
'Camelot.' *See* grandiflora
Campsis radicans. See trumpetvine
cantaloupe, 162
candytuft, 127, 184
cankers, 172
canna, 133
carbon, 19–20
cardinal flower, 35
Carissa holly. *See* holly
carnations, 120, 127

Carolina jessamine, 108
carpet bugle, 53
carpetgrass, 38
carrots, 154, 162, 179–85 passim
Carya illinoinensis. See pecan trees
cast iron plant, 53, 171
catalpa, 70
Catalpa speciosa. See catalpa
caterpillars, 34–35, 163, 170, 175, **175,** 179–80
cauliflower, 162, 179–84 passim
'Cécile Brünner.' *See* climbing roses; poly-
    anthas
cedar elm, 70, **71,** 173
cedar sage, 34
Celeste. *See* fig trees
'Céline Forestier.' *See* old roses
celosia, 182
Celosia cristata. See cockscomb
Celtis occidentalis. See hackberry, common
cenizo, 92, **93,** 93, 115, 171
Centaurea cineraria. See dusty miller
Centaurea dealbata. See Persian centaurea
century plant, 54, **55**
Cercis canadensis var. *texensis. See* Texas
    redbud
Chaenomeles japonica. See Japanese flow-
    ering quince
chemical fertilizers, 167–73. *See also* fertil-
    izer
cherry laurel, 70, 93
chill factor, 84
Chilopsis linearis. See desert willow
chinaberry, 173
Chinas. *See* old roses
chinch bugs, 39, 46, 181
Chinese elm, 70
Chinese parasol tree, 70
Chinese photinia. *See* photinia
Chinese pistachio, 70–71
Chinese tallow, 71, 173
Chinese wisteria, 108, 109, **109**
Chinquapin oak, 71
'Chipper.' *See* miniature roses
chives, 163

chlorine, 16, 173
chlorosis. *See* iron chlorosis
chromium, 20
chrysanthemums, 7, **123**, 127, 176–83 passim
Chrysanthemum superbum. See shasta
    daisy
'Chrysler Imperial.' *See* hybrid tea roses
'Cinderella.' *See* miniature roses
clay, 1, 14, 92, 107, 122, 145. *See also* soil
clematis, 109
Clematis drummondii. See clematis
Clematis texensis. See clematis
Clematis viticella. See clematis
cleome, 116, 180
Cleome hasslerana. See cleome
cleyera, 93
Cleyera japonica. See cleyera
climate, 3–10 passim, 144, 148
climbers. *See* vines
climbing fig, 110
climbing roses, 141
cobalt, 16
cockscomb, 117, 181
cold fronts, 4
coleus, 117, 176, 181–82
color, 31, 114
Color in Your Garden, 25
columbine, 127
common camellia. *See* camellias
'Compacta.' *See* cenizo
companion planting, 168
Complete Guide to Texas Gardening, 25
Complete Guide to Texas Lawn Care, The,
    25
Complete Pond Builder, The, 25
compost, 12–15, 18–20, 178–83 passim; and
    annuals, 122; and cannas, 133; and pe-
    rennials, 122; and roses, 142; and veg-
    etables, 145–59 passim. *See also* sludge
'Comtesse de Bouchard.' *See* clematis
coneflower, 32, 127
Confederate jasmine. *See* star jasmine
copper, 16, 20, 183; and gardenias, 95; and
    soil pH, 15

copper plant, 117, 181
coral bells, 35
coral honeysuckle. *See* honeysuckle
coralvine, 110
coreopsis, 127, **137**, 138, 180
Coreopsis lanceolata. See coreopsis
corkscrew willow. *See* weeping willow
corms. *See* bulbs
corn, 154, 162, 180
Cornus. See dogwood
Cornus florida. See dogwood
Cortaderi selloana. See pampas grass
cosmos, 117, 181
cotoneaster, 50, 173
cottonless cottonwood, 71
cotton root rot, 165, 172–73
cottonseed meal, 15
cottonwood, 172, 173
county extension agent, 24, 27, 46, 174, 179;
    and fruit trees, 84; and pruning, 64; and
    soil testing, 16
coverings, protective, 5
crape myrtle, 31, 65, 72, **73**, 168, 173–74, 182
creeping juniper, 50, 54
creeping myrtle. *See* periwinkle, common
crimson barberry, 171
crimson pigmy barberry, 94, 115
crinums, 133, 135
crocus, **125**
crop rotation, 168
Cross Timbers, 12
cucumbers, 154–55, 162, 182–83
cultivator, 23
Cuphea hyssopifolia. See Mexican heather
cupheas, 35
Cupressus arizonica. See Arizona cypress
Cycas revoluta. See sago palm
cyclamen, 120, 186
Cyclamen persicum. See cyclamen
Cynodon dactylon. See bermudagrass
Cyrtomium falcatum. See holly

daffodil, 133, 185
daisies, 181

damping off, 173
Dasylirion texanum. See Texas sotol
daylily, **123,** 127, 179–84 passim
decomposed granite, 29, 49
dehorning, 65
Delphinium grandiflorum. See larkspur
desert willow, 72
design, garden, 25
Desirable. *See* pecan trees
Dianthus, 180, 184. *See also* carnations
diatomaceous earth, 169, 177
dibble, 21
dieback, 172
dill, 163; and butterflies, 175; and caterpillars, 35
Dillo Dirt, 44
Diospyros texana. See Texas persimmon
dirting, 158
disbudding, 122, 124
diseases, 167–68, 171; properties of various kinds, 172–74; and roses, 142–43; and silver maple, 78; and vegetables, 152. *See also speciWc kinds*
dividing, 127, 131, 180, 184; perennials, 124
Dixieland. *See* peach trees
dogwood, 72
Dolichos lablab. See hyacinth bean
'Don Juan.' *See* climbing roses
'Double Delight.' *See* hybrid tea roses
double dig, 150
drainage, 10–12, 101, 116–18, 131, 184; and annuals, 121; and bulbs, 124; and carnations, 127; and fruit trees, 84–85; and ground cover, 49, 50; and landscaping, 29, 41; and perennials, 122; and roses, 142
drip irrigation, 34, 149
Dryopteris erythrosora. See autumn fern
dusty miller, 117
Dutch iris, 185
dwarf burford holly. *See* holly
dwarf Chinese holly. *See* holly
dwarf yaupon, 94

earworms, 154

Eastern red cedar, 72
Echinacea purpurea. See coneflower; purple coneflower
edgers, 21, 23
Edwards Plateau, 12, 109
elaeagnus, 62, 65, 94
Elaeagnus pungens. See elaeagnus
elbon rye, 176, 178
Elements of Garden Design, 25
elm, 173
El Niño, 9
'El Toro.' *See* zoysia
'Emerald.' *See* zoysia
'Enchantress.' *See* Indian hawthorn
English ivy. *See* ivy
Entomosporium maculatum, 101, 173
environmental attitudes, xi
equipment. *See* tools, gardening
Eriobotrya japonica. See loquat
erosion, 11
Erythea adulis. See Guadalupe palm
euonymus, 94, 174, 182, 185. *See also* wintercreeper
Euonymus fortunei. See wintercreeper
Euonymus japonica. See euonymus
Euonymus japonicus. See euonymus
Euonymus kiautschovica. See euonymus
'Europeana.' *See* floribunda
evaporation, 9
evergreen euonymus. *See* euonymus
evergreens, 4, 63, 67–75 passim, 92–10 passim, 179–81; and fertilizer, 17; and pruning, 65
evergreen sumac. *See* sumac
Extoxnet, 27

'Fairy, The.' *See* old roses
fall: flowers suitable for, 120–36 passim; plants suitable for, 153–54. *See also* gardening calendar
fall aster, 127, 180
fatshedera, 94
Fatshedera lizei. See fatshedera
fennel, 163

ferns, 48, 50. *See also specific kinds*
fertilizer, 16–20, 33–34, 107, 165, 178–85
passim; and disease, 168; and flowers,
116–25, 142; and ground cover, 44–50;
and trees and shrubs, 58–64 passim, 84;
and vegetables, 146–61 passim
fescue, 40
Ficus pumila. See climbing fig
fig trees, 84, 176
fire ants, 175–76
fire blight, 173; and pear trees, 85; and pyracantha, 104
firebush, 128
'Fire King.' *See* floribunda
firethorn. *See* pyracantha
firewheel, **137**
Firmiana simplex. See Chinese parasol tree
'First Prize.' *See* floribunda
flameleaf. *See* sumac
'Floratam,' 39
floribunda, 140–43
flowering peach, 72
flowering quince, 181
flowers, 114; annuals, 115–22; bulbs, 124–25,
133–36; perennials, 122–24, 126–32;
wildflowers, 136–39. *See also specific
kinds*
foliar spraying, 18, 61, 172, 174
fork, 21–22, 124
fountain grass, 52
four nerve daisy, 128
four o'clock, 128
419 Tifway. *See* bermudagrass
foxglove, 7
fragrant sumac. *See* sumac
Frank. *See* peach trees
Fraxinus velutina. See Arizona ash
freezing, 4–7, 22, 74, 90; dates, **6;** and lawns,
41; and potatoes, 158; and pruning, 65
French mulberry. *See* American
beautyberry
friable soil. *See* soil: friable
fruit gardening, 165–66
fruitless mulberry, 72–73

fruit trees, 32, 84–86, 179–80
fungi, 78, 101, 172–73
fungicide, 47, 181
Funginex, 143
fusarium wilt, 160

gaillardia, 128
Gaillardia pulchella. See gaillardia; Indian
blanket
Gala. *See* apple trees
Garden Bulbs for the South, 25
garden centers, 5, 32, 150, 157, 180
garden clubs, 13
garden design, 25
Gardenia jasminoides. See gardenias
Gardenia radicans. See gardenias
gardenias, 61, 94, **95,** 95, 176, 181
gardening calendar, 178–85
gayfeather. *See* liatris
gazania, 117
Gazania rigens. See gazania
Gelsemium sempervirens. See Carolina jessamine
'Gene Boerner.' *See* floribunda
geranium, 180
gerbera daisy, 128
Gerbera jamesonii. See gerbera daisy
'Ginger.' *See* floribunda
ginkgo, 73
Ginkgo biloba. See ginkgo
gladiolus, 133, 179, 182
Gladioulus. See gladiolus
Gleditsia triacanthos var. *inermis. See*
thornless honey locust
globe amaranth. *See* gomphrena
glossy privet. *See* ligustrum
glyphosate herbicide. *See* Roundup
gold dust. *See* aucuba
'Golden Girl.' *See* grandiflora
goldenrain tree, 73
goldenrod, 7
'Golden Showers.' *See* climbing roses
'Golden splendor.' *See* lily
gomphrena, 117

Gomphrena globosa. See gomphrena
'Granada.' *See* grandiflora
grandiflora, 141, 143
Granny Smith. *See* apple trees
grapefruit, 176
grapes, 165. *See also* wild grapes
grass: and fertilizer, 44; and wildflowers, 137. *See also* lawns; *specific kinds*
grass seed, 41, 42
'Green Cloud.' *See* cenizo
'Green Leaf.' *See* cenizo
greens, 185
ground covers: care of, 48–49; and ivy, 111; ornamental grasses, 52; spacing for, 50
ground covers, other, 53, 55–56. *See also specific kinds*
ground fill. *See* soil: imported
growing season, length of, 7
grubworms, 46, 153, 182
Guadalupe palm, 74
Gulf Coast, 7
'Gulf Stream.' *See* nandina
gypsum, 12, 14; and vegetables, 145

hackberry, common, 74
Hall's Japanese honeysuckle. *See* honey-suckle
Hamelia patens. See firebush
'Handel.' *See* floribunda
hand tools, 23
harbour dwarf. *See* nandina
hardscape, 48
havard penstemon, 128
heading, 62
heat: and compost, 19; plants suitable for, 110, 117–19
heat stress, 122
heavy soil, 11
Hedera. See ivy
Hedera canariensis. See ivy
Hedera helix. See ivy
hedges, 87–99 passim, 104
'Helen Traubel.' *See* hybrid tea roses
Helianthus. See sunflower

Hemerocallis. See daylily
herbicides, 41, 46
herbs, 163–65. *See also specific kinds*
Herperaloe parviflora. See red hesperaloe
hibiscus, 7, 181
Hibiscus syriacus. See Rose of Sharon
Hill Country, 9, 12, 30, 78–79, 89
Hinkley columbine, 34
Hippeastrum. See amaryllis
hoe, 22
holly, 51, 65, **96**, 96–97, 173, 185
hollyhock, 184
'Hollywood Juniper.' *See* juniper
honey mesquite, 74
honeysuckle, 110, 173
'Honor.' *See* hybrid tea roses
hoses, 2, 21
huisache, 74
humidity, 9; and disease, 172; and leaf spot, 173
hummingbirds, 34, 35
humus, 12, 14; and fruit trees, 84; and roses, 142; and wisteria, 108
hyacinth, **125,** 134
hyacinth bean, 110
Hyacinthus. See hyacinth
hybrid tea roses, **140,** 140, 143
hydrangea, 97
Hydrangea macrophylla. See hydrangea
Hydrangea quercifolia. See hydrangea
Hymenocallis. See spider lily
Hymenoxys scaposa. See four nerve daisy

Iberis amara. See candytuft
Iberis pinnata. See candytuft
Iberis sempervirens. See candytuft
Iberis umbellata. See candytuft
Ibervillea linadheimeri. See balsam gourd
Ilex. See holly
Ilex cornuta burfordii. See holly
Ilex cornuta burfordii compacta. See holly
Ilex cornuta rotunda. See holly
Ilex cornuta var. carissa. See holly
Ilex decidua. See yaupon holly

Ilex decidua. See possumhaw
Ilex pendula. See dwarf yaupon
Ilex vomitoria. See dwarf yaupon; yaupon
	holly
Ilex vomitoria 'nana.' *See* dwarf yaupon
Ilex x hybrida. See holly
impatiens, 117, 181, 185
Impatiens wallerana. See impatiens
Indian blanket, 138
Indian hawthorn, 30, 95–96, 173, 181
indica azalea. *See* azalea
Indigo Spires, 128
inorganic fertilizers. *See* fertilizer
insecticides, 44–46, 170–81 passim
insects, 74, 78, 82, **175;** properties of vari-
	ous kinds, 174–77; and vegetables, 152
integrated pest management (IPM), 167–
	77
Internet, 26–27, 36
iris, 124, 134, 184
iron, 16, 173; and gardenias, 95; and Japa-
	nese black pine, 75; and vegetables, 146
iron chelate, 173, 182–83
iron chlorosis, 95, 173, 183; and St. August-
	ine, 39; and soil pH, 15, 61; and sy-
	camores, 79
iron sulfate, 61, 182, 183; and soil pH, 15
irrigation: and fig trees, 84; and landscap-
	ing, 30; and lawns, 43–44
Italian jasmine. *See* primrose jasmine
ivy, 34, **51,** 54, 110–11; as groundcover, 48

'Ja Mur.' *See* zoysia
Japanese black pine, 74–75
Japanese flowering quince, 97
Japanese lawn grass. *See* zoysia
Japanese littleleaf box. *See* boxwood
Japanese painted fern, 51
Japanese privet. *See* ligustrum
Japanese silver grass, 52
Japanese yew, 31, 97, **98**
jasmine, 176
jasmine, Asiatic. *See* Asiatic jasmine
Jasminum humile. See primrose jasmine

Jasminum mesnyi. See primrose jasmine
Jerusalem thorn. *See* retama
Johnny-jump-up. *See* violas
Joseph's coat. *See* alternanthera
'Judy Fischer.' *See* miniature roses
juniper, 49, 50, 97–98, **99,** 171, 173, 179
Juniperus ashei. See ashe juniper
Juniperus chinensis. See juniper
Juniperus horizontalis. See creeping juniper
Juniperus virginiana. See Eastern red cedar
Justicia spicigera. See Mexican honeysuckle

kale, 179, 184. *See also* ornamental cabbage
'Katie.' *See* Mexican petunia
Kelthane, 176
Kieffer. *See* pear trees
Kocide, 173
Koelreuteria paniculata. See goldenrain tree
Korean lawn grass. *See* zoysia
kurume azalea. *See* azalea

'Lady Banksia.' *See* climbing roses
Lady Bird Johnson Wildflower Center, 27,
	137
Lagerstroemia indica. See crape myrtle
landscaping, **29;** planning for, 28–31; plant
	selection, 31–32; and ponds, 35, 36; and
	xeriscaping, 33, 34
lantana, 49, 129, 171; and butterflies, 35
Lantana camara. See lantana
Lantana horrida. See lantana
Lantana montevidensis. See lantana
larkspur, 117
lattices, 106
laurestinus viburnum. *See* viburnum
lavender tree. *See* vitex
lawn(s), 41–47, **51,** 179–84 passim; alterna-
	tives, 37–38, 48; and chlorosis, 173; and
	ground cover, 49–50; ground cover,
	other, 53–56; ornamental grasses, 52
lawnmowers. *See* mowers
lawn mowing. *See* mowing
'Lawrence Pink Rosette.' *See* floribunda
leaf curl virus, 161

leaf spot, 173, 174
leaf stalks, 106
leatherleaf mahonia, 98
lettuce, 155, 162, 179, 184–85
Leucophyllum frutescens. See cenizo
liatris, 129
Liatris elegans. See liatris
ligustrum, 65, 99, **100,** 173, 181
Ligustrum japonicum. See ligustrum
Ligustrum lucidum. See ligustrum
lilac chaste tree. *See* vitex
Lilium. See lily
Lilium candidum. See lily
Lilium regale. See lily
Lilium tigridum. See lily
lily, 134
lime, 15
Lindheimer's Muhly grass, 52
liriope, 54, 184; as ground cover, 49; and
    xeriscaping, 34
Liriope muscari. See liriope
little bluestem, 52
live oak, **75,** 75, 173, 174, 180
loam, 11–12
Lobularia maritima. See alyssum
Logic, 176
Lombardy poplar, 75, 172
Lonicera. See honeysuckle
Lonicera japonica var. *chinensis. See* hon-
    eysuckle
Lonicera japonica var. *halliana. See* honey-
    suckle
Lonicera sempervirens. See honeysuckle
loquat, 76, 173; and soil pH, 61
Louisiana iris, 124
low-growing plants, 48
Lupinus. See bluebonnets
lycoris, 134
Lycoris radiata. See lycoris

Madonna. *See* lily
magazines, recommended, 26
'Magic Carrousel.' *See* miniature roses
magnesium, 16

magnolia, 68, 181; and soil pH, 61
Magnolia grandiflora. See southern mag-
    nolia
Mahonia bealii. See leatherleaf mahonia
maidenhair tree. *See* ginkgo
'Majestic Beauty.' *See* Indian hawthorn
Malathion, 176–77
Malaviscus arboreus var. *drummondii. See*
    Turk's cap
mandevilla, 181
manganese, 16
Manhattan euonymus. *See* euonymus
manure, 12, 159; and bulbs, 125; and com-
    post, 20; and vegetables, 145, 150, 158
'Marie Pavie.' *See* polyanthas
marigolds, 118, **121,** 168, 180–82
'Mary Marshall.' *See* miniature roses
Matthiola incana. See stock
'Maulei.' *See* Japanese flowering quince
Maxine. *See* pear trees
mealybugs, 176
Melampodium leucanthum. See blackfoot
    daisy
Melia azedarach. See chinaberry
melons, 155
mescal bean. *See* Texas mountain laurel
Methley. *See* plum trees
Mexican buckeye, 76
Mexican bush sage, 129
Mexican hat, 129
Mexican heather, 129
Mexican honeysuckle, 129
Mexican marigold mint, 129, 180
Mexican oregano, 129, 171
Mexican petunia, 130
Mexican plum, 76
Mexican sunflower. *See* tithonia
mildew, 181–82; and annuals, 122; and
    beans, 153; and melons, 155; and onions,
    156; and roses, 142–43; and sulfur, 170;
    and zinnias, 119
milkweed, 35
mimosa, 76
miniature roses, 141

mint, 163

Mirabilis jalapa. See four o'clock

'Mirandy.' *See* hybrid tea roses

Miscanthus sinensis. See Japanese silver grass

molybdenum, 16

Monarda citriodora. See purple horsemint

mondo grass, 52. *See also* monkey grass

monkey grass, 52, 54; as ground cover, 48–49

Monterrey oak, 76

'Montezuma.' *See* grandiflora

Morus alba. See fruitless mulberry

Morus rubra. See red mulberry

mosaic virus, 157

moss phlox, 130

moss rose. *See* portulaca

mowers, 21–23

mowing, 39–46

'Mrs. B. R. Cant.' *See* old roses

Muhlenbergia lindheimeri. See Lindhemier's Muhly grass

mulberry, 172, 175

mulch, 20–33 passim, 49–50, 59–61, 156, 181–82; and annuals, 122; and bulbs, 125; and perennials, 124; and roses, 142; and vegetables, 149, 151

mustang grape. *See* wild grapes

'Mystery.' *See* gardenias

nana dwarf. *See* nandina

nandina, 99, 100; and pruning, 65; and xeriscaping, 34

Nandina domestica. See nandina

narcissus, 7. *See also* daffodil

Native Texas Plants: Landscaping Region by Region, 26

naturalization, 124, 133–36

Neighborhood's Garden, The (website), 27

Neil Sperry's Garden, 26

'Nellie R. Stevens.' *See* holly

nematodes, 160, 176; and beets, 153

Nerium oleander. See oleander

'New Dawn.' *See* climbing roses

nickel, 16

nierembergia, 118

nitrogen, 15–20; and daylilies, 127; and fertilizer, 44; and perennials, 122; and vegetables, 146

Noisettes. *See* old roses

nozzles, 22

nursery. *See* garden center

nutrients, 12–16; and vegetables, 144–48

nut trees, 84–86, 179–80

oak. *See specific kinds*

oak-leaved hydrangea. *See* hydrangea

oak wilt, 63, 75, 78, 174

obedient plant, 130, 180

okra, 176, 181, 183

'Old Blush.' *See* old roses

'Old Gold.' *See* juniper

old man's beard. *See* clematis

old roses, 139, 143

oleander, 100, **101**

onions, 155–56, 162, 179, 185

Ophiopogon japonicus 'nana.' *See* monkey grass

oregano, 164

organic fertilizers. *See* fertilizer

organic matter, 12, 14, 18, 180, 184; and flowers, 120–31 passim; and vegetables, 145–57 passim

Orient. *See* pear trees

ornamental cabbage, 120

ornamental date palm, 76

ornamental grasses, 48, 52. *See also specific kinds*

ornamentals, 17, 179

ornamental trees, 68–83. *See also specific kinds*

'Over-the-Rainbow.' *See* miniature roses

oxalis, 130, 134

Oxalis crassipes. See oxalis

Oxalis regnelli. See oxalis

oxygen. *See* aeration

paint, wound, 64, 174

'Palisades.' *See* zoysia

palm. *See specific kinds*

pampas grass, 52, **53,** 171

pansies, 120, 180–85 passim

Papaver. See poppy

Parkinsonia aculeata. See retama

parsley, 164, 185; and butterflies, 175; and caterpillars, 35

Parthenocissus quinquefolia. See Virginia creeper

Passiflora. See passionflower

passionflower, 111, 176; and butterflies, 35

Pavonia lasiopetala. See rock rose

'Peace.' *See* hybrid tea roses

peach trees, 64, 85, 181

pear trees, 85, 173, 179

peas, 156, 162, 179, 185

peat moss, 12, 14, 178, 185; and azaleas, 90; and bulbs, 136; and chlorosis, 173; and perennials, 122; and roses, 142; and transplanting, 61; and vegetables, 145

pecan trees, 60, 64, 77, 86, 173, 175

Penstemon havardii. See havard penstemon

Penstemon 'Red Husker.' *See* Red Husker

Penstemon tenuis. See Brazos penstemon

pentas, 35, 118

Pentas lanceolata. See pentas

peppermint. *See* mint

peppers, 156–57, 162, 179–81

peppervine, 111

Perennial Garden Color, 26

perennials, **123,** 122–24, 179–84 passim; properties of various kinds, 126–32

periwinkle, common, 55

periwinkle, vinca, **51,** 54–55, 118

perlite, 14, 185

Persian centaurea, 130

pesticides, 27, 34, 41, 170–76; and vegetables, 152

petunias, 118, **121,** 180, 184

Petunis. See petunias

'Pfitzer.' *See* juniper

pH level, 14, 15. *See also* soil

phlox, 118, 180; and hummingbirds, 35

Phlox divaricata. See moss phlox

Phlox drummondii. See phlox

Phlox paniculata. See summer phlox

Phlox subulata. See moss phlox

Phoenix canariensis. See ornamental date palm

phosphorus, 15–20 passim; and vegetables, 146

photinia, 100–101, 173, 181–82; and pruning, 65

Photinia fraseri. See photinia

Photinia serrulata. See photinia

Physostegia virginiana. See obedient plant

pillbugs, 169, 176–77; and lettuce, 155

pinching, 63–64

'Pink Lady.' *See* Indian hawthorn

'Pink Powderpuffs.' *See* ageratum

pinks. *See* carnations

Pinus eldarica. See afghan pine

Pinus thenbergii. See Japanese black pine

Pistacia chinensis. See Chinese pistachio

Pistacia texana. See Texas pistachio

pittosporum, 101–102, **120,** 181

Pittosporum tobira. See pittosporum

planting, 185; and disease, 168; flowers, 121; schedule, 178–85; trees and shrubs, 57–66; vegetables, 150–51

plant selection, 31; and balled trees, 32; and IPM, 167–68; and transporting, 33

Platanus occidentalis. See sycamore

plugs: and aeration machines, 42; and bermuda, 39; and St. Augustine, 38; and zoysia, 40

plumbago, 130; as ground cover, 49

Plumbago ariculata. See plumbago

plumeria, 181

plum trees, 85–86

Podocarpus macrophyllus. See Japanese yew

poison ivy, 20

Polliomintha longiflora. See Mexican oregano

polyanthas, 141

Polygonum aubiertii. See silver fleecevine

pomegranate, 102

ponds, 27, 35–36, 182
'Poodle Ligustrum.' *See* ligustrum
poppy, 119
Populus deltoides. See cottonless cottonwood
Populus nigra var. *italica. See* Lombardy
poplar
portulaca, 119, **121**, 180–82
possumhaw, 102–103
possumhaw holly. *See* yaupon holly
post oak, 77
Post Oak Savannah, 12
potassium, 15–16; and compost, 20; and fertilizer, 17, 44; and vegetables, 146
potatoes, 157–58, 162, 179–84 passim
powdery mildew. *See* mildew
primrose jasmine, 103
'Pristine.' *See* hybrid tea roses
Prosopis glandulosa. See honey mesquite
pruners, 23
pruning, **62,** 61–66, 107–10, 179–84; and disease, 168–69; and dividing, 124; and fruit
trees, 84; and oak wilt, 174; and roses,
143; and shrubs, 88
Prunus caroliniana. See cherry laurel
Prunus cerasifera. See purple plum
Prunus mexicana. See Mexican plum
Prunus persica. See flowering peach
pumps, water, 36
Punica granatum. See pomegranate
purple coneflower, 131
purple horsemint, 138
purple Japanese honeysuckle. *See* honeysuckle
purple plum, 77
purslane, 182
Purslane oleracea. See portulaca
pyracantha, **103,** 104, 173
Pyracantha coccinea. See pyracantha
pyrethrum, 170
Pyrus calleryana 'Bradford.' *See* Bradford
pear

'Queen Elizabeth.' *See* grandiflora

queen's wreath. *See* coralvine
Queen Victoria maguey. *See* century plant
Quercus macrocarpa. See bur oak
Quercus marilandica. See blackjack oak
Quercus muhlenbergii. See Chinquapin oak
Quercus polymorpha. See Monterrey oak
Quercus shumardii. See shumard oak
Quercus stellata. See post oak
Quercus texana. See Spanish oak
Quercus virginiana. See live oak
quince, 173

radishes, 158, 162, 179, 184–85; and caterpillars, 35
rainfall, Central Texas, 9, 43
raised beds, 12, 14, 146
rakes, 22
'Raleigh.' *See* St. Augustine
'Ramona.' *See* clematis
ranunculus, 4, **125**, 135, 185
Ranunculus asiaticus. See ranunculus
Raphiolepis indica. See Indian hawthorn
Ratibida columnaris. See Mexican hat
redbud, 173
red cedar, 173
Red Delicious. *See* apple trees
red hesperaloe, 55–56
Red Husker, 131
red mulberry, 77
red oak, 173–74
redskin. *See* peach trees
red-tip photinia. *See* photinia
red yucca, 171. *See also* red hesperaloe
'Regal.' *See* lily
retama, 77
rhizomes. *See* bulbs
Rhododendron. See azalea
Rhododendron indicum. See azalea
Rhododendron obtusum. See azalea
Rhus. See sumac
Rhus aromatica. See sumac
Rhus copallina. See sumac
Rhus sempervirens. See sumac
river fern, 51; as ground cover, 49

Robinia pseudoacacia. See black locust
'Robusta.' *See* juniper
rock rose, 131
root rot, 174–75
root shock, 58
rosemary, **164,** 164, 171; as groundcover, 48
Rose of Sharon, 104
roses, 173–85 passim; properties of various
    kinds, 139–43. *See also specific kinds*
rose soil, 142
rotenone, 170
rototilling. *See* tilling
roughleaf dogwood. *See* dogwood
Roundup, 41
Rudbeckia masima. See coneflower
ruellia, 35
Ruellia brittoniana. See Mexican petunia
rust, 153
rye, 40

Sabal texana. See Texas palm
SAD, 39, 47
safety, chemical, 170–71
sago palm, 104
St. Augustine, 23, **38,** 38–47 passim, 181, 184;
    and wildflowers, 137; and xeriscaping,
    33
St. Augustine Decline. *See* SAD
Salix babylonica. See weeping willow
Salvia coccinea. See scarlet sage
Salvia elegans, 126
Salvia farinacea. See blue sage
Salvia gregii. See autumn sage
Salvia guarantica, 126
Salvia 'Indigo Spires.' *See* Indigo Spires
Salvia leucantha. See Mexican bush sage
salvias, 7, 171, 180–83; and hummingbirds,
    35
sand, 11–14, 178; and perennials, 122; and
    roses, 142; and vegetables, 145. *See also*
    soil
sandankwa viburnum. *See* viburnum
'San Gabriel.' *See* nandina
sanitation, 168–69

Sapindus drummondii. See Western soap-
    berry
Sapium sebiferum. See Chinese tallow
'Sarabande.' *See* floribunda
sasankwa camellia. *See* camellias
sawdust, 19–20
saws, 23
scab, 158
scale, 176, 185; and landscaping, 31
scalping lawns, 45
scarlet clematis. *See* clematis
scarlet sage, 131
schefflera, 176
Schizachyrim scoparium. See little bluestem
'Sea Green.' *See* juniper
Secrets to Great Soils, 25
seed, 181–85; and buffalograss, 40; and flow-
    ers, 115–22 passim; and St. Augustine,
    38; and vegetables, 151–59 passim
selecting plants. *See* plant selection
Sentinel. *See* peach trees
'Seville.' *See* St. Augustine
Sevin, 154, 177, 180
sewage sludge. *See* sludge
shade, 7; and grass, 39–40; and ground cov-
    ers, 49; and landscaping, 30; plants suit-
    able for, 54, 93–136 passim, 163, 181; and
    vegetables, 148; and xeriscaping, 34
shade trees, 68–83. *See also specific kinds*
shasta daisy, **123,** 131, 184
shovels, 21–22
shrubs, 87–105, 179–85 passim; buying, 65;
    pruning, 65–66; siting, 88. *See also spe-
    cific kinds*
shumard oak, 77, 174
'Silver Dragon.' *See* liriope
silver fleecevine, 111
'Silver King.' *See* euonymus
silverlace vine. *See* silver fleecevine
silver maple, 77–78, 173
'Silvery Sunproof.' *See* liriope
Sioux. *See* pecan trees
site selection, 5, 7; and water, 9
609. *See* buffalograss

sludge, 44–45; and vegetables, 145

slugs, 169, 177

snails, 169, 177

snapdragon, 120, 184

soaker hose, 34, 60, 122

sod blocks, 38–42

sodium, 16

soil, **13,** 15–20, 25, 31–33, 49, 61, 69–72, 84, 107, 124; acid, 12, 91–97 passim; alkaline, 97, 109, 173; and flowers, 121–22, 136–37; friable, 14, 145, 154; and grass, 42; imported, 14, 41, 44–45, 58, 171; sand, 11–14, 92, 97, 142, 178; and vegetables, 144–50

soil preparation, 11–14, 178–85 passim

soil testing, 16, 30, 41, 46

Sophora secundiflora. See Texas mountain laurel

southern magnolia, **78,** 78

southern maidenhair fern, 51–52

sowbugs. *See* pillbugs

spacing, 50

Spanish dagger. *See* yucca

Spanish oak, 78, 174

spearmint. *See* mint

spider flower. *See* cleome

spider lily, 135. *See also* lycoris

spider mites, **175,** 176, 181; and junipers, 97; and marigolds, 118; and peppers, 157

spinach, 7, 158–59, 162, 185

spirea, 104

Spirea bumaldo. See spirea

Spirea cantoniensis. See spirea

Spirea reevesiana. See spirea

spring: flowers suitable for, 116–36 passim; plants suitable for, 155. *See also* gardening calendar

Springold. *See* peach trees

sprinklers, 22, 34

squash, 159–62, 180–83

staking, 60, 123

star jasmine, 111

stem rot, 174

Stenotaphrum secundatum. See St. Augustine

Step by Step Landscaping, 24

stock, 120, 180

stokes aster, 131

Stokesia laevis. See stokes aster

strawberries, 166

suckers, 63

sugar snaps, 156, 185

sulfur, 16; and disease, 170; and potatoes, 157, 158

sumac, 104

summer: flowers suitable for, 116–36 passim. *See also* gardening calendar

summer grape. *See* wild grapes

summer phlox, 131; and butterflies, 35

'Summer Snow.' *See* ageratum

'Sundowner.' *See* grandiflora

sunflower, 119

sunlight, 4, 30, 51, 88; and annuals, 121; and fruit trees, 84; and ground covers, 42, 44, 49, 52; plants suitable for, 7, 31, 56, 72, 92–164 passim; and vegetables, 149

'Sunray.' *See* coreopsis

sun scald, 157

superphosphate: and bulbs, 125; and roses, 142

swan river daisy, 119

sweet acacia. *See* huisache

sycamore, 79, 173, 179

Tagetes. See marigolds

Tagetes lucida. See Mexican marigold mint

taproots, 60

Taxodium disticuem. See bald cypress

temperature, 4–7; and plant selection, 31

tendrils, 106

ten o'clock dirt, 145

terraclor, 174

Testurf 10. *See* bermudagrass

Texas A&M Agriculture Extension Service, 24–25, 151

Texas A&M University; as information source, 24; and soil testing, 16; website, 27

Texas everbearing. *See* fig trees

Texas Gardener, 26
'Texas Gold.' *See* columbine
Texas mountain laurel, 31, **79,** 79
Texas palm, 79
Texas Parks and Wildlife Department, 27
Texas persimmon, **80,** 80
Texas pistachio, 80
Texas redbud, 80, **81**
Texas sage, 171
Texas sotol, 56
Thelypteris kunthii. See river fern
thermal kill, 19
thinning, 62, 65
thornless honey locust, 74
threadleaf. *See* coreopsis
thrips, 156, 177
thyme, 165
'Tiffany.' *See* hybrid tea roses
'Tiger.' *See* lily
tilling, 12, 14, 183; and vegetables, 149
tithonia, 119
Tithonia rotundifolia. See tithonia
tobacco mosaic, 160
tomatoes, 160–81 passim
tools, gardening, 21–24
topping, 63
Trachelospermum asiaticum. See Asiatic jasmine
Trachelospermum jasminoides. See star jasmine
Trachycarpus fortunei. See windmill palm
transpiration, 9, 59
transplanting, 178, 183–85; flowers, 121; and onions, 155; trees and shrubs, 59–61
transporting plants, 33
treated wood, 20
tree planting, 57–66
trees, 185; fruit and nut, 84–86; pruning, 61–65; selecting, 67; shade and ornamental, 68–86 passim. *See also specific kinds*
tree well, 171
trellises, 106, 109; and beans, 153; and peas, 156; and vegetables, 149
trimmers, 21–23

trowel, 23
trumpetvine, 111
tubers. *See* bulbs
Tulipa clusiana. See tulips
tulips, 135, 185
Tulipa saxatilis. See tulips
turfgrass, 137, 180; and lawns, 37; and water, 43; and xeriscaping, 33
Turk's cap, 131, **137;** and hummingbirds, 35; and xeriscaping, 34
twining, 106, 108
twistleaf yucca. *See* yucca

Ulmus carssifolia. See cedar elm
Ulmus parvifolia. See Chinese elm
underground watering system, 9
Ungnadia speciosa. See Mexican buckeye

varnish tree. *See* Chinese parasol tree
Vegetable Book, The, 24
vegetables, **147,** 147–51, 178–85 passim; and fertilizer, 17; properties of various kinds, 152–62; and soil, 144–46; and temperature, 5, 7. *See also specific kinds*
vegetational designations: of Texas, 12
verbena, 132; and butterflies, 35
Verbena hybrida. See verbena
vermiculite, 136
verticillium wilt, 160
VFNTM, 160
viburnum, 105
Viburnum rufidulum. See viburnum
Viburnum suspensum. See viburnum
Viburnum tinus. See viburnum
'Ville de Lyon.' *See* clematis
Vinca major. See periwinkle, common
Vinca minor. See periwinkle, vinca
Vinca rosea. See periwinkle, vinca
vine borer, 159
vines, 106–12. *See also specific kinds*
violas, 120
Viola tricolor. See violas
violets, 184
Virginia creeper, 111–12

vitex, 81

Vitex agnus castus. See vitex

Vitis. See wild grapes

Vitis aestivalis. See wild grapes

Vitis berlandieri. See wild grapes

Vitis candicans. See wild grapes

'Vogue.' *See* floribunda

warm season, length of, **8**

Warren. *See* pear trees

Washingtonia filifera. See Washington palm

Washington palm, 81

Washingtonia robusta. See Washington palm

wasps, 183

water, 9–10, 31–34, 60, 90, 108, 179–84; and annuals, 116–22; and fertilizer, 17; and fruit trees, 64; and lawns, 39–50 passim; and perennials, 123; and roses, 142; and vegetables, 144–55 passim

water garden. *See* ponds

water lilies, 36

watermelons, 180

water stress, 84

waxleaf ligustrum. *See* ligustrum

weather. *See* climate

websites. *See* Internet

webworms, 175, 183

weedeaters. *See* edgers

weeds, 46, 49, 182; and compost, 19–20; and disease, 168; and fruit trees, 84; and ground cover, 50; and imported soil, 45

weeping willow, **82,** 82

weeping yaupon. *See* dwarf yaupon

weevils, **175**

Western soapberry, 82

Wheeler's dwarf. *See* pittosporum

whitefly, 170, 177

white rust, 159

wildflowers, **137,** 136–39, 184

wild grapes, **112,** 112

Will Fleming yaupon. *See* dwarf yaupon

willow, 172–73

windmill palm, 82–83, **83**

winecup, 132

winter, 4; flowers suitable for, 120. *See also* gardening calendar

wintercreeper, 56

winter grape. *See* wild grapes

wireworm, 153

Wisteria sinensis. See Chinese wisteria

wood fern. *See* river fern

wood sorrel. *See* oxalis

worms, 18, 20

wound paint, 174

xeriscaping, 33–34

yarrow, 132

yaupon, 31; and pruning, 65; and xeriscaping, 34

yaupon holly, 83

yucca, 56

Yucca aloifolia. See yucca

Yucca rupicola. See yucca

Yucca treculeara. See yucca

zinc, 16; and vegetables, 146

Zinnia linearis. See zinnias

zinnias, 119, 180–82; and butterflies, 35

zoysia, 23, 37, **38,** 39–40, 180

Zoysia japonica. See zoysia

Zoysia matrealla. See zoysia

Zoysia tennuifolia. See zoysia